CW01501923

HAMISH MACBETH

THE MAKING OF A BBC TV CLASSIC

JONATHAN MELVILLE

FOUNTAINBRIDGE PRESS

First published in 2025 by Fountainbridge Press

Copyright © 2025 by Jonathan Melville

All photos © Jonathan Melville or person named in caption

Larger photos:

Pages 46-47: Looking along the foreshore to Plockton. © VisitScotland/Paul Tomkins

Pages 140-141: Looking down to Plockton on the south side of Loch Carron. © VisitScotland/Paul Tomkins

Page 156: Shooting a key scene with Alex from the end of 'Radio Lochdubh', 20th October 1995. Photo by permission of Deirdre Keir

Page 205: Andrew Keir and Stuart Davids take a break from filming 'The Lochdubh Deluxe'. Photo by permission of Deirdre Keir

Cover by Ben Morris

ISBN: 978-0-9933215-2-8
eBook ISBN: 978-0-9933215-3-5

ALSO BY JONATHAN MELVILLE

Seeking Perfection: The Unofficial Guide to Tremors

A Kind of Magic: Making the Original Highlander

Local Hero: Making a Scottish Classic

COMING SOON

Rainbow Connections: Volume One: Meeting the people who
brought Jim Henson's vision to life

UPDATES

Sign up to my newsletter at jonathanmelville.substack.com

Contact me direct via linktr.ee/jonathanmelville

CONTENTS

INTRODUCTION

In the mid-1990s, TV's view of Scotland rarely seemed to stray far from the mean streets of Glasgow. When Jim Taggart growled 'There's been a murder' or Rab C. Nesbitt philosophised from the streets of Govan, they reinforced an image of urban Scotland that dominated the nation's screen identity.

The Highlands, when they appeared at all, seemed to exist in a parallel universe, a place of misty glens and shortbread tin romanticism.

But on 26th March 1995, BBC One viewers encountered something different in *Hamish Macbeth*. The series followed the adventures of its eponymous Highland police constable, played by Robert Carlyle, in the fictional village of Lochdubh for 20 episodes across three series.

Filmed in the picturesque coastal village of Plockton, the series blended crime, comedy and romance while building an ensemble cast of memorable characters. Though loosely based on author M.C. Beaton's novels, the show carved its own distinctive path under writer Daniel Boyle.

Hamish Macbeth stood out from other so-called 'cosy' Sunday night dramas such as *All Creatures Great & Small* (1978-90) or *The Darling Buds of May* (1991-93). Seconds into its first episode, Hamish oversaw a poaching expedition by his friend TV John McIver, before kicking in a car's headlight and smoking a joint with the local doctor. It was a show that felt unmistakably Scottish, yet its appeal was universal.

Cosy Sunday night TV? Not exactly.

For me, the journey to this book started long before I knew I'd be writing it. As a homesick student in Edinburgh in 1995, I sat down to watch the first episode, curious about this new series set in a part of the country where I'd spent much of my childhood and teenage years. What I saw was a Scotland rarely portrayed on screen: a vivid, eccentric version of the Highlands that felt authentic yet heightened, familiar yet surprising.

Years later, that same curiosity led me to seek out the voices of those who made *Hamish Macbeth* a reality. Over nearly two decades, I've interviewed cast, crew and locals from Plockton, the village that became Lochdubh. Their stories, shared over Zoom, emails and the occasional pub table, form the heart of this book. It's perhaps worth noting that Deirdre Keir, Nicholas Renton and Julia Duff all spoke to me together over lunch, so at some points you'll 'hear' them talking to each other in the text.

Hamish Macbeth stood apart not just for its setting, but because it was created by a primarily Scottish team. Executive producer Scott Meek and producer Deirdre Keir had already brought the quintessentially English *Inspector Morse* (1987–

2000) to TV, while writer Daniel Boyle contributed a handful of episodes. With *Hamish Macbeth*, they shifted their focus to the Highlands, bringing the same meticulous approach but with a uniquely Scottish twist.

Although Robert Carlyle, whose unforgettable performance defined the series, declined to take part—'I don't like looking back,' he told me at the 2012 Edinburgh International Film Festival—his presence is felt throughout via archive interviews and the recollections of those who worked alongside him.

This book is partly an oral history, a chance for the people who lived and breathed the series to share their memories in their own words. You'll hear from producers who fought to get the show made, actors who embraced its eccentricities and locals whose lives changed as Plockton became a filming hotspot. I've lightly edited some quotes for clarity, but in the main these are their words.

With *Hamish Macbeth* attracting a new generation of fans on streaming platforms, I hope this book offers fresh insight into the series' creation and enduring legacy. Whether you're revisiting Lochdubh or discovering it for the first time, take a deep breath—you might just smell the pomade—and step into a world where the future, and the past, always seem just around the corner.

Jonathan Melville
Edinburgh
February 2025

THE INTERVIEWEES

This book wouldn't exist without the generous contributions of the following cast, crew and locals who shared their memories. Below is a guide to their roles in the series and on set, helping you get to know the people who brought Lochdubh, and this book, to life.

Cast (Alphabetical by Surname)

- David Ashton – Major Roddy Maclean
- Tam Dean Burn – Black Bob Roberts
- Jimmy Chisholm – Tartan Salesman/Christie McMurray
- Stuart Davids – Lachlan McCrae Jr
- Ron Donachie – Zoot McPherrin
- Duncan Duff – Doc Brown
- Valerie Gogan – Alex Maclean
- Shirley Henderson – Isobel Sutherland
- Philip Jackson – Malachi McBean
- Phyllida Law – Vicky Jeffreys

- Edith MacArthur – Belle Carter
- Michael Mackenzie – Ferdinand McLopez
- Alasdair MacQuarrie – Danny MacLellan
- Forbes Masson – Tam Flood
- Stuart McGugan – Barney Meldrum
- Brian Pettifer – Rory Campbell
- Barbara Rafferty – Agnes Meldrum
- Ralph Riach – TV John McIver
- Dallas Young – Houston Old
- Jimmy Yuill – Lachlan McCrae Sr (Series One)

Crew and residents

- Daniel Boyle – Writer
- Sarah Bruce – Stand-In and Runner
- Andrea Calderwood – Head of Drama, BBC Scotland 1994–97
- Dougie Craig – Plockton resident
- Julia Duff – Casting Director
- Bryan Elsley – Writer
- Colin Finlay – Local resident
- Mandie Fletcher – Director
- James Fraser – ex-Kyle of Lochalsh resident
- Jonas Grimås – Director
- Toby Hefferman – Third Assistant Director
- Stuart Hepburn – Writer/Actor
- Ming Ho – Script Editor
- Deirdre Keir – Producer (Series One and Two)
- Ian Knox – Director
- John Lunn – Composer
- Calum Mackenzie – Plockton resident
- Charlie MacRae – Plockton resident
- Scott Meek – Executive Producer

- Dominic Minghella – Script Editor and Writer
- Donald Murdoch – Musician
- Jon Older – First Assistant Director
- Nicholas Renton – Director
- Charles Salmon – Producer (Series Three)
- Mike Shucksmith (Chairman, Balmacara Community Trust)

ONE
THE BIRTH OF HAMISH MACBETH

MANHATTAN 1983

MARION GIBBONS STROLLED along Fifth Avenue beside her editor, discussing her latest idea. After publishing dozens of romance novels under her maiden name, Marion Chesney, she was proposing something different: a detective story set in the Scottish Highlands.

'And who's your detective?' her editor asked.

'The village bobby,' Gibbons replied simply.

The idea had taken root during a fishing holiday in Sutherland, a county in the far north of Scotland that had so captivated the Glasgow-born author and her husband, author Harry Scott Gibbons, that they'd purchased a croft there.

Their subsequent attempts at Highland farming had provided more material than she'd expected. The locals' response to these city newcomers, from sabotaged fences to mysterious sheep incidents, had given her plenty of inspiration for the kinds of stories she wanted to tell.

Her editor suggested that a Scottish pen name might help sell the series. Drawing from an old Scottish ballad—'The queen she had four Marys, Mary Seaton, Mary Beaton, Mary Carmichael and me'—M.C. Beaton was born.

By 1985, that Manhattan conversation had manifested as *Death of a Gossip*, the book that introduced readers to Hamish Macbeth, a lanky, red-headed village constable living in the village of Lochdubh [pronounced 'Loch-doo'] who solved crimes, avoided promotion and indulged in a spot of poaching. Hamish is accompanied by a colourful cast of Lochdubhians, including love interest, Priscilla Halburton-Smythe, and his loyal dog, Towser.

For almost a decade, Hamish existed purely on the page, his adventures attracting a devoted following among readers who appreciated gentler whodunnits, more commonly known today as 'cosy mysteries'. Then, in the early 1990s, another New York encounter would transform Hamish from literary character to TV star.

Scott Meek, director of production at Zenith Productions, found himself with time to spare while working on a film in Manhattan. At the time, Zenith was one of Britain's most successful independent production companies, having made its name with films such as *Prick Up Your Ears* (1987) starring Gary Oldman and the hit ITV series *Inspector Morse*.

On a whim, Meek stopped by New York's The Mysterious Bookshop and picked up M.C. Beaton's *Hamish Macbeth* novels. 'I'd never seen or heard of them, which I found to be profoundly peculiar,' says Meek.

What caught his attention wasn't the cosy mystery trappings or even the setting, but something more fundamental: here was a detective whose greatest challenge wasn't solving crimes, but avoiding credit for doing so. 'That, along with the notion of maybe liking a drink along with a bit of poaching and liking the ladies, seemed to me an appealing character,' Meek adds.

The concept of a capable policeman actively sabotaging his own advancement to stay in his beloved village struck Meek as the perfect foundation for a different kind of police drama. Reading the novels on his flight back to London, he began to see possibilities that went far beyond their gentle tone and traditional mystery plotting.

Back in the UK, Meek had recently been introduced to a struggling young actor named Robert Carlyle by mutual friend David Hayman. Convinced he was the most talented actor he'd met since Gary Oldman—'I thought he could do anything'—Meek cast Carlyle in an episode of the police drama *99-1* (1994), before actively searching for a project that could showcase his talents.

Over lunch in Glasgow with screenwriter Daniel Boyle—who had written several acclaimed episodes of *Inspector Morse* and shouldn't be confused with his near-namesake Danny Boyle, the English filmmaker who would soon direct 1994's *Shallow Grave*—Meek pitched his newest idea: a contemporary Scottish version of Dickens' *A Christmas Carol*.

'John Thaw would play Scrooge, with the mean person being English and all the other sweet and generous people Scottish,' says Meek. 'Dan thought it was a terrible idea, so he asked me if there was anything else we could work on together. I said I'd optioned a series of novels about a policeman called Hamish Macbeth and Dan just laughed and laughed and laughed. He thought I was joking because he thought the name was so incredibly stupid.

Daniel Boyle (Writer): I thought the name was preposterous. There was something about the name that, in order for *Hamish Macbeth* to exist, it had to be in a world that's not quite real.

Deirdre Keir (Producer, Zenith Productions): Daniel and I had worked with Scott on *Morse*, I'd done two scripts with him. *Morse* was quite strict in its concept, but I just loved them. He could take it away from the centre, so Scott went to him and that was a really good idea.

Scott Meek: Dan said, 'I'm not much interested in writing this *Miss Marple* type of whodunnit, but I really like some of the ideas you talked about, so can I just go off and write something?' I gave him free rein and said, 'Let's have some fun.' He then read the books which Zenith had optioned, and we agreed to only take a very few elements to use. Oddly, *Maverick* [1957–62] was the programme we most discussed, [with its] different tonal pleasures from week to week.

APART FROM HAMISH, Daniel Boyle avoided carrying over characters and plots wholesale from M.C. Beaton's novels, though he found something of interest in book three, 1988's *Death of an Outsider*.

In Beaton's version, Hamish is sent to the village of Cnothan to cover for another officer who is on holiday. There, he investigates the death of the despised Mr Mainwaring, whose skeleton is found in a tank of lobsters. The novel unfolds as a leisurely paced mystery with carefully placed red herrings, fitting neatly into the cosy mystery tradition where violence happens offstage and justice arrives without much bloodshed.

The team at Zenith had originally been steering the series towards a more traditional police procedural, but it soon became clear that *Hamish Macbeth* would not be a simple adaptation of the novels.

Daniel Boyle's first script, 'The Great Lochdubh Salt Robbery', took the lobster plot strand from *Death of an Outsider* and introduced domestic abuse and filicide, ending with the entire village becoming accidental participants in perhaps the most roundabout case of cannibalism in TV history; eating lobsters that had fed on a murder victim. Where Beaton's novel spread its revelations across multiple chapters, Boyle condensed his mystery into a tight 50 minutes, using flashbacks to deliver both the 'how' and 'why' in the episode's final moments.

The changes weren't just about plot, they reflected a fundamental reimagining of what a Highland police drama could be.

Deirdre Keir: [We knew we were] way, way out on the edge. It wasn't, 'Let's make a show that would frighten the wits out of everybody.' It was just a lovely script and this guy who got eaten by the lobsters.

DANIEL BOYLE'S SECOND script, 'Wee Jock's Lament', referencing Hamish's on-screen dog, Wee Jock, saw ghosts and the second sight—an ability to perceive future events through supernatural visions—play a part in Hamish's latest investigation.

Speaking to *Scotland on Sunday* in 1997, Robert Carlyle emphasised that realism hadn't been the goal for *Hamish Macbeth*. 'It was never meant to portray a Scotland as it is today. Lochdubh is a bizarre place and bizarre things can happen there. The programme works best when it's dark.' This wasn't meant to be a documentary-style portrayal of contemporary Highland life, but rather something more akin to a modern folk tale.

Ming Ho (In-house Script Editor, Zenith Productions): The mystical elements were unusual for a TV detective show, but were not a complete invention by Daniel. They had their roots in actual Highland myths/legends and beliefs that persist anecdotally in these parts to some extent today: second sight, ghosts and selkies, half seal/half woman sea creatures akin to mermaids. Daniel was fascinated by such stories and they were organic to his conception of Lochdubh.

BOYLE'S APPROACH CREATED a notable contrast with previous screen depictions of Highland mysticism, most notably Robin Hardy's cult film *The Wicker Man* (1973). It saw a Christian policeman from the Scottish mainland, Sergeant Howie (Edward Woodward), arrive on the island of Summerisle to investigate the disappearance of a young girl, only to encounter pagan rituals and human sacrifice.

Thankfully for BBC executives, *Hamish Macbeth*'s take on the supernatural and spirituality was much more suited to a Sunday evening TV slot, though Daniel Boyle's plans to kill off Hamish's dog in 'Wee Jock's Lament' did lead to concerns among the production team.

Deirdre Keir: Daniel had a Wee Jock, and he'd speak to people with his dog. So he wrote the script about what would happen if someone ran your dog over when it's your best friend. I read the script and thought, *Holy moly*. I'd done a regular police series in *Inspector Morse*, and we'd done some weird stuff. I loved the weird stuff. Having done two scripts with Daniel on *Morse*, I could just hear him in them. People who didn't know Daniel would pick up the script and say, 'Where's the rest of it? It's very thin,' and I'd say, 'No, that's the script.' It's usually a page a minute on a script, but Daniel doesn't do big chunks of description, not of the character or the place.

I went to Scott and said, 'If you don't give me this [to produce], I'll never speak to you again!' When Daniel gave him the 'Wee Jock' script he said, 'I've had a really good time writing this, but it'll never get made.' He knew it was wacky, ghosts and everything else.

Scott Meek: I received the first draft and called Dan to say, 'There are some things you just can't do on television, the audience won't let you, and you can't kill the dog. On a Sunday night we can't kill the dog, people will just crucify us.' Dan said, 'It's my dug, and if I want to kill it, I will.'

Daniel Boyle: I said that if the dog couldn't die, I wouldn't be involved. I'd leave. It was at one point suggested to me that the problem was because it was a wee dog. If it had been an Alsatian, it would have been OK. I've done similar stuff since then. I like that tone, black comedy.

Scott Meek: We had a barney about it and eventually I said, 'Alright, we'll kill the dog. But if we're going to kill the dog, Dan, we have to have a puppy and a moment of sentiment,' which is how we end up with Jock's lament.

Daniel Boyle: Hamish goes to the city to meet the parents who give him the new dog. People bought into it, it's not Chekhov.

LOOKING BACK ON the situation in 1997, Boyle managed to retain his sense of humour, telling *The Box*: 'Every time I hear a politician say there's too much violence on TV, I think of the trouble I had trying to get a dog killed on BBC One.'

Ming Ho: The pilot script by Daniel had already been commissioned: there may initially have been some debate over whether to go with Daniel's distinctive take on the idea or to aim for something closer to the books, which already had a readership following.

Scott Meek: By this time I'd spoken to Bobby [Carlyle] and said 'I think I've found something you should do.'

WHEN LATER ASKED about his initial reaction to the role, Carlyle told *The Box* he had bristled at the idea of playing what seemed, on paper, to be just another 'Scottish country copper'. But his trust in Zenith gave him confidence that there would be more to Hamish than met the eye.

Scott Meek: Bobby ran [theatre company] Raindog with Stuart Davids and Caroline Paterson, but he had no money and was looking for a career as an actor. He'd done a film with Ken Loach [1991's *Riff-Raff*]. We deliberately put him in *99-1* before *Hamish* to see him on television. Zenith wanted to set up a partnership with a Scottish company so that we wouldn't be seen as 'carpetbagging' north of the border. We had worked with Steve Clark-Hall before and he was a partner in [Edinburgh-based independent production company] Skyline and *Hamish* seemed like a good idea to do with them. Skyline knew Marion Chesney, and they didn't much like the direction we took the show in.

I put *Hamish* into development and then went to the BBC. Michael Wearing was the Head of Series in London and there was no Head of Drama at the BBC in Scotland.

GETTING PAST THE GATEKEEPERS

It was in August 1993 that Bill Bryden abruptly left his role as BBC Scotland's Head of Drama, with his replacement, 28-year-old independent producer Andrea Calderwood, announced in early November. Calderwood was known at the time for producing short films, including 1994's *Marooned*, starring Robert Carlyle.

Andrea Calderwood (Head of Drama, BBC Scotland 1994–97): I had no expectation that they would give me the job. It was all credit to [BBC Scotland Head of Television] Colin Cameron and [BBC Scotland Controller] John McCormick that they went for it. It was very controversial at the time and it was incredibly bold of them. I was 28, I was making short films. For whatever reason, they felt I would go for what they wanted, which is to get as many bold commissions from Scotland as I could.

I guess I had that fearlessness of youth, but also I just felt really clear as a Scottish producer what I wanted to see. People like Scott, Deirdre and Michael Wearing were incredibly generous, because God knows what they must have thought when I rocked up as a child producer, but they took me seriously. We collaborated and we went for it.

THE NEWS OF Calderwood's appointment wasn't met with universal positivity. Veteran playwright Peter McDougall told *The Herald*, 'I am not a sexist, but personally cannot believe that Bill Bryden's replacement is a lassie.' *Hamish Macbeth*'s future executive producer Trevor Davies wrote to the paper in Calderwood's defence, calling out the 'lassie' jibe: 'Andrea Calderwood is tough enough and smart enough to chew up him and his moustache.'

Andrea Calderwood: When I got the job there was a Scottish BAFTA event and some older male members of the industry poked me in the chest and kicked me in the shins, saying 'Nobody's going to take you seriously. How are you qualified for this job? Those people in London will just undermine you.'

But they didn't, particularly Michael Wearing and [Head of Single Drama] George Faber, who were the two execs I worked with a lot. They absolutely weren't like that and were really keen to do fresh, original stuff from Scotland.

CALDERWOOD ANNOUNCED HER first commissions, including 'a one-off ghost story starring Emma Thompson... *The Negotiator*, a 90-minute thriller starring Brian Cox; and *McBeth [sic]*, a six-part series about a Highland police constable written by Danny Boyle', at the end of November, just a few weeks after starting the job.

Andrea Calderwood: *Hamish* was in development when I arrived at BBC Scotland. Danny Boyle had helped me on a short film, so I knew him and his sense of humour. Colin Cameron gave me the first couple of scripts and I read them late at night, thinking *Bloody hell, I actually like these.* They were original, fun and they made me laugh out loud. Bobby Carlyle was already attached.

Scott Meek: The BBC tried to persuade me to leave the independent sector and come and do [the Head of Drama] job. I explained I thought they were out of their minds and somewhere in that conversation with Colin Cameron I think *Hamish* got commissioned largely as an act of trust through Michael Wearing.

Andrea Calderwood: It was presented to me that I had a choice. Now, that might just have been Colin Cameron being very political and appropriate because I was taking over as the head of drama, but my memory is that he said, 'Look, this thing is ready to go, we're really hoping it's going to go and hopefully you'll like it.' I thought, *If it makes me laugh, I'm sure it's going to make a section of the audience laugh, so let's go for it.*

Then I went to my first offers meeting in London before I officially started. I didn't know what an offers meeting was, but it's when the internal execs at the BBC pitched to [Controller of BBC One] Alan Yentob and all the other BBC executives. I went in with Colin Cameron and it was very intimidating, it was a U-shaped table and there were around 20 people sitting around it. I tried to sit at the side, but Colin said, 'No, you sit here in Alan's eyeline.' Alan said, 'It's not going to be like *Heartbeat* [1992–2010], is it?' I hadn't watched *Heartbeat* and had no idea, but said, 'No, it's not going to be like *Heartbeat*.'

I remember using the inimitable phrase, 'It's going to be really romantic and charming, and there's shagging in the heather.' Alan then said yes. In my head, I helped get it over the line and Michael Wearing was very supportive of it.

Deirdre Keir: Nowadays everyone does one episode of something and it all hangs on that, so it was a big commitment from BBC Scotland to give us six based on two scripts.

Andrea Calderwood: There was a real push to do more in Scotland and I think, having hired me, they needed to back me. But also, with Scott wanting to do the show and Bobby Carlyle being the star that he was, I think it was the right combination. The fact that Danny had set it up with that tone, it was almost like you could do anything. There was a lot of optimism, boldness and confidence, people brought that from other things: Bobby was confident from his theatre work and films, Scott is always confident and was doing distinctive films and Deirdre had her brilliant TV experience.

PRODUCER DEIRDRE KEIR soon began her search for a lead director who could handle the show's delicate balance of comedy and drama. 'I sat with the scripts and thought about whose work I'd done that I really liked,' she remembers, 'but none of the directors I'd worked with were weird enough.'

The recommendation of Nicholas Renton, a director with several single BBC plays under his belt and episodes of ITV's *Maigret* (1992-93), came from a trusted colleague. Renton's understanding of the material was immediate, particularly regarding *Hamish Macbeth*'s more outlandish elements.

Nicholas Renton: Deirdre gave me the 'Wee Jock' script and said, 'If you understand this, you'll understand anything.' That was the bible. You could see from those two scripts where you had to be. You had to be real, you had to be in a community, you had to have a kind of thrill, but it wasn't meant to be a specious thriller and it was very character driven.

Scott Meek: Nick directed a lot of the best episodes and he was the director who started it off. *Hamish* was very much a thing in and of itself, tonally, and Nick was very responsible for that.

TWO
RAINDOGS AND RISING TALENT

WHEN JULIA DUFF took on her first job as an independent casting director in 1993, she faced a challenge. The BBC had commissioned a new Scotland-set police drama and needed a cast who could navigate the tricky balance between comedy and darkness that writer Daniel Boyle was crafting, while maintaining authentic Scottish voices.

Duff had already encountered Robert Carlyle's particular approach to choosing roles while working as a casting assistant on Mel Gibson's *Braveheart* (1995). 'Gibson was absolutely determined to have Bobby,' she says, 'but he refused to do it because he didn't trust what someone like Mel would do with that story. More money? Nope. He wouldn't do *Rob Roy* [1995] either.'

This principled stance was characteristic of Carlyle's career choices. 'I wasn't really interested in being a hairy-arsed Highlander running up a hill,' he told the *Sydney Morning Herald*. 'If you're going to make films about Scotland in Scotland, there are issues you can talk about that are current. You're in danger of romanticising the whole thing if you go too far back.'

The show's star had already been chosen by the time Duff joined *Hamish Macbeth*. As an actor whose reputation primarily rested on intense dramatic roles, the idea of an edgy Glasgow performer playing a laid-back policeman raised eyebrows. But executive producer Scott Meek had spotted something in Carlyle that others hadn't yet recognised, a versatility that could transform this unlikely choice into something special.

'We didn't have to seek casting approvals,' says Meek, 'otherwise it's possible the BBC would have said, "Can you not get somebody known?"' Andrea Calderwood, then Head of Drama at BBC Scotland, remembers her first meeting with Controller of BBC One, Alan Yentob. 'Alan was a bit sceptical. Because I'd just made a short film with Bobby in which he was incredibly charming, I said, "I think he's gorgeous and all my friends fancy him."'

For Carlyle, the decision to take on a Sunday night BBC drama wasn't straightforward. 'I thought long and hard before I accepted the project,' he told *Time Out* in 1996. 'But Hamish appealed to me because here was someone who'd grown up through the Thatcher years and become one of the favoured few—a policeman—yet he has absolutely no ambition.'

'I didn't know who he was,' admits lead director Nicholas Renton. 'I spoke to a producer friend of mine who said he was the "Al Pacino of Scotland". Bobby was well known in Scotland as an extraordinary young actor. He'd done *Cracker* [1993–96] just before and you think, *This guy's going to go into something that has wit and ambiguity, how's he going to fit into that?*'

CARLYLE HAD MADE an impact in the ITV crime drama *Cracker*, starring Robbie Coltrane as the abrasive but brilliant criminal psychologist, Dr Eddie 'Fitz' Fitzgerald. The three-part story 'To Be a Somebody', broadcast in October 1994, featured Carlyle as Albie Kinsella, a man driven to murder after his father's death. It was an emotionally raw performance that stood in stark contrast to the gentler humour of *Hamish Macbeth*.

In interviews during early 1995, Carlyle addressed the apparent disconnect between his intense dramatic roles and this lighter, Sunday-night fare. Speaking to *Radio Times*, he explained, 'I don't find it difficult to go from Albie to Hamish. It's about an attitude, about understanding the character.' As he told *The List*, traditional casting would never have led to him: 'If you went looking for an actor to play a conventional cop, Bobby Carlyle would be the last person you went to.'

This choice resonated with writer Daniel Boyle, who told *The Box* that the casting of Robert Carlyle meant that, 'Hamish could not be a voluble, excitable character.'

Director Nicholas Renton remembers an early meeting where Carlyle's commitment to understanding the role became clear: 'I had a drink with him and he asked me this really difficult question: "Why do you think I should be Hamish Macbeth?" He was asking for some kind of confirmation of something within him.'

This thoughtful approach impressed Daniel Boyle, who noted in *The Guardian* that '[Bobby] asks you questions that you'd never even considered about what a character might be thinking.'

For Carlyle, even commercial television needed to have deeper purpose. 'The most important thing for me is that a project has some kind of social worth,' he explained to *The Guardian*. 'At its base level, acting is such a frivolous thing to do, so you want to try and use that skill on something that has something to say. *Hamish Macbeth* is different, that's commercial television. But it does have its wee bits of subversion—the two most respected members of the village, for example, they are the hash-smokers.'

The actor's careful consideration of roles had become something of a trademark. Casting director Julia Duff notes that 'he was very aware of his standing in the acting fraternity in Scotland,' with Daniel Boyle adding that Carlyle was 'completely wrong but right [as Hamish]. He's got a desire to be the psychopath, but with an edge.'

It's telling that even at an early stage, Carlyle spoke of his role in *Hamish Macbeth* in terms of survival rather than opportunity. 'The stuff that I've been doing over the past three years has been, for want of a better word, the arthouse circuit,' he told *The List*, before adding with characteristic intensity, 'I felt that the canon of work I'd produced so far was strong enough to do this [*Hamish Macbeth*], that I could survive it.'

For an actor already making his mark in edgier productions, the prospect of leading a BBC Sunday night drama seemed to represent not a career breakthrough but a potential artistic compromise that would require careful navigation.

WIDENING THE SEARCH

Writer Stuart Hepburn remembers his initial scepticism about Robert Carlyle's casting: 'Scott Meek told me about reading M.C. Beaton's books and saying he was going to make it. He said, "Do you know what the premise is? It's a Highland cop who doesn't want to get promoted, and I've got Bobby Carlyle." I thought, *Bobby's the crook, the ducker and diver. He's the guy that gets into trouble. Cop?!* Of course, what you do is create a group of people around him that makes sense: it was a work of genius to put Bobby in the middle of that.'

With the 32-year-old Carlyle secured as their unconventional leading man, the production team faced the challenge of building an equally distinctive ensemble around him.

Producer Deirdre Keir knew they needed to look beyond the usual channels: 'I hadn't worked with Julia Duff before, but I'd heard she knew her Scottish actors. I said to her, "It'd be good to get faces we don't know. This is comedy/tragedy so they're not going to be mugging and if they're straight actors, they need to know timing."'

At a time when Scottish actors typically had to travel to London for auditions, Duff took the unusual step of meeting them in Glasgow. 'It was quite tough,' she recalls, 'because you had to spend a lot of time at the Tron [and other theatres] trying to make them believe it was worth doing, selling it.' Nicholas Renton notes the political dimension: 'Julia said, "It's like Scottish politics, there are little cliques." There were the Scottish actors who had gone to London to make a living and stayed down there. There was a big north/south thing.'

One rich source of talent came from Robert Carlyle's own theatre company, Raindog. 'When *Hamish* first came up,' Carlyle explained to an audience at the Belfast Film Festival in 2019, 'the casting people asked me, "Who do you think we could cast?" I'd been directing for many years before that and we had an ensemble with Raindog, about 20 of us that came and went. I think just about every single person in *Hamish*

Macbeth was in Raindog, nearly all of them. I was able to work with my friends.'

'Julia brought people in to meet us,' explains Deirdre Keir. 'It was very free flowing, and that's difficult for an actor if they don't know what they're coming to read for. She said, "Just get a feeling for these people." She had ideas of who she thought could play what, but most casting directors won't say, "I think you should have him or her."'

The resulting ensemble would blend established Scottish TV talent with emerging theatrical performers, creating a cast as eclectic as the Lochdubh residents themselves.

'I would never really have been interested in playing the front man for a series if it was only about him,' revealed Carlyle to *Radio Times* during filming in 1995. 'The great thing about *Hamish Macbeth* is that there are seven or eight other characters who we could quite easily base an episode around and it would be entertaining viewing. So I knew the pressure would be taken off me to a certain extent.'

'Producers can cast, hoping that the chemistry will work, especially a thing like *Hamish* where you're creating a community,' adds Sutherland-born actor Jimmy Yuill, best remembered for his role in *Local Hero* (1983), who won the part of local wheeler dealer, Lachlan McCrae Sr, while appearing concurrently in ITV's *Wycliffe* (1993–98). 'You can get a wee one, a tall one, a fat one, a thin one, but that doesn't mean that the chemistry will work. But I really think it did.'

Stuart Davids, a co-founder of Raindog, took on the role of Yuill's on-screen son, Lachie McCrae Jr, while Ralph Riach, familiar to TV audiences from *Chancer* (1990–91) and *Doctor Finlay* (1993–96), would bring gravitas as TV John, so-called because he was the first person to own a television set in Lochdubh.

Shirley Henderson, whose intense performance in *The Advocates* (1991–92) had marked her as a rising star, was cast as determined reporter Isobel Sutherland, while Valerie Gogan, who had previously worked with producer Scott Meek on the mini-series *Heart of the High Country* (1985) became Hamish's on-off girlfriend, Alex Maclean.

With family roots in the Highlands, Edinburgh-born Duncan Duff brought authenticity to Doc Brown, while veteran character actor Brian Pettifer, whose career stretched back to *The Vital Spark* (1965–74), was paired with Anne Lacey, respected for her extensive stage work, as the endearingly romantic Rory Campbell and Esme Murray.

Stuart McGugan, known for roles in comedy series *It Ain't Half Hot Mum* (1974–81) and the 1987 drama *Tutti Frutti*, joined *Rab C. Nesbitt*'s (1988–2014) Barbara Rafferty as publicans Barney and Agnes Meldrum, while actor and writer David Ashton, took on the recurring role of Major Roddy Maclean.

Duncan Duff (Doc Brown): I was just going for a meeting and I met Nick Renton. I thought it was brilliant, it was like the police show set in a small community, but with that delicious sort of twist on it and that darkness that Danny Boyle brought to it. I was recalled, and I met Deirdre and Nick was there again, and Julia Duff. [When they later offered me the part] I was absolutely delighted. It was my first time as a regular and I thought, *Yeah, this is great.* It gives you a certain amount of stability, which is very much in short supply in an actor's life.

Somebody mischievously put a rumour around that the only reason that I'd got the job was because Julia Duff was my cousin. I remember several people were outraged, as if there was some sort of nepotism going on. But there's actually no relation between Julia and me whatsoever.

Nicholas Renton: One or two actors came in and you knew they didn't want to be in it, you didn't know why.

Deirdre Keir: They were frightened they were going to be in something that was an embarrassment.

Julia Duff: I don't think people got it.

Duncan Duff: My father was born in Portmahomack and brought up in Dingwall, so I used to go up every year and I know a little what the Highlands is about. I know that it's completely the opposite of what most people's impressions are, all being very light-hearted and people are a bit stupid and a bit soft. It's a tough environment, let alone people's lives are pretty tough as well. But there is that kind of twinkle in the eye and a wee bit of, 'You may think I'm stupid, but...' and I love that.

Jimmy Yuill (Lachlan McCrae Sr): I'd never read the books. It looked like a fantastic job and it was a chance to go home, genuinely home [to the north of Scotland]. It was a chance to not have to hide your voice. It's not your accent, it's your voice. I think of three people I know for every part. I write down every single thing about them and eventually come down to one. I'm really playing somebody I know, through me. That's the base camp. Then you have the lines from the writer, which the person you're based on will never have said.

David Ashton: Jimmy [Yuill] was terrific. I've used him in one of my stage plays. He had it in his bones because he was from up there.

Jimmy Yuill: I was doing *Wycliffe* at the time and they were paying me stupid money for that. My agent said 'No' to *Hamish*, but eventually they said, 'Yes, but you have to be the dialect coach as well.' I said, 'I'm sorry, I'm not telling Brian Pettifer how to put on an accent. Ralph Riach's from Elgin for God's sake.'

Deirdre Keir: Julia had visited Raindog and knew that there was some very good talent in there. Stuart Davids came from there, but there was no obligation [to cast anyone]. That's not the way Bobby does things, but then you're off to a flying start as far as he's concerned because he already has actors around him who know him.

Stuart Davids: I went to drama college when I was 18, had done *Taggart* [1983–2010] and worked with various theatre companies. Myself, Robert [Carlyle] and Caroline Paterson were living together at the time. Robert had read the script and said he thought there was a part that was right for me, so I just went up for it one day and I got it the next. Suddenly, I was up in Plockton.

Julia Duff: Stuart Davids wasn't technically a screen actor, but he grew. We had quite a few people in and it wasn't gelling, and we remembered Stuart.

Deirdre Keir: He was tremendously willing and eager.

Julia Duff: And his naivety was useful.

Jimmy Yuill: I loved that casting. I'm 5-foot-8 and I thought, *He's obviously not my son, he's 6-foot-4!* I said to Nick Renton, 'It's great. You cast people who look nothing alike.' 'How do you mean?' 'Well, he's obviously not my boy is he?' 'How do you mean?' I'm not saying somebody 5-foot-8 can't have a 6-

foot-4 child, I'm just saying people in the village would have been asking questions.

Valerie Gogan: I was living with my best friend Susannah. Her dad was a very famous actor called Tony Doyle who was in *Ballykissangel* [1996–2001], and suddenly I was going up for this series called *Hamish Macbeth*. I'd met Scott Meek before because I'd done a big mini-series just six months out of drama school, which I went to New Zealand to shoot. Scott really championed me and I got that part, so we were good friends, although I hadn't seen him for years.

I felt quite relaxed going in. Scott was there and Nick [Renton] and I remember it had been nice weather, so I went in maybe not as nervous as I might've normally been. I don't think I'd even read any of the script. I think we just chatted. Looking back, I don't know how I got it. I didn't have to prove myself.

Shirley Henderson: I don't remember the audition, but I remember walking along Baker Street. I got the job not knowing what was going to happen with her.

Stuart Hepburn: I knew Shirley from *The Advocates*. She gave one of the most astonishing performances I'd ever seen, a pocket battleship. She's like a quiet volcano.

Shirley Henderson: I wasn't involved in all the early shenanigans, it was dotted about and so I don't think they had very much for me to go by, so maybe it was just a chit chat at the audition. It was just, 'Be yourself and see what happens with it.'

Valerie Gogan: I only knew I'd be in one episode at that point. I knew she was the laird's daughter. I knew that Hamish and her had a relationship beforehand and that she liked him, but it was not plain sailing, so to speak. I also knew that there would be two love interests. I came down to London to go to drama school, so I'd left Scotland, anyway. Not that I have a particularly posh accent, but I also don't have a strong Glaswegian accent. So I was more the posh girl that was coming back to the village.

David Ashton: I wasn't one of the main characters, for want of a better word, but I was in quite a few episodes. There were some that I had a very strong narrative part in, which was very rewarding. Danny has this knack of somehow getting through to feelings that are deceptively simple. You think it's simple, but it's not at all. There's a great deal of craft in the writing, but it doesn't advertise its cleverness.

Brian Pettifer: There was an audition in London. It seemed to go alright. I was enthusiastic about the series and they offered me the part of Rory.

Anne Lacey: They were seeing lots of people, trying to match them up. There was no script. I just met them, got offered it and sent the scripts. At first I remember thinking that it wasn't a fun part, but I was so glad I did it.

Brian Pettifer: They mentioned there'd been books but not to bother reading them. The series would be completely different. I said it sounded a bit like *Twin Peaks* [1990–91] and they said, 'That's exactly the sort of thing we're looking for.' I'm not a great reader of scripts, so I probably didn't read them, I just do the bits that I'm in and that's it. You knew which episodes were better than others, the cast would say, 'This is a really good episode,' and that's kind of how it went.

Anne Lacey: They wanted to pair [Brian Pettifer and I] up. I think if Brian hadn't done it they might have gone without me, chosen someone more suited to another actor.

Stuart McGugan: My agent put me up for it and I went to see Deirdre Keir. I met her and the director just before I was off to France on holiday, and I got called in to speak about playing the guy who runs the bar, which is ironic as I'm a non-drinker. The premise was great, I could relate well to it being from Letham in Forfar and the characters were recognisable.

Barbara Rafferty: I'd worked with Bobby a lot in the theatre with Raindog. These fun, quirky scripts would come in from Danny Boyle.

Stuart Hepburn: When you see folk like Anne Lacey and Barbara Rafferty getting parts, you know the producers aren't going for the obvious and they're going for authentic Scots and good actors. You knew you had folk who could deliver the lines. Both actresses have great depth and the ability to show real emotion.

Ralph Riach: [For *Hamish*], I remember a costume designer friend was going to be working on the show, so I just vaguely heard the name [*Hamish Macbeth*]. Then I got a call to go and see Deirdre Keir and Nick Renton at the BBC on Queen Margaret Drive in Glasgow, and they talked a lot about the series and TV John and it was a big part. They gave me a couple of scripts to take home, and I read them and wondered what part they had in mind. It couldn't be TV John, as I'd never been up for anything of that size.

A week later, I went through to see them and I thought they'd ask me to read for them and they didn't. We talked about the scripts, and at the end of it they said, 'Thanks very much.' There was a train strike, and I was on the bus home. I thought *Ah well*, and when I got home, there was a call from my agent to say, 'Ye bugger, they've given you TV John!' I was over the moon.

Stuart McGugan: I didn't know many of the cast. I didn't know Babs Rafferty and didn't even know Bobby Carlyle. I remember him coming up to me in the bar and me asking him who he was playing. Not a very diplomatic thing to do, but he took it well. Though he remembered it three years later at the farewell party. But you float in and hope it's going to be a good gig.

Ralph Riach: As far as Bobby was concerned, I'd met him before and knew him, not that well, but every time I saw him there was a hug. He's such a generous actor, so easy to work with.

Shirley Henderson: It felt very equal. Everything linked back to Bobby and the police station, but the rest of it felt very ensemble, very even, which is what we liked about it.

Nicholas Renton: [With Bobby] we learned as we went and we got something that was reciprocal and we grew together. He grew, we grew and the cast grew around him. But you have to be blessed with all the people in the right place to start with.

David Ashton: As a cast, I don't remember us having crossed words, and I don't mean it was lovey-dovey, but we respected each other and that gave it a real flavour.

Andrea Calderwood: *Hamish* captured that sense of a really distinctive community. Small communities have a whole range of characters. You don't need to be in a city to have a massive range of characters, because all the characters are there in microcosm.

Deirdre Keir: Had we not had Julia getting people in regardless where they lived, worked, how much telly or theatre they'd done, that show wouldn't have [been what it was].

HAMISH'S CAST WAS rounded out by the addition of one more performer who would go on to achieve even more fame than some of the humans around him.

Seven-year-old West Highland Terrier Zippy may have played a character called Wee Jock on screen, but according to his owner Helen, the 'big softie at heart' was a natural performer. His role demanded a complex range of behaviours, from pricking up his ears and following Hamish devotedly to acting jealous and growling menacingly on command.

Producer Deirdre Keir was impressed by how quickly Zippy mastered these tasks, noting that once he understood what was required, he became a reliable 'one-take performer'.

THREE
A TALE OF TWO HAMISHES

STANDING at her kitchen window in the Cotswolds, M.C. Beaton stared at the morning's post. Among the usual letters lay a thick BBC contract, its legal language granting away the TV rights to her books.

The fee seemed modest: £5,000 per episode for the first two, dropping to £2,500 thereafter with no repeat fees or residuals for foreign sales. But after nearly a decade of Hamish living solely on the page, perhaps it was time to let him find a new audience.

She couldn't have known then how unrecognisable her creation would become in others' hands. Zenith Productions would soon reimagine the tall, red-headed constable she'd crafted through multiple novels. Her mysteries, beloved by readers who appreciated their crimes cosy and their violence minimal, were about to take a sharp turn.

The first warning signs came with the announcement that a relatively unknown young Glaswegian actor would be the small screen Hamish. As Beaton told *Woman's Hour* in 2014, 'I wrote about a 6-foot, laid-back Highlander and I got a 5-foot-8 Glaswegian with a chip on both shoulders.'

Though Beaton would be more involved in the later TV adaptation of her *Agatha Raisin* book series, for *Hamish Macbeth* the baton was being passed and the recipient was running in an entirely different direction. As she later explained to *Radio Times*, 'I had to let go of [my Hamish]. You do when something is adapted for film or TV. What is it Hollywood says about writers: "Writers are on the same level as hookers." Ah well.'

Ming Ho (In-house Script Editor, Zenith Productions): M.C. Beaton was not involved in the development of the scripts. This is par for the course for a series of books optioned for TV, particularly detective stories: the author licenses the underlying rights in the property for adaptation in another medium. Unless that original author also adapts the work for the screen, the TV series then becomes an entity in its own right, based on the characters and 'world of the show' as established by the lead screenwriter, which may be quite different for production reasons. Some novelists can be more pragmatic about this; it's harder if you're expecting your work to be faithfully transferred to screen, exactly as it appears in the books.

Andrea Calderwood (Head of Drama, BBC Scotland 1994–97): I never met the author of the books, but there was a bit of discussion that she wasn't 100% happy about it being quite a left-field spin on her stories. She was concerned that Hamish didn't have red hair. I think she possibly wanted it to be more literal than the approach that Danny [Boyle] had taken.

Duncan Duff (Doc Brown): The talk at the time was that these books were not selling huge amounts, and she was getting a decent amount of money for something that would otherwise never have been picked up. Nobody was going to turn the book into a TV series in a literal way. They're very light.

Stuart McGugan (Barney Meldrum): She's lucky that her books were picked up.

Mandie Fletcher (Director): I suspect it's because she wasn't involved. She was really involved in *Agatha Raisin* [2014–22] and nobody enjoys being held at arm's length. In my experience, that's what it's about. I don't know many people who didn't like the series, so I suspect that goes deeper.

Ming Ho: As soon as Daniel [Boyle] came on board it was his show, based on his take on Highland sensibility—mystical, otherworldly and his own particular style of black humour. Once the BBC became involved and the other scripts for series one were commissioned, we were clear that we were making Daniel's *Hamish*. Within Zenith, we never tried to push it down another road.

Andrea Calderwood: Danny put a surreal spin on the genre. It wasn't a straightforward, cosy detective series. It had things like the death of Wee Jock, and it was very distinctive, in the way that Danny's mind works.

Deirdre Keir (Producer): Dominic Minghella came in as my PA on the comedy-drama I did for Zenith before *Hamish*. That took a bit of training, as he hadn't been in a production office. He'd sit working away on things and phones would be ringing and everyone would look at him to answer them. Going onto *Hamish*, he asked if he could be promoted to script editor and I said, 'OK, and when we go up [to Plockton] you'll come up too.'

Dominic Minghella (Script Editor, Series One; Writer): It was clearly a quality idea from a great scriptwriter. I loved the dark, understated humour and it was exciting to contemplate working on something that wasn't too earnest.

A HIGHLAND MAVERICK

Early discussions between Daniel Boyle and Scott Meek had led the pair to settle on US Western series, *Maverick*, as a template for the small screen *Hamish Macbeth*. The show had cleverly subverted the traditional hero: James Garner and Jack Kelly played brothers Bret and Bart Maverick, charming gamblers who outsmarted their adversaries with cunning rather than brute force. Each week would see the brothers alternate as lead, the other absent until the following week.

A more recent reference point had been the US comedy-drama series *Northern Exposure* (1990–95), which showcased a small Alaskan town where eccentric locals and their outsider protagonist navigated themes of identity and belonging. With storylines featuring a local election spiralling into chaos and another where a DJ's poetic radio broadcasts sparked unexpected ripple effects among the townsfolk, the show's tone became a comparison for *Hamish Macbeth*.

Dominic Minghella: *Hamish* stands in a tradition of 'straight guy in wacky world' shows like *Northern Exposure*, which I very much admired and was a touchstone for me as we put series one together.

Nicholas Renton: *Northern Exposure* was lurking in the background, so if you're going to go into that territory, one thing you can't be is funny, nor can you be straight. There's a kind of blend.

Dominic Minghella: These shows take the audience to a far-flung, particular place, with its own geography and community. They're hard to do without patronising the locals, and without asking the central character to always wear a 'What the hell!?' expression... but there will always be a pleasure to them. Transporting the audience should always be something we aspire to do.

Stuart Davids (Lachie McCrae Jr): It was very much inspired by *Northern Exposure* and it could have gone that way. Had it been post-watershed, it would have been much more quirky. It was like creating a world where anything could happen to these people living in a small village.

Stuart McGugan: There was the *Northern Exposure* influence: they had the moose, we had the Highland cows. There was also a big Western influence.

SPEAKING AT THE Belfast Film Festival in 2019, Robert Carlyle recalled his childhood ambitions. '[I had] no notion really of being an actor. Maybe a notion of being a cowboy, that would have been something I wanted to do.' Hamish presented him with the opportunity, as he told *The Herald* in 1995: 'Hamish Macbeth sees himself as the sheriff of a one-horse town, with the role of keeping the peace.'

Duncan Duff: It was set in a West Highland village, but all the tropes and stock characters that you see in Westerns were there. The saloon owner, the store owner, the doc and the sheriff.

Barbara Rafferty (Agnes Meldrum): That's exactly how the series was set up, about the Wild West [of Scotland], the locals were a law unto themselves. All those undercurrents made it fabulous. I think it could have got darker. I think the BBC were a bit scared at just how dark Danny wanted to make it, so they brought in the other writers to balance it out. They were all good, but Danny had that darkness.

Daniel Boyle: I kept the name of the village: that was a legal requirement. In the books, Hamish is a big lump that wanders around talking to people, and there are always murders; to have murders every week [on TV] was impossible.

Ming Ho: I don't recall Daniel being restricted to keeping only Hamish and Lochdubh from the books. My impression is those were the elements that were fruitful for him, along with the basic idea of a love triangle between Hamish, the laird's daughter and a news reporter rival.

Scott Meek (Executive Producer): We did *Inspector Morse* for seven years and honestly, the murder mysteries aren't what sustains a show like that either. *Morse* was basically a character comedy between Morse and Lewis and the murders were incidental.

ROUNDING-UP THE WRITERS

Having established the world of *Hamish Macbeth* in his first two scripts, Daniel Boyle was joined by four more writers charged with replicating the series style while also adding their own spin on the characters and setting.

Ming Ho: *Hamish* was commissioned as a cop show, although it soon became apparent in development that it was really a character comedy-drama, not a whodunnit or police procedural.

Deirdre Keir: We said to the writers, 'We've got Lochdubh and these characters and each week majoring one character who gets their moment in the sun.' They read Daniel's scripts and as soon as there was footage, we showed it to them. We showed them photographs so they could see how it was shaping up. They had Daniel's take on who TV John was and who Barney was.

Ming Ho: Series one's writers were drawn principally from detective drama. Daniel had worked on *Morse*; Stuart Hepburn came from *Taggart*.

Stuart Hepburn (Writer): When Scott Meek comes to you and says, 'Do you want to write two episodes of this new Scottish comedy-drama?' you don't say no. I thought [Dan's scripts] were tremendously irreverent. I felt I was in the middle of a really good thing. The idea of an irreverent cop was just wonderful, so when Bobby kicked the headlamp in, that for me was the magical moment, I thought, *That's the sort of cop show I want to write. I want to be part of this.*

Deirdre Keir: Stuart got the tone right away.

Stuart Hepburn: I like to think I can seed in who did what, and I like the idea there's a wee secret you discover at the end. I blame my father. He was a member of the crime club, so by the time I was 10 I'd read John Creasey, every *Miss Marple* and I loved whodunnits. Subverting the audience's belief in who had done it really interested me. I tend to do that, then I ask, 'Why should I care emotionally about that?' That would be the secondary thing to be planted under the whodunnit.

You've got three levels: the cheeky chappie story, the whodunnit and under that the emotional bang of lost love. And usually you're writing it back to front, so you come up with the surface thing first. Most ideas are just fragments and you've got to deliver that to the audience in a way that they want but don't expect. Audiences love it. Ming would say, 'I've put the rewrites in, see what you think of them,' and they'd be better than my version. Very clever.

Ming Ho: Bryan Elsley had a track record in popular drama such as *Casualty* [1986–] and *London's Burning* [1988–2002]. I think he was known to Scott and Deirdre from his original BBC play, *Govan Ghost Story* [1989], and may also have come to us via BBC Scotland executive producer Andrea Calderwood, for whom he adapted Iain Banks' *The Crow Road* [1996], which was probably in development around the time we were starting *Hamish*.

Bryan Elsley (Writer): I'd been doing quite a lot of work with BBC Scotland one way and another, not all of it seeing the light of day, but I was around and about in Glasgow. By then I'd moved to the Lake District, but I'd been working in Scotland fairly consistently. I was quite interested in the idea of a Scottish comedy-drama that wasn't kooky or was vaguely taking the piss out of itself.

Ming Ho: Dominic Minghella was the script editor for series one and Julian Spilsbury was the wild card for the final episode, which was more of an action drama. I think we did explore a couple of others to storyline stage, but didn't go to script.

Dominic Minghella: I think I was always asking to write. Who wouldn't want to write *Hamish Macbeth*?

Ming Ho: There was no overall storylining for either the individual episodes or each series, beyond general character arcs for the triangle of Hamish/Alex/Isobel—which would be very unusual today, where series are heavily storylined by the showrunner/production team before the episodes are assigned to writers.

Stuart Hepburn: I'd never met Dan; we all met together in London and there were eight of us round a table. I knew Dan had written [the 1989 *Screen Two* drama] *Leaving*, which I loved: I wondered, *Which one is Danny Boyle?* I'd read the script and liked it, but somebody asked what we thought about it. Silence. I started talking, saying, 'I loved the tone, structurally I'm a bit worried about this bit...' and in walks this man. Very dapper, raincoat and briefcase. 'The weather's dreadful out there. Sorry I'm late folks.'

I'm halfway through this sentence, pontificating what I think about this script, and it's obvious that this is Daniel Boyle. I paused, then thought I better keep talking. Danny is sitting across from me and he doesn't know me from Adam: 'Is that right? Is that what you think?' 'Aye.'

So we start giving it this chat and the producer thought a fight was going to start between these two Scottish 'alpha males'; me and Danny knew everything was cool, and Danny and me ended up staying and getting drunk and having the most brilliant time. Danny told me he thought I was the producer. Deirdre thought there might not be a fight, but wasn't sure. We got on like a house on fire, but he's much more iconoclastic than me: he has much more balls to do the big thing differently than me, and he sticks to it. I'm more of an equivocator.

Stuart Davids: Danny's scripts are tremendous and you always enjoyed working on a Danny Boyle script more than the others just because you knew he was going to do something that was quirky. I think it was hard for the other writers to emulate that.

Daniel Boyle: People took to the heightened style and it emboldened me. Maybe I went too far?

LOBSTERS, A LAMENT AND A LEAP OF FAITH

Ming Ho: Some episodes were notably more 'plotty' than others, but the plots could be bizarre because the style was not social realism. The whole thing came together more organically than a new series would be developed now.

Dominic Minghella: For the ensemble, I felt as though we ought to be respectful of the locals; although their behaviour was sometimes daft, I wanted it to be grounded in something human. I hope we got some of that right.

Ming Ho: *Hamish* evolved very organically, with each episode being quite a separate film; this was a reflection of the way we worked at Zenith in general. The process tends to be much more industrial nowadays, with series built from the outset for longevity and uniform marketing. Tone, and consistency thereof, was always the challenge on *Hamish*. Daniel's scripts were very original and often quite different from each other, let alone the other writers; it really wasn't a uniform show.

Stuart Davids: As the series progressed, the scripts got better. Danny would also go up to Plockton to write the scripts, so it was like being in a theatre company, which you don't always get in TV.

Deirdre Keir: The scripts went to a script editor at BBC Scotland, and Colin Cameron, Head of Television at BBC Scotland, read them as well. I didn't get lots of notes. God, it was wonderful, partly because we were very far away. There were fax machines but no mobile phone reception, so if I wasn't sitting at my desk, nobody could reach me, and most days I was out.

KEIR HAD MADE the decision early on to film the fifth episode, 'Wee Jock's Lament', first rather than the episode that would be broadcast first, 'The Great Lochdubh Salt Robbery'.

Deirdre Keir: I was absolutely adamant we weren't going to shoot episode one first, because if we didn't know who we were when we started out then it's really hard to expect the actors to find their feet for the first episode for something like this. So we started with something very outré with Ken Hutchison and Billy McColl [as escaped convicts Harry Dobbs and Francie McGilp in 'Wee Jock's Lament'].

Duncan Duff: The thinking was that the production would have found its feet by the time you're shooting the first episode. It's going to be the first impression that people are going to get of the show and you want to make sure that everybody in every department is completely on top of what they're doing by that stage.

Julia Duff: It was a great leap of faith on the part of the actors because they didn't know what they were buying into. [Usually] if you cast a series then they know what their journey is, but they didn't have a clue.

Stuart McGugan: You don't see any of the scripts before it starts, it's a huge leap of faith.

Nicholas Renton: Often the complaint on more conventional series by episode three is, 'Where are the other scripts, we don't know who we are or where we're going. How can I play it?' They never once did that.

Deirdre Keir: Because in those first scripts there's just a tiny look at Hamish, Shirley did once come to me and said, 'I don't know what I'm doing.' It's not easy if you start with episode five.

Shirley Henderson (Isobel Sutherland): I remember there not being much to go with and they couldn't tell me the story-line or where it was going to go.

Deirdre Keir: All I could say is, 'This character is going to have quite a hard time because no sensible woman would choose to fall in love with Hamish but it is going to burn and burn. I promise you I'm looking after it and it'll go up and down.' I could see her thinking, *I wish I hadn't started this conversation...*

Shirley Henderson: It's daft what people think. I was probably very keen, listening hard, very shy, trying to do my best... I was just trying to get any clues into what this thing was. They're the writers and producers beavering away in the background and revealing things on a need-to-know basis.

Ming Ho: Daniel created the central relationship between Hamish and TV John, who I think was based on someone he had known, who had been the first person in his community to get a TV in the 1950s/1960s.

Ralph Riach (TV John McIver): We worked out this thing where maybe TV John was Hamish's godfather. We reckoned that his parents were from Lochdubh and had moved to Glasgow where he was born. Something in his life must have happened where he said, 'I've got to get away from this, I just want to be an ordinary bobby. I don't want any promotion, I just want to live here and have a quiet life.' There was also a notion that TV John might have been in the Merchant Navy, he'd been to all sorts of foreign climes and knew lots of things.

ROBERT CARLYLE DISCUSSED Hamish and TV John's relationship in a 1997 interview with *The Herald*, stating the latter 'was Hamish's surrogate father and, in a way, Ralph almost became that for me. We had known each other before we started the series and, during the filming, we struck up this really fantastic friendship.'

The actor expanded on his backstory for Hamish in a 1995 interview with the *Daily Express*. Hamish was born in Lochdubh where his father served as the local policeman. When Hamish was just three-years-old, the family relocated to Glasgow, and he eventually followed in his father's footsteps by joining the police force. After working in the city for a decade, an unspecified incident prompted Hamish to return to his birthplace. As Carlyle explained, Hamish's self-appointed mission became 'to protect this little town from any of those outside influences', a motivation that informed much of the character's actions throughout the series.

WEE DOG, BIG PROBLEM

Hamish's other enduring relationship throughout the series was with his canine sidekick, Wee Jock, though it wasn't always harmonious.

Robert Carlyle questioned whether a West Highland Terrier was the right choice for the character. Speaking to *The Sydney Morning Herald* in 1997, he explained, 'I've always said that if Hamish is going to have a dog, a West Highland terrier is the last dog he'd have. He'd have a collie. A whopping dog. That was Danny. Because Danny Boyle has a dog that happens to be a West Highland terrier and happens to be called Jock. He wrote his own bloody dog in!'

Writer Stuart Hepburn recalls the weekly production updates from producer Deirdre Keir, which sometimes included unexpected tidbits about the show's canine star. 'Deirdre would phone you every Monday and let you know what was happening,' he says. 'I've worked on things for two years and never had a phone call. "Hello, just thought I'd tell you we're doing this or that, Zippy bit Bobby." Bobby hated the fucking dog.'

Even Brian Pettifer acknowledges the dog was not exactly a beloved presence on set. 'I think everyone hated the dog. I didn't hate it—I like dogs. But when there was publicity to be done, there would more likely be a photograph of the dog than of you. So that got a bit irritating.'

For Hepburn, the appeal of Wee Jock was more of a mystery. 'All I saw of Zippy is that he was a pain in the neck, but the audience loved him.'

FOUR
FACING THE MUSIC

ONE IMPORTANT ELEMENT of the series playing on producer Deirdre Keir's mind was *Hamish Macbeth*'s title sequence, designed to pull viewers into an episode before they tried to change the channel.

Keir wanted to signal to viewers that they were about to watch something completely different from typical Sunday night TV, setting the tone for everything that followed. Just as Daniel Boyle's scripts walked a fine line between reality and dark comedy, Keir felt that the opening credits needed to both embrace and subvert Scottish stereotypes.

Deirdre Keir: I got a lot of stick about the titles. It was the only time I had to have a conversation with Colin Cameron and I completely respected his position as Head of Television. He said, 'These titles are inappropriate, you can't do this.' I said, 'Why?' and he said, 'You wouldn't understand because you live in the south [of England], but there are a lot of people up here who'd like the show to fail, there's a lot riding on it and you're taking every single icon and...' I said, 'Taking the piss?' and he said, 'Well however you want to put it.' He was extremely unhappy and he hadn't been to visit. He trusted Andrea to get on with it and she said, 'I know why you've done the titles like that but Colin's not having it.'

Andrea Calderwood: Colin Cameron and John McCormick, who were running BBC Scotland, were very determined to put BBC Scotland on the map, to increase the output and to do bold series, not apologetically Scottish or traditional Scottish stuff. Because it was a play on tartan and Scottishness in the titles, I think Colin was worried it would be a bit too twee and self-consciously Scottish. But Deirdre loved the titles and was convinced we should go for it because it was a kind of tongue-in-cheek spin on Scottishness.

Ming Ho: [The titles] establish the quirky nature of the show and offbeat sense of humour; Deirdre's name appears over a shot of a Highland cow and there are clacking lobsters and lemon segments around the frame, referencing the comedy macabre pilot story, 'The Great Lochdubh Salt Robbery'. There may have been some initial frisson that they didn't look like traditional Sunday evening titles.

Deirdre Keir: I'd worked with Christine Butner on the titles. She's a very clever woman. I brought her up, and she spent three days looking at what we were doing, at the footage and at the place and she said, 'This is so exciting,' and got a lot of stuff together then went down and did a cut. What I wanted was that when people were watching the titles, they'd immediately get a whiff of the fact this was going to be fun and out there.

I kept saying to Colin, 'If you want me to do something that's straight down the middle, the audience isn't going to get a starter for 10. Just think about the first episode, about Geordie being fed to the lobsters. Please don't do this, please stick with it and give them an in. I know you're going to get stick about it, people saying, 'These are southerners taking the piss, these are not homegrown talent.' It went on for a few weeks and bless him, he must have agonised about it because there were pressures from BBC Scotland and he didn't make me change a frame.

Andrea Calderwood: Because the entire show was tongue-in-cheek, the titles worked. I think if it had been a much more traditional Scottish show, then maybe the titles wouldn't be right. But because it was being ironic about a quaint Scottish village, I think that's why everybody felt confident to have ironically Scottish titles. They fitted in perfectly with Bobby Carlyle's image because he was seen to be a kind of cutting-edge, cool, young star. He trusted Scott [Meek] to make something that wasn't conventional and traditional and that would work for him.

THE TITLE SEQUENCE performed a clever sleight of hand. At first glance, it seemed to embrace every Highland cliché imaginable—the tartan, the Highland cow, the scenery, the West Highland Terrier—all packaged like the lid of a shortbread tin. But as *The Herald* observed in April 1995, this was no simple capitulation to stereotypes. The show was deliberately playing with these tropes, using them knowingly. 'No doubt southern viewers will miss much of the joke and take it all at face value,' claimed the paper.

Robert Carlyle understood exactly what the titles were doing. 'People who don't watch it, who see the titles, think it's all scenery,' he noted in 1997. 'But there's something very subversive going on most of the time.'

The Herald went further, suggesting this approach offered a refreshing alternative to what it called Scotland's 'obsession with "realism" and authenticity' which it suggested had 'become a vice, as though truth can only be approached via the factual record.'

Stuart Davids: I remember seeing the opening credits for the first time and thinking they were quite strange, but the more you saw it, the more you see how perfect it is for it.

Ming Ho: In my opinion, the titles and John Lunn's music were very much instrumental in establishing the identity of the series. Lunn's distinctive and haunting theme for *Downton Abbey* [2010–15] is now indivisible from our impression of that series.

John Lunn (Composer): I had just finished working on *Finney* [1994], a thriller produced by Zenith. *Hamish Macbeth* was quite different: I was Scottish and knew Scottish music, but they were nervous about giving me the job because I'd done relatively little comedy. In reality, there was very little comic music in the show; the comedy came from playing things for real. I was given two or three months to get the first episode right, which is a luxury by today's standards. There was a lot of talk about Scottish folk music obviously, but there was also a feeling that in some ways it was actually a Western.

I didn't see the title sequence [before I started]; I wrote that music to a certain length and they put the pictures to it. I had been using that tune in the first episode itself and I think everyone thought it had captured the show very well. I was unaware that there was any nervousness about the titles though I can see why now that there might have been. I think that after watching the first episode, there would never have been any doubt that we were not making fun of Scotland. Quite the opposite in fact.

I wrote some of my most moving and profound music for the show. I also had a pretty good budget. If I needed an orchestra, I got it, if I needed eight bagpipes, etc. Every episode had a blend of themes that ran throughout the series, but also some new elements. I don't think I ended up writing much conventional Scottish music. In some ways, it was really only the title music which came anywhere close.

I approached the music by taking recognisable film genres—like Westerns, Hitchcockian suspense and film noir—and 'Scotifying' them. I played banjo, double bass and some guitar, recording at home before mixing at Lansdowne Studios in London. I developed great working relationships with Deirdre Keir and Nick Renton; together with Danny Boyle, they defined what *Hamish Macbeth* was about. I'd like to think that I contributed to that as well in some small way.

It was a pivotal moment for me: the show took my career to another level, and my son was born while I was working on the first series. I can still remember my first recording session, nervously asking the sound engineer, Paul Golding, not to solo the banjo parts—partly because I was uncertain of my playing and partly because my son might be heard crying in the background. And what was the first thing he did? Very *Hamish Macbeth*!

FIVE
FROM PAGE TO PLOCKTON

SPRING 1994

THE PALM TREES stopped Deirdre Keir in her tracks. After weeks of scouting locations along Scotland's west coast to find the real-world version of Lochdubh, the producer hadn't expected to find New Zealand Cabbage Palms flourishing in a Highland fishing village. Yet here they were, lining Plockton's Harbour Street as improbably as the production she was trying to establish.

Acutely aware that most TV crews would typically film exterior shots on location before retreating to studios for interior scenes, Keir knew this approach wouldn't work for *Hamish Macbeth*.

'Everyone expected it to be in Inverness,' says Keir. 'You'd do your locations, then you'd pull back somewhere and you've got the studio house and the police house in a set and other standing sets. While reading the scripts, I quickly realised that we needed weather cover where our locations were. It wouldn't work if we were doing all the exteriors and then going back to studios in Glasgow for the rest of it.'

Situated on a sheltered bay in the northwest Highlands, Plockton nestles on a promontory jutting into Loch Carron, its palm-lined Harbour Street curving along the waterfront. Forested hills that rise to the dramatic Plockton Crags back the village, while views stretch across to the Applecross Peninsula and, on clear days, to the Isle of Skye and Outer Hebrides beyond.

Palm trees line Harbour Street

Those palms that had caught Keir's attention had been planted in the 19th century and flourished due to the warming effects of the Gulf Stream and the bay's sheltered position.

The village had its first brush with screen fame when director Robin Hardy chose its sheltered waters to film scenes for *The*

Wicker Man in late 1972. By the 1990s, Plockton was a National Trust for Scotland conservation village, its traditional character preserved in its Thomas Telford-designed church, whitewashed cottages and working harbour.

For a TV production, this preserved slice of Highland life seemed almost perfect. There was just the small matter of logistics.

Plockton lay over 600 miles from the BBC's London headquarters and a five-hour drive from Scotland's production hub in Glasgow. The village was reachable only by a single-track road or the Kyle of Lochalsh railway line, with Inverness, the Highland capital and nearest major city, two hours away by car. While Plockton offered basic amenities—a general store, post office, village hall and three hotels with pubs—housing and feeding a television crew would present challenges.

Would the community accept such disruption to their lives?

Deirdre Keir: We started talking to the locals, then I found that the National Trust owned the foreshore, which nearly got us back in the car and driving away again.

Nicholas Renton: They were very expensive.

Deirdre Keir: So that nearly didn't work. I went to Edinburgh to talk to [the National Trust] and we weren't on the same page when it came to what this might cost. I said it was a TV series and not a feature film and I didn't have a lot of money and we are not going to just be in Plockton so can we talk some sensible fees? It wasn't working at all. Then, when *Braveheart* went to Ireland, I had another conversation and this time the National Trust worked out. The locals were happy as long as we didn't get in the way of the holiday trade. We were shooting in September at Attadale House, so we stayed in the wilderness.

I had a meeting at BBC Scotland with Andrea Calderwood, Daniel [Boyle] and Skyline's Trevor Davies. We all sat down and everyone looked at me. I said, 'This is not *MacHeartbeat*. I think we've got the place, Plockton, and I think we're going to shoot the whole thing up there.' And they all said, 'Why?' and I said, 'Because I think it'll work better. We can duck and dive between exteriors and interiors. We're at the coast and weather will come in from Skye, and by the time we've moved the crew it's a waste of time.'

Andrea Calderwood: That was a big deal. I made the case for shooting it in Plockton and fought to get another £150,000 per episode. It was a specific additional cost that we had to insist on. Deirdre was brilliant at knowing what the production needed and putting all the money on screen. Plockton was a great choice; it wouldn't have been anything as distinctive as it was without it. I think the year after we did *A Mug's Game* [1996], a mini-series that was set in Tarbert, and Alan Yentob saying, 'Why would an audience want to watch something set on the West Coast of Scotland? Isn't it very parochial?' I was thinking, *Everybody around this table lives within one square mile of London. What's more parochial?*

Stuart Davids: Scott Meek made movies and I think he was ambitious. They could have filmed it somewhere much more accessible, but they went for the most beautiful place they could, and that's just Scott.

Scott Meek: There was a huge advantage in that there was no mobile signal whatsoever, so nobody at the BBC could contact us, they could contact the production office [in London].

Duncan Duff: My first memory of Plockton is as a kid in the back of a car, driving around hither and thither. It was a windy night, but we were going to see this place where there were palm trees. I remember looking out the window, and it was blowing a gale, but there were palm trees. What I didn't realise until I went back there for *Hamish* is that it's a dead end. I always assumed it was a through road, but it's actually the end of the line. You reach the end of the village and you have to do a U-turn and drive back out again.

IN 1866, SCOTTISH businessman and MP Sir Alexander Matheson built Duncraig Castle a few miles east of Plockton. With its stunning views across the Applecross Peninsula, 29 bedrooms, 10 bathrooms, chapel, boathouse, two islands and purpose-built train stop, it was the very picture of Victorian excess.

Looking across Loch Carron to Duncraig Castle

By late 1994, as Zenith Productions began planning to move staff from their London production office to Plockton, the castle had fallen into disrepair. The local council had leased it for a nominal £1 to David Balfe, former keyboardist with Liverpool band The Teardrop Explodes, who had recently sold his successful record label Food Records to EMI.

'It was a big Victorian pile,' recalls Deirdre Keir. 'The council didn't know what to do with it. David saw an opportunity to make a media college up there. It had been a catering college at one point.'

Exterior of Duncraig Castle. Photo by Ron MacKenzie

The production team negotiated to use Duncraig as their base of operations, with the fee helping Balfe maintain the increasingly leaky building. 'There were buckets everywhere,' Keir remembers. 'But I had the most glamorous production office in the world. It was huge—there was a 20-yard walk to the desk and huge windows overlooking Loch Carron.'

Writer Bryan Elsley already knew David Balfe from a previous life. 'I'd done a comedy act with Harry Enfield for a number of years and we used to hang out at David Balfe's studio in London and lust after the girls from Strawberry Switchblade.

He seemed like a rich rock star and he had indeed bought a very big house in the country.'

'We said to Plockton and environs, "We've got 50 or 60 crew and artists up here for weeks, can we block book your bed and breakfasts (B&Bs) and will you do their laundry for them and let them live with you?"' adds Deirdre Keir.

Charlie MacRae, chairman of Plockton and District Community Council, distributed a leaflet to every villager setting out the terms: £100 per day to the village, £40 a day for every extra, £100 a week for 10 weeks for the sailing club. The village's response was enthusiastic.

The production initially guaranteed 20 days of filming with a £2,000 payment, the largest single payment Plockton had ever received. This eventually extended to 34 days, bringing in £3,400 toward the village hall's £20,000 renovation target. The arrangement proved mutually beneficial.

Cast and crew settled into their B&Bs for up to 16 weeks, getting their laundry done and boots dried while integrating into village life.

SIX
BECOMING LOCHDUBH

AUTUMN 1994

BETWEEN SIPS of his hot toddy, Robert Carlyle gazed out from the Creag-Nan-Darach Hotel, contemplating the unfamiliar rural rhythms of his new temporary home.

He'd never spent much time in the country before, now here he was spending four months living in the Highlands, getting used to being stopped in his police Land Rover by tourists asking for directions. Though Plockton didn't have a real-life policeman, the locals seemed happy for him to play the part.

Through the doors, he could see Bill Rae, the hotel owner, greeting yet another arrival. The rooms that would normally be emptying out as tourist season wound down were still full—six of them at £45 a night, with breakfast for two. The dining room that had seen 20 meals a night in summer was now serving 40, as cast and crew mingled with the last of the season's visitors.

Around every corner, reality and fiction were beginning to blur.

Morag Mackenzie's Highland cattle—Morag, Kirsty, Albanach, Hector and Annie—had unexpectedly found themselves appearing as non-speaking extras in the production. They'd amble past Mary Jane Campbell's house, now freshly emblazoned with 'LOCHDUBH HOTEL' across its facade. Campbell's West Highland Terrier, Canach, was offered the chance to star as Wee Jock, but his owner declined when she realised it would mean three months of intensive training for her dog.

Morag Mackenzie and her Highland cattle prepare for a scene. Photo by Morag Mackenzie

The building was also doubling as the exterior of the Stag Bar, though locals knew the real bar scenes would be filmed a few miles away in the Balmacara Hotel, where manager Shelley Woodward was already considering making the fictional name permanent.

John O'Kane from the local takeaway was standing in for cast members in long-distance shots from helicopters, while at the craft shop Edmund and Irene MacKenzie watched their premises turn into a general store.

The village had seen change before, from fishing boom to tourist haven, but this transformation would prove different. In the autumn of 1994, Plockton wasn't just hosting a TV show, it was becoming Lochdubh.

SETTLING IN

For 10-year-old Alasdair MacQuarrie, the transformation was happening quite literally on his doorstep. As the son of the High School janitor, he would wake each morning to find the production's makeup trucks and caravans lined up in the school car park.

When the original choice for a young actor to play Danny MacLellan in episode three, 'The Big Freeze', fell through, the production team visited Plockton Primary School looking for a replacement. MacQuarrie, who was already involved in school drama, landed the role after a quick audition.

Alasdair MacQuarrie: I remember getting the script in a white padded envelope and sitting down to learn it. I was alright with that kind of thing because I was always good at learning and memorising words, but I had no idea what I was getting myself into. They told me I'd get something like £180, and I remember thinking, *If I do this, I'll get to buy myself a mountain bike.* My mum was offered the chance to be my mum in the show. She didn't want to be on TV, so Anna Rowe, who was the mother of the other boy that had gone for the job, ended up being my mum.

Bryan Elsley: The people who lived in Plockton embraced the series. There were production vehicles everywhere and things being shot in every corner of the town. That was a kind of golden era of Scottish drama production. The 90s was a time when there was a kind of sense of confidence and spirit in the thing. There were great crews, creative people around and some emerging stars like Bobby [Carlyle] and Shirley [Henderson].

Deirdre Keir: We were very lucky that the whole area welcomed us and stayed on side, not because we threw them thousands of pounds, but because they liked it. Which I was surprised by, because they'd had years of tourists because it's such a beautiful place, but also because it was in the Autumn when things run down.

Charlie MacRae (Plockton resident; former Chairman of Plockton and District Community Council, Secretary and Treasurer of the village hall and member and former Secretary of the sailing club): If a resident didn't want the crew in their garden, they just upped the fee. A few people were annoyed at getting stopped for a time in their cars, but as many became extras and with the hall, sailing club, etc. all benefitting, it was mostly OK. As I have broad shoulders, they didn't bother me.

Calum Mackenzie (Plockton resident; Owner, Calum's Seal Trips): My children used to have stickers in their window, and when they were filming, they paid them £20 to take the stickers off. So I think the children soon realised how to make some money. We got paid around £25 or £35 as extras, whether you were there for five minutes or all day. We got the catering and the food was incredible.

Alasdair MacQuarrie: There was a buzz to the place. You could always head down into the village and on the odd day they'd be paying people to be an extra in the background. You could make yourself 10 or 20 quid just by playing or kicking a ball about on the beach. Plockton is a great place in its own right, but at the time it really put it on the map. People moaned a little bit about the traffic and how busy it was, but all in all I think everybody has very fond memories of it being filmed there.

Colin Finlay (Local resident): Most people were hired by speaking to somebody else in the pub. There was a guy called Gordon from Camuslongart who would drive round all the pubs in the area if he was short of extras for the next day's filming.

Duncan Duff: Travel was time consuming. Because I was based in London, I flew to Inverness, then someone picked me up, and we drove to Plockton. If you were based in Glasgow, you could drive, or take a train to Fort William, and someone could pick you up. But I think because of the constraints and because of the difficulty of getting there, the production made sure that they got all their stuff done within a certain period and they stayed.

Nicholas Renton: Once we were there shooting it was 11-day fortnights, so there was no way you could go south.

Stuart McGugan: Because the hotels were full, they billeted us all in bed and breakfasts, and each morning I'd think, 'Just the toast, just the toast,' and my landlady, Lexie, would ask, 'Breakfast, Stuart?' and I'd say, 'Yes, the works.' My mouth was saying something different from my brain. They were very kind to us.

Ralph Riach: It was a great set to be on. The first series started in September: I was due to go to Inverness on the Sunday, be met there and driven to Plockton. On the Saturday, there was a phone call to say my mother died. I went up and there was a party at the castle and it just seemed strange to be drinking wine with people I hadn't met before while my mother was lying dead in Elgin. They were very good about it and rearranged the schedule; it was Thursday when I was able to go to Elgin. Vince drove me across, the best driver I ever had. He'd been a rally driver.

Valerie Gogan: I hadn't really worked in Scotland and a lot of [the cast] knew each other. I think I'd sort of lost my Scottish sense of humour a wee bit. I was very nervous and worrying about everything and I felt a wee bit like a fish out of water the first year. That's why it was quite nice being with Pip Torrens [as Peter Peterson] in the first episode, because he'd come up from London as well and we were staying in the same hotel.

You always worry what you look like and Ralph would tease you, 'Have you been in makeup? Oh, you've been in already?' I would sort of go, 'Ha ha' and then I'd think, 'Oh, I look like shit.' But then I realised it was that Scottish thing, which is if people tease you, that means they like you. I really settled in the second year, I felt much more comfortable.

Shirley Henderson: I was a late arrival, and it was all up and running by then. It was an extraordinary looking little village with the palm trees and that one little street and the cattle used to roam about freely. Everybody knew everybody and it was proper village life, the nosiness... the characters in our stories would be nosy, eavesdropping on other characters' lives, and it's so easy to happen in a village.

Duncan Duff: Everybody mingled and there were basically two places to go in the village. There was the Plockton Hotel, which was on the main street, they had great food. It had a pool table, so that was the main watering place. We had some great nights there; karaoke, lots of pool played, lots of whisky drunk. Initially, I used to spend most of my time in the Plockton Inn. I was staying in an extraordinary B&B opposite, it was run by a retired Eton schoolmaster and his wife. We had breakfast in the morning with a roaring fireplace. And the poached haddock... you would not get better in the Savoy Hotel. That's where I was staying and then over the road was the pub.

Shirley Henderson: I think there were two pubs and the little fish and chip shop that was the size of a toilet, it was so tiny.

Barbara Rafferty: It was one of the best jobs ever. We did that for three years and it was sunny in the summer... it was wonderful. The people of Plockton were fabulous. I stayed with a great couple.

Duncan Duff: Loads of people were always up for a drink and my rule at the time was that I would not go to the pub if I was shooting the next day. If you'd had a really good day shooting and went to the pub, you were never on your own. There'd be different waves. There'd be people that would go in straight after work, but then they'd go back to their digs and phone their partners and speak to their kids. At that stage I was married but had no children. Then you'd get the second wave of people that had gone home, showered and hit the pub. Then there were the ones that had gone for the posh dinner around the corner at the Plockton Hotel, they'd come in near closing time. We had some seriously good nights. Relations with the community were absolutely brilliant, there was no kind of us and them and no resentment of us being there.

Jimmy Chisholm (Tartan Salesman, 'Pillar of the Community'/Christie McMurray, 'The Lochdubh Deluxe'): There were no mobiles in those days. It was the guy behind the bar going, 'Anyone here called Jimmy Chisholm?' Simple but perfect.

Shirley Henderson: It was a cosy atmosphere, so perfect for a *Hamish Macbeth* setting. It was joyous up there.

Jimmy Chisholm: That was quite early in my career and everything was exciting. In those days, if you worked for the BBC, when you arrived at Plockton they gave you a little brown envelope with your expenses in it and that was it, you wouldn't see the rest of us for being out at the pub that night.

Valerie Gogan: The first year I was staying in a few different places. It's pretty, but there's not really enough places for everybody to stay in Plockton. Bobby, because he was going to be in it all, he was in the hotel and they got him a house later on. I was in Dornie with Pip at this sort of hotel, it had the castle right across the road from it. They'd ship us into Plockton and back out again. There's no public transport, so you couldn't get anywhere. When I came back, I stayed with a couple in a cottage right on the front in Plockton. I gave them my crew jacket in the first year and they bought me some little tartan bowls in return, I've still got them. In the second year I lived with Anne Lacey. They put us in a cottage. I'm still friends with Anne.

Anne Lacey: For the first year I was in a hotel then into a holiday home. It was beautiful. The house I stayed in was on a point, look out of any window and you see the sea. Series one was best, the tourists didn't know who anybody was.

Brian Pettifer: It's just a fantastic place, it's the best location you could find and the people in Plockton were fantastic. Doing a good series made all the difference.

Jimmy Chisholm: The locals loved it, especially by the time of the second series. The first time they didn't know what to make of it, but it was hugely successful from the start.

Duncan Duff: [I knew Robert Carlyle] a little bit. Initially, apart from working and hanging out on the set, we didn't properly bond for about a month or so. I think probably because he had a lot on his plate. Then he said, 'Do you want to come over?' I enjoyed getting to know him properly.

Stuart Davids: There was a real ensemble feeling to it. I think it was because we were all staying in this tiny place. We all had to get on well and share houses together. You were there for months and that binds you together. There was a real camaraderie between the actors.

Jimmy Yuill: I really enjoyed working with Stuart. He had a theatre company with Bobby and there was a nice shorthand between them. Bobby was quite distant, and that's fine. [Being] number one is a lot of work; he's in every scene, I completely get that. But it was a nice company. I knew Bobby wouldn't be doing more than two or three series. You could see that the camera loved him and he was very talented.

Jimmy Chisholm: Bobby and I were friends for many years, we lost touch when he moved to the States. He was very focused, very quiet, never any bother. He always had a lot to do, he was in almost every scene in every episode.

ROBERT CARLYLE ALWAYS spoke fondly of his time in Plockton, telling one newspaper in 1996 that he could see himself moving there in later life 'because it's such a beautiful place. One of the nicest things is the community spirit and I think it's lovely the way they look after each other.' He recalled that one of his favourite memories of the village was from Guy

Fawkes Night in 1994: 'The production company contributed some money for a fireworks display and the whole village was there. It was a magical night.'

Scott Meek: I came and went because I had other things to do in London, but I went there as often as I could. It became very much a shared adventure in which they were making something they felt was going to be really good. And they all got on really well.

David Ashton: On the very first day of filming I walked up the main street to find a paper. I met one of the locals and asked him, 'Is there anywhere I can get the paper?' and he said, 'Oh yes, the supermarket's just up there on the left', and I said thanks. I'm then looking for the supermarket, but he meant this wee grocery shop. He was winding me up, but he did it deadpan and instantly.

Nicholas Renton: There were some extraordinary people in that village. There was one lady in her 80s who was a racing driver and a speed freak. There was the man from Skye who was divorcing his wife. Something had happened in the dentists in Kyle of Lochalsh.

David Ashton: We were doing a scene in the village hall and was sitting next to this old fellow and he said, 'You wouldn't like a salmon would you?' and he undoes this big coat and has a salmon he's obviously poached from the river. I said, 'No thanks, I don't have the cooking facilities.'

Dominic Minghella (Script Editor, Series One; Writer): I was mostly in Plockton. I remember the terror of production supervisor Annie Rees, who had a heart of gold, but no idea what a script editor did. I remember the wonderful community of Plockton; how they embraced (and quite possibly fleeced) us.

I remember being awed by the talent of Bryan Elsley. I remember Shirley Henderson sitting shyly in the pub with a book or a script and wishing I knew how to talk to her. I remember royal visits from Scott Meek and Julia Duff, always bringing energy and wisdom with them. Most of all, I remember Deirdre's maternal kindness and confidence in me, which will never be forgotten.

Duncan Duff: Somebody pointed out to me the very first time I drove into the village, 'Oh, that's funny, there's a B&B called Nessun Dorma,' and I said, 'Why is that funny?' He said, 'Because that means *None shall sleep.*' Did the owners know it meant none shall sleep, or had they been watching the World Cup in 1990 and thought Nessun Dorma was a really cool thing? That's sort of a *Hamish Macbeth*-type joke. You'd also go past the sign near Plockton that says Stromeferry, and in brackets it says 'No Ferry'. That was a sign: Turn right here to Stromeferry (No Ferry).

CAPTURING THE LOCAL CHARACTER

One of *Hamish Macbeth*'s greatest achievements was capturing the unique character of Highland life, what David Ashton calls its 'otherness'. As someone who, like writer Daniel Boyle, came from Greenock, a town in the west central Lowlands of Scotland, Ashton was particularly struck by how well Boyle captured this distinct world despite having no direct connection to it. 'It's got its own laws and way of doing things,' says Ashton, 'and I became more aware of that 'otherness' during the three years we did it.'

The key to this authenticity lay in Boyle's personal experience. 'I've travelled the West Coast of Scotland and visited many of the villages,' he explained to *Radio Times* in 1997. 'They've a different outlook there.' Rather than merely observe from a distance, Boyle had immersed himself in Highland life, working as a deckhand alongside men from Harris and Barra. This gave him insight into local contradictions, like the strongly Presbyterian islanders who would gather for illicit drinking sessions in shebeens on Sundays.

Boyle took these real experiences and, in his words, 'raised it [two feet off the ground],' creating something that was both authentic and heightened. As David Ashton adds, 'He found that kind of strange otherness expressed well in both humorous and dramatic terms that I think made it completely individual.' This distinctive tone set *Hamish Macbeth* apart from other shows, though Ashton believed the BBC never fully appreciated just how individual it was.

For Boyle, this deep knowledge of the location was crucial to understanding the character at the heart of the show. 'It was important for me to have been there, seen this and taken part,' he reflected. 'Knowing Macbeth's patch helps me know him.'

Lead director Nicholas Renton helped ensure the landscape became as much a character in the series as any of the cast, though capturing its majesty required a different approach to conventional television filming.

Nicholas Renton: I directed half of the episodes in the end. When you go into that landscape you can't go into a conventional job on it, you can't do a wide, close and mid shot because the weather defeats you. [Cinematographer] Fred Tammes and I are both Europeans and don't like just having three people sitting around a table and that landscape absolutely tells you not to do that. Then there's Dierdre [Keir] on the other end of the phone going, 'If the weather changes, you shoot, don't wait for the sun!'

Stuart Davids: It felt as though it was quality right from the word go in the sense that they were spending so much money on it. It was shot on film and you were getting driven up mountains in Land Rovers. You felt that Scott [Meek] really wanted to throw the money at it, and I think they knew it would have a good international audience as well with the scenery.

Nicholas Renton: There was never a pressure of including scenery for foreign sales. I did a shot of a line of cars going up the hill and we chose that bit of road because you had this vast landscape behind it. It's there without you being forced to look at it the whole time, it just seeps into the whole thing. We never really talked about that style, it was just the obvious thing to do.

THE HIGHLAND MENACE

While the scenic beauty of Plockton provided the perfect back-drop for *Hamish Macbeth*, the production faced an unexpected nemesis: the Highland midge. These biting flies, barely visible to the naked eye but notorious throughout Scotland, proved to be a recurring challenge during filming.

The tiny terrors were particularly active during early morning shoots and around water, precisely when and where much of the filming needed to take place. The crew took to wearing special headgear that, as Duncan Duff recalled, made them look like they were at 'some weird Italian funeral' with their black pillbox hats and gauze veils. Yet even these defences weren't enough to fully protect against the determined insects.

'They don't really show up on camera,' Duff says, 'but god almighty there were times that they were a complete pain in the arse and most of your effort was going into trying to put the bloody midges out of your mind and not swipe across your face to get rid of them or slap your cheek.'

'We used to say the midges and the rain kept the tourist population at a good level in Plockton,' joked Charlie MacRae to the *Sunday Mirror* in 2004. 'Visitors have gone away before because of them.'

Robert Carlyle was particularly vocal about his hatred of the midges, later telling an audience at the Belfast Film Festival that they were 'the worst thing about *Hamish*'. He noted that you wouldn't find warnings about midges in Scottish Tourist Board literature: 'Come and see the lovely mountains, the fucking midges are going to bite you to death.'

GOING WILD IN THE WEST

Despite being hidden away in the far north of Scotland, quietly filming their first six episodes far from the prying eyes of BBC executives, the production team was aware they'd have to meet them at some point. It was while shooting the fourth episode that Deirdre Keir was informed of the imminent arrival in Plockton of BBC One's recently appointed Head of Drama, Nick Elliott.

Deirdre Keir: Nick Elliott came up in his suit on 'West Coast Story' and it was terribly wet and he got a chill. We went to the castle, sat him down and asked if he wanted to see a cut [of an episode]. He had no idea what it was about, as it was BBC Scotland's production and he was BBC London. I said: 'This is 'Wee Jock's Lament'. It's not the first episode. This is down the end [of the run], so it's a bit wild.' He was frowning away and I thought, *This isn't going well*. When they ran over Wee Jock and put him in the fridge, Nick got up and walked away. I thought, *Oh God, I'm going to get fired!*

'You can't do that,' he said.

'I did say this is quite far down in the series.'

'You can't kill a dog. Do you know how many people love their dogs? I've got a dog and that really upset me. You killed a dog.'

'No, no, we didn't.'

'The dog was dead in the fridge.'

'We did not kill the dog and put it in the fridge. It's a stuffed dog.'

'You stuffed a dog?!'

It was bad.

Daniel Boyle: Nick Elliott hated it and said we had our 'heads up our own arses'.

Bryan Elsley: I remember the big shot BBC executive arriving, seeing his shiny shoes as he got out of the car and thinking, 'Oh, that's not going to last very long.' He sort of tottered around for the day and then was ushered away. I think there was a kind of sense that we were up there and no one was particularly paying that much attention to what the show was. Deirdre just quietly went about putting it on and nobody really interfered with it, which was obviously very good.

Scott Meek: There was a conversation with senior execs in London after they'd seen the first episode: 'It's all very well made Scott, and we wouldn't expect anything else, but there are two things wrong with it. You're asking the audience to laugh and cry at the same time, and they can't do both.' I said, 'I have a higher opinion of the audience than you do.' They then criticised Robert Carlyle's casting: 'He may be a good actor, but he's not tall and he's skinny and not classically handsome. You can't have a TV star on a show like this who's not tall and handsome.' I replied, 'Yes, but he's very sexy,' something the straight men at the BBC in London didn't understand at all.

I explained: 'Have you ever been at a party where you've seen a blonde across the room who's not the most classically beautiful woman in the world, but there's something deep inside you that tells you she'd be great in bed? When women look at Bobby, that's what they think.' They were shocked by my coarseness, but Andrea [Calderwood] collapsed in a fit of giggles and said, 'It's true.'

THE TEAM RECEIVED a lukewarm response from M.C. Beaton, who visited Plockton towards the end of production on the first series.

Daniel Boyle: Beaton hated the show and the producers kept us apart. She also hated the dog. She was appalled [with Robert Carlyle] and suggested Duncan Duff for Hamish. I never met her, but she was friendly with Anne Robinson, who said in one of her columns that her friend's work was better.

WEE JOCK'S SUNDAY LAMENT

There was much curiosity from the Scottish press about Andrea Calderwood's initial slate of programming. The recently appointed drama head told *The Herald* that her target was 'to get about 20 hours of network drama a year coming from Scotland', including series such as *Cardiac Arrest* (1994–96), *A Mug's Game* and *Hamish Macbeth*.

The paper stated that *Hamish* would likely air in the important early Sunday evening slot, and that an audience of between six million and 10 million would effectively guarantee a second series.

Calderwood explained *Hamish* could do well because although it was mainstream TV, it was 'also highly original... People who haven't seen it say "Well, it must be like *Heartbeat*" or "It's just another *Taggart*." But it's not. As soon as you see it you realise that it is a very different and original piece of work.'

Kind courtesy of The List Archives

Scottish culture magazine *The List* promoted Robert Carlyle's move from 'cop killer to village bobby' on 24th March with a front cover and a new interview between the actor and journalist Eddie Gibb, who noted that without Carlyle, the series 'could so easily have turned out to be *Heartbeat* meets *Whisky Galore!* [1949]'.

Speaking to the *Daily Express*, Deirdre Keir made it clear what her priorities were: 'It's incredibly important that Scotland likes this series. We made this for Scotland, we made it for the rest of the country and we made it for overseas sales—in that order.'

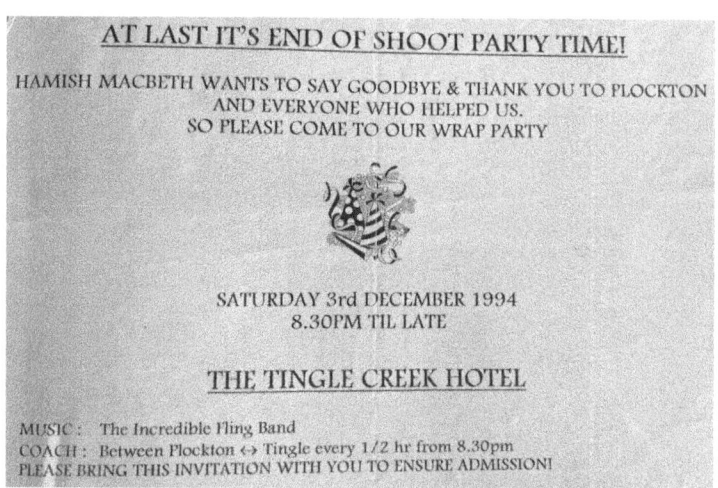

Invitation to series one's wrap party. Courtesy Charlie MacRae

When it came time to broadcast the first episode on BBC One on Sunday 26th March, scheduled between an episode of *Only Fools and Horses* (1981–2003) and the *Nine O'Clock News* (1970–2000), *The Herald* turned its attention to an unexpected angle: with Sunday television viewing taboo among members of the Free Church, Free Presbyterian Church and Associated

Presbyterian Church, how would Plockton's devout religious community approach watching *Hamish Macbeth* on the Sabbath?

The answer was that many local homes would simply boycott the series premiere. Plockton's Free Church minister, the Rev. Roddy Rankin, acknowledged that 'Some people will choose not to watch the programme, preferring to spend the time in more worthwhile worship.' However, he took a pragmatic view on recording the show, noting it would be 'up to individual consciences' whether to watch it on Monday instead: 'I will not be lambasting anyone from the pulpit on Sunday about the use of videos.'

According to Associated Presbyterian Church minister Johannes Van Woerden, 'Watching TV on the Lord's Day is not something we do. In any case, the series sounds like pretty cheap entertainment.' Community council chairman Charlie MacRae, a member of the Free Church, was conflicted. 'To watch or not to watch... I have two teenage sons who are eager to watch the programme and I would be very unpopular if I said No.'

For younger residents like Alasdair MacQuarrie, such concerns seemed removed from daily reality: 'That wasn't really a thing. I think the older, more traditional people in Plockton would perhaps have views about that kind of thing, but that was never the case for us. Plockton on Sunday was just like a Saturday.'

Jimmy Yuill: My dad was a churchgoer and so much of the telly I did was on Sunday night telly. *Wycliffe* was on Sundays as well, so he could never admit to people that he watched it. He did see it though, because one day somebody was walking along the Main Street [in Golspie] and said, 'Hi Alan, I saw James last night,' and my dad said, 'Ah yes, did you see the bit...'

SEVEN

SERIES ONE OVERVIEW

REGULAR CAST

Robert Carlyle (Hamish Macbeth), Shirley Henderson (Isobel Sutherland), Valerie Gogan (Alex Maclean), Ralph Riach (TV John McIver), Jimmy Yuill (Lachlan McCrae Sr), Stuart Davids (Lachie McCrae Jr), Duncan Duff (Doc Brown), Brian Pettifer (Rory Campbell), Anne Lacey (Esme Murray), Barbara Rafferty (Agnes Meldrum), Stuart McGugan (Barney Meldrum), David Ashton (Major Roddy Maclean). With Zippy as Wee Jock and Zack as Wee Jock II.

1. THE GREAT LOCHDUBH SALT ROBBERY

Writer: Daniel Boyle
Director: Nicholas Renton
Original broadcast: 26th March 1995, 8pm

Kenny Ryan (Big Geordie Robb), Julia Wallace (Alice Robb), John Grieve (Whisky Bob), Anne Lannan (Lucy Robb), Pip Torrens (Peter Peterson), Jon Croft (Malkie Clunie), Rab Christie (Jimmy Soutar), Bill Leadbitter (DI Willie Bruce), Greer Gaffney (DS Sandra McDonald).

SUMMARY

'The Great Lochdubh Salt Robbery' introduces viewers to Hamish Macbeth's unique approach to Highland law enforcement, as he and Wee Jock begin their night assisting TV John with some poaching.

The next morning brings two disruptions to Lochdubh's peace: the theft of half a hundredweight of salt from Rory Campbell's shop, and the return of Hamish's ex-girlfriend Alexandra Maclean with her publisher Peter Peterson in tow. When Peterson's casual mockery of Hamish's name leads to the latter kicking in his Mercedes' headlights, it's clear our hero isn't your typical TV policeman, a point reinforced when he later shares a contemplative joint with Doc Brown in the police cell.

After father-son handyman duo, the McCraes', discover Geordie Robb's empty car near the Devil's Humph (passing a 'No more than three sheep abreast' road sign on the way), Hamish finds himself conducting his investigation with DI Bruce and DS McDonald from Inverness. While trying to solve the salt theft, Hamish pieces together a darker mystery. With Rory entertaining Esme upstairs, the McCraes stole the salt (using makeshift disguises of socks over their heads instead of stockings) to preserve lobsters they'd acquired from Robb's fish company. But these weren't ordinary shellfish.

When traces of blue wool and lemon fabric are found in the lobsters' digestive systems—matching the clothes Robb was last seen wearing—the truth emerges: Robb had returned home in a rage and attacked his wife Lucy, leading his mother Alice to kill him in her defence. With Whisky Bob's help, she disposed of the body in the company's lobster tanks.

The episode ends with two revelations: Alice Robb's confession to protecting her daughter-in-law from her son's abuse, and the villagers' horrified realisation that they've been unknowingly dining on lobsters that had been feeding on Big Geordie, leading to an unprecedented run on Rory's supply of laxatives.

COMMENTARY

Duncan Duff: There's an outtake of Hamish sitting in the Land Rover, he rolls a cigarette and he's brooding. Wee Jock is patiently at his master's side and it all looks great and you have music over the top of it. Of course what you don't see is the animal handler going, 'Zippy, Zippy, over here, Zippy, Zippy!' How the hell Bobby remained brooding...

ROBERT CARLYLE MADE no secret of his feelings about working with the West Highland Terrier. 'I hate dogs,' he told *Time Out*. 'Imagine sitting in a Land Rover at 6:30am, in December, with a dog who farts continuously and has smelly breath to boot. When they shoot my point of view out of the car, the dog has to appear to notice what I'm looking at, so what I actually see is the entire crew waving squeaky toys and standing on their heads to keep it interested.'

Anne Lacey: Deirdre Keir's mother [Julia Wallace] was in the first episode as the mother. John Grieve was fantastic. I saw him live on stage and he was so funny. You were always pleased when you heard who was coming in to do a guest part.

Deirdre Keir: I think my mother and John worked together in the Citizens [Theatre]. So when she came up to Plockton, she couldn't believe that's who she was going to be playing scenes with.

Nicholas Renton: John Grieve trying to drink his gin with a straw, that was undirectable. He just picked it up and it went round and round.

Duncan Duff: We were shooting at the fish farm and these lovely scenes with poor Whisky Bob. Bobby and I had to do a house visit because the daughter was getting beaten up. I came out and Hamish was having to give me a lift because I didn't have a car. So we've been up there shooting some scenes, and we were hanging around in between setups and somebody said, 'Oh, this is just fantastic.' And I was like, 'Oh, thank you', and he said, 'Yeah, the scenery, the wee dog...' and it dawned on me that there's some great writing here and some fantastic actors and great performances, but there's also this amazing scenery and this fucking little dog that in reality was a pain in the arse.

THE EPISODE ESTABLISHES Esme and Rory's romance, perhaps Lochdubh's worst kept secret. The bath sequence that takes place during the McCrae's robbery was an opportunity for visual gags from the cast, including a suggestive fire engine ladder...

Ralph Riach: I love that in the first episode when Rory's in his bath, and she's outside playing with the crane. That was brilliant. Cheeky. They missed that at the BBC!

Anne Lacey: Putting the ladder up was my idea. The designer on the first series [Zoe MacLeod] was ingenious, bringing in all the Tunnocks teacakes and the toys, that was her inspiration.

David Ashton: The idea of the erotic overtones between Rory and Esme worked. I don't think Brian would mind if I described him as not necessarily George Clooney. You're watching it thinking, *This is very sexy, these two getting up to this.*

The scene of the McCrae's salt robbery

Calum Mackenzie (Plockton resident; Owner, Calum's Seal Trips): Esme's house at the pier was owned by a lady called Jessie and she got her living room decorated for the filming. They said they would paint it back and do whatever she wanted afterwards and she said, 'No, I'm very happy with what you've done.' So she kept it the same.

Jimmy Yuill: I totally believed [the McCraes wearing socks over their head]. We kept corpsing while we were doing that.

WHAT SET THE episode apart from its Sunday night contemporaries was its willingness to push boundaries, particularly around the use of recreational drugs.

Deirdre Keir: BBC Scotland left us to it. Scott [Meek] knows Scotland, has nous about a whole lot of stuff and has a tremendous sense of humour. The scripts would come in and you never got someone grabbing you by the throat and saying, 'You can't do this.' All I needed to know was whether it was pre or post-watershed because that really affects the tone of it and where you go with it. Things like Bobby smoking in the cell in the first episode.

Scott Meek: I think *Hamish* had such a big audience watching it and seeing entirely different shows. The text was available to be read in two different ways. There was an older audience who watched it and saw a Sunday night BBC programme with fabulous scenery, good acting and little stories. Then there was a younger audience who saw, as it were, the dope smoking version that was slightly hip and subversive.

Ming Ho: There was some nervousness about the pot-smoking and the black humour, both unusual at that time for the Sunday night BBC One slot. Tone was the issue; would the audience for that slot take it on board?

Duncan Duff: The pipe was a great prop and it was very funny, the whole idea that the doctor is filling it with something more interesting than tobacco, to slip that in on a Sunday evening... I'm sure that it went sailing over the heads of the vast majority of viewers. They just didn't get it. It was never pushed in anybody's face, but for those people that were sharp, they just thought, *How fantastic is that?* Hilarious.

Valerie Gogan: *Hamish* was so innocent and lovely. They had all of that with him smoking dope, but it wasn't seen as a crime, it was a quirk of that character. It wasn't grass. They broke up an oxo cube.

Duncan Duff: At the time I was a kind of dabbler in smoking; I would have the odd smoke when I'd reached a certain level of intoxication. But this bloody pipe, to get it going and then have it going so you could get a nice puff of smoke on cue, was a nightmare: I was smoking masses of this Old Holborn or whatever it was shoved in there. Early on I got the scunners because it was really, really strong pipe tobacco. I wasn't drawing it down into the lungs, even so you're getting it in the mouth or whatever. And of course with filming you don't just do it once, you do it again and again and again.

Ralph Riach: We had a great thing with the dope smoking, all quite underplayed. You didn't see him taking a puff, but you did see him exhale, and the Doc was always puffing away at his pipe.

Duncan Duff: We were playing a scene where we're smoking dope together in the police cell. We weren't going to prepare the joint on screen, melting it down, crumbling it or making a big three-skinner. We also weren't going to be going, 'Hey man,' that weird thing American actors do when they smoke anything. We wanted to avoid signalling it in an obvious or clichéd way. We were smoking and at one point my voice went a bit weird and Hamish started going off on a wee reverie which involved Alex. It was all very oblique. We did it in a couple of different ways and they must have had their options in the editing, they could be a bit more or less obvious about it.

Nicholas Renton: I wrote a memo to [Controller of BBC

One] Alan Yentob trying to vindicate an additional three seconds showing him sitting in the cell smoking.

Barbara Rafferty: I thought Bobby was brilliant in it, all these wee spliffs... we were hoping to sell it to America, but they said they wouldn't buy it because of the smoking.

THE DRUG CONTENT wasn't the only aspect of *Hamish Macbeth* that raised eyebrows at the BBC. The moment when Hamish deliberately kicks in the headlights of a Mercedes also sparked controversy. While the BBC's *Points of View* reported 33 complaints about both the drug use and vandalism, viewers seemed especially exercised by the headlight incident, with some questioning the logistics of how repairs could be carried out in such a remote village: 'Lochdubh, which hasn't got a dry cleaners never mind a McDonald's, was nevertheless able to supply spares for the silly Englishman's vintage Merc so the headlight that Hamish took his foot to could have been fixed by the time the policeman kicked in the other one.'

The Herald reported that Northern Constabulary was quick to distance itself from what it called the BBC's 'light entertainment', issuing a statement emphasising that the show was 'far removed from the realities of policing, professionally, and in many other ways'. The situation became particularly awkward for PC Finlay MacBeath, a real Highland officer who had gone to school in Plockton and now found himself the subject of workplace 'ribbing' due to sharing his fictional counterpart's name. MacBeath was sufficiently concerned to have 'informal discussions' with his Police Federation representative, finding it 'embarrassing being mixed up with the fictional character'.

Not everyone took such a serious view. The *Daily Record* reported that some police officers were 'taking legal advice' about their own similarities to TV cops, with one comparing his situation to Erik Estrada's in *CHiPS* (1977–83): 'The series is set in California, where hippies sit in tents, make free love and smoke dope. I was raised in Glenelg where this behaviour still exists. Erik Estrada had a tall blond idiot for a partner with homicidal tendencies. So did I.'

Looking down Innes Street, where Hamish kicked in Peter Peterson's headlights

Despite the show's popularity, there were attempts to rein in some of its more controversial elements. According to *The List*, 'Hamish was written as a character who enjoys the odd spliff, but cuts had to be made before the first series was transmitted and, according to [Daniel] Boyle, word came from the higher-ups in the BBC that this was not a storyline to be explored in subsequent series.'

Robert Carlyle would later reflect that the show's success lay in its ability to balance these edgier elements with its more traditional aspects. 'With Hamish, you've got the shortbread and the tartan and you've got the policeman smoking cannabis,' he told *The Box*. 'If it was all cannabis and kicking headlights in, it wouldn't get so many viewers. If it was all shortbread, it'd probably get millions more f***ing viewers!' He also touched on Hamish's views on poaching in a 1995 *Daily Express* interview, explaining that 'if someone is poaching fish, it's "Well, you give me one and you keep the rest but put that one back," rather than say "Right, we'll lock this guy up."'

Ralph Riach: Some of the critics picked up on Hamish smashing in the lights on the first episode, saying a policeman wouldn't do that. But why wouldn't he? It was done with great wit.

Andrea Calderwood: We did want to push a bit. I mean, it seems quite tame now. He's mildly breaking the law, he's taking direct action.

Deirdre Keir: [The BBC] do take that seriously. If you're pre-watershed language, sex, violence against women, it's all down there in a book.

Nicholas Renton: On the other hand, feeding someone to lobsters isn't on the list!

Ming Ho: Today these elements look pretty mild, but back in 1995 it was a show ahead of its time.

WHILE SOME CRITICS were quick to point out the show's seemingly stereotypical Highland imagery, *The Herald* recognised that *Hamish Macbeth* was 'playing with caricatures and making caricatures come to life'. The series managed to both embrace and subvert expectations; what might appear as cliché to outsiders often reflected genuine Highland life.

Take the sign warning 'No more than three sheep abreast'—it perfectly captured the show's ability to find humour in authentic details. Similarly, as the paper noted, while 'Highland cattle might seem like the most risible of Caledonian imagery,' in Plockton, standing in for fictional Lochdubh, 'they really do have them wandering around. The cliché just happens to be perfectly true.'

Nicholas Renton: There was a review very early on that said, 'And then there were these cattle coming down the main street...' as though we'd staged it. Now you go to Plockton and sometimes you have to sit waiting because these beasts are there. We never moved away from the truth, that really happened.

Bryan Elsley: I remember reading in Danny's first script that there would be a shot with a sign in it on a trail that said 'No more than three sheep abreast' and thinking that was hilarious.

Nicholas Renton: That was pure Danny. I had conversations with the designer asking, 'How do we do this sign? Do you have four sheep on it with a red line across it, so three sheep with a line across it is only two sheep?' It was like the phone box. You always carry a phone box with you and on the last day you sometimes get the phone box shot. We had to carry this bloody thing. We had to stick it all over the place. 'Now we do the shot?' 'No, stick it here.' 'Now we do the shot?' 'No, there's a little road here.' Bobby didn't have his driver's licence, so in series one he had this rickety car and he always had to be shot on roads which weren't public.

DESPITE THE EPISODE'S subject matter, it was the clever nature of Daniel Boyle's script that let the production team get away with it all. There's nothing bloodthirsty, graphic or gory here, just the dawning realisation that the entire village has been eating one of their neighbours for dinner.

As Robert Carlyle told *The Herald*, 'I think it always worked best when it was dark. When it became lighter, that was when it began to lose its soul. If I'm honest, I think there were maybe one or two episodes which didn't quite come up to the mark. But when Danny Boyle was writing and Nick Renton was directing, it was a drama which said a helluva lot more than a 7.15 on a Sunday night show had a right to.'

Special mention should go to John Grieve, in one of his last TV roles before his death in 2001. A star of stage and screen for over 50 years, it was as the canny shipman Dan MacPhail in BBC Scotland's *The Vital Spark* that brought him his greatest fame. Whisky Bob doesn't get to say much, but has a look in his eyes that suggests he could tell a hundred stories.

His final, lopsided, run after Alice Robb's car as the police take her to Inverness is as sad an ending as you would expect. Though Grieve didn't return as Whisky Bob, who, used sparingly, could have been a welcome returning character, he made a cameo appearance in *Hamish Macbeth*'s final episode, 'Destiny–Part II' as a different character.

Barbara Rafferty: I always loved John Grieve. He was in a [*Rab C.*] *Nesbitt* as well. I was on tour and went to a matinee of his in Aberdeen and told him how pleased I was to meet him.

FINAL THOUGHTS

From its opening scene featuring Hamish quietly observing TV John poaching in the river, Daniel Boyle's 'The Great Lochdubh Salt Robbery' set the tone for what viewers could expect from this corner of Scotland. Boyle weaves together the latest scam perpetrated by Lachlan Sr and Lachie Jr with Geordie's family problems, while also introducing Hamish and

Alex's complicated relationship and giving various members of the Lochdubh community moments to shine.

We learn early on that Hamish's parents moved from Lochdubh to Glasgow when he was very young, before he then joined the force and moved back to Lochdubh. As well as adding some backstory to the character, it's also a neat way to address the fact that Robert Carlyle's accent is more Maryhill than Mallaig.

Hamish deliberately letting another officer take credit for solving the case initially seems like simple career avoidance. Only later will we understand how his fear of leaving Lochdubh shapes every decision he makes. All-in-all, the first episode efficiently and entertainingly sets the tone for a series that is anything but conventional.

2. A PILLAR OF THE COMMUNITY

Writer: Stuart Hepburn
Director: Nicholas Renton
Original broadcast: 2nd April 1995, 8pm

GUEST CAST

Phyllida Law (Vicky Jeffreys), David Ryall (Paul Jeffreys), Ken Drury (Cameron Dicks), Dolina MacLennan (Flora), Jimmy Chisholm (Tartan Salesman), John McLean (Wee Boy), Kay McLean (Wee Girl), Linda Ormiston (Evadne McTurk), Willie Beaton (Willie Muirhead), Ceilidh Band (The Incredible Fling Band).

Summary

When newcomer Vicky Jeffreys decides to reinvent Lochdubh Day, the village's annual celebration, she sets off a chain of events that threatens to tear the community apart. Her plans to replace the traditional bouncy castle and ceilidh (a traditional Scottish social gathering with live music and dancing) with historical reenactments and Gaelic cookery competitions don't sit well with the locals, particularly when she starts implementing changes without consultation.

The situation takes a darker turn when dead crows begin appearing nailed to Vicky's door, followed by threatening letters. Vicky's husband, Paul, also reveals his secret identity to Hamish: Chuck Sadler, author of popular Western novels. Tensions escalate when Vicky clashes with Lachlan McCrae Sr over his plans to demolish an old blackhouse for a septic tank. She sees precious heritage being destroyed; he sees a 'pile of stones' standing in the way of modern plumbing.

Meanwhile, the village divides into factions, with Agnes convinced Vicky has designs on Barney, while others resent her attempts to 'improve' their way of life. Even the normally unflappable Esme bristles at having her choir arrangements altered.

The mystery unravels when Hamish realises Paul is behind the threats, not out of malice, but desperation. He's watched his wife organise community after community into submission, leading to a pattern of moving on when locals inevitably resist. Rather than press charges, Hamish engineers a reconciliation that brings everyone together at the ceilidh, where traditional music and dancing prove more powerful than any carefully planned 'authentic' entertainment. The evening ends with the sight of Vicky and Paul joining in the Eightsome Reel, while Hamish slips away with Wee Jock for a spot of poaching.

COMMENTARY

Like many a frontier town, Lochdubh sat on the edge of civilisation, its saloon-style pub doors swinging in the Stag Bar. This wasn't accidental—the production team had deliberately infused *Hamish Macbeth* with the spirit of the American West, seeing parallels between Scotland's remote coastal communities and those dusty outposts where justice often came down to one person's interpretation of right and wrong.

Years later, Robert Carlyle would tell *The Telegraph* that many of his characters could be seen as cowboys—loners, outsiders, drifters—with Hamish being 'the first one that I played as a cowboy, even down to his drawstring pouch'.

Deirdre Keir: We said from the beginning, it was probably something Daniel [Boyle] said, the West Coast is the Wild West, so in terms of John Lunn's music, Stuart's script, the guy who wrote the cowboy stories... I had an uncle who absolutely loved cowboy stories and he knew every Native American tribe. That worked really well.

Stuart Davids: The Wild West theme was very important to Danny. It was important to have this character with a moral compass that was set at north, yet was flawed and could push the limits like in Wild West movies, where the sheriff isn't always the most law abiding and yet still gets the bad guys. I think we all picked up on the theme. The bar had the swing doors, that was very deliberate.

Stuart Hepburn: 'Pillar...' was the idea of an incomer who tried to work hard to become a pillar of the community. I had this idea that we'd think it was everyone in the community. I think that probably came from my experience in Ardfern in Argyll and of the people who come into the community and try to out-Jock the Jocks. My sister-in-law, my brother-in-law, my mother-in-law all lived in Ardfern and there were a lot of incomers, so I understood the world.

INCOMERS WERE ALSO very much a part of Plockton, with Charlie MacRae telling journalist Ian Black in 1994 that 'We wouldn't have a village if it wasn't for the incomers, and 95% of them have fitted in very well. The chairman of the village hall is an Englishman, but he's been here for 25 years. He's beginning to fit in fine.'

Shirley Henderson: [*Hamish*] was for all ages. It doesn't matter how old you are, there's room for everybody. The amazing faces and the wealth of experience were lovely. Phyllida Law was fantastic to work with, such an eccentric character and we had such a giggle.

Phyllida Law: I come from Glasgow, which is not immediately obvious. I didn't know everybody, though I knew Jimmy Yuill, we'd done Shakespeare together. I taught David Ryall at drama school. Plockton was the most beautiful village I'd ever seen. I was staying at a wee hotel, they were very nice people.

Nicholas Renton: Jimmy Chisholm is in the first episode selling shortbread red tartan and he had lots and lots of fluffy hair. Then he came back in series two as the undertaker ['The Lochdubh Deluxe'].

Jimmy Chisholm (Tartan Salesman): My agent must have got a ring that said, 'Does Jimmy want to come and sell tartan?' That first time it was very short. I think I was there for two days altogether because it took a while to travel up there in those days. I think we went up on the Saturday and started filming on the Monday, so I was finished by the end of Monday. Everything was a lot smaller in those days. I knew almost everyone who was in it. It was great to be on it and very exciting, something up in the Highlands of Scotland. Being from Inverness, there really wasn't a lot up there. We were all hanging on to see what [*Hamish*] would be, though I still had no idea after doing my part because I wasn't in it for very long at all.

Shirley Henderson: I was at the end of a sequence, there was a lot of filming before they got to me, and just before they reached me the donkey stood on my foot and the pain was just... I was so unsure what you do. Do you stop filming? Do you keep going? Now I'd shout, 'Stop, there's a donkey on my foot!' but then I didn't.

Phyllida Law: We did a bit of Scottish dancing, which I've never been any good at because I can't count. Ralph [Riach] used to twirl me around the room, he was fierce. It's the only way to do it to get me to move. I loved him, he was very good fun.

Shirley Henderson: Vicky was a sad character in the end, desperate for attention. They brought something special, all those people. I loved the balance of all these different age groups.

David Ashton: The thing about *Hamish* that worked best was that the main director, Nick Renton, took it tremendously seriously. He was directing it as if it was a drama. The comedy was incidental as far as he was concerned. That was one of the strongest points to it that somehow made it very popular, because although people looked at it and thought, *Here we are in the Highlands and here are all these colourful people*, there was a kind of reality underneath, as there is in the actual Highlands that Nick was absolutely spot on about. Nick would never let us stray off the ball.

Deirdre Keir: When we did the launch at the Royal Society of Arts in London, we got The Incredible Fling Band to come down and I don't think they'd ever been to London. They came and played and the TV critics were invited. We had bits and pieces of Scottish food. Bobby didn't come, but it was a bit of an occasion.

Donald Murdoch (Accordion, The Incredible Fling Band): We appeared in a few episodes of *Hamish Macbeth*, including 'A Pillar of the Community' and 'Radio Lochdubh'. I felt bad about barging past the esteemed actress Phyllida Law, but it was only acting! Sadly, we lost our fiddle player, singer and raconteur Willie Beaton, but the band's still playing.

Dougie Craig (Plockton resident): My Dad Norrie was the classical accompaniment, playing piano, in a scene where an opera singer gets ousted by some more local tunes by way of the Fling Band boys. While rehearsing what was ultimately a very small part, he met the lady playing the starring role. He took delight in a wee wind up when he finished playing something for the lead lady at Duncraig where they had a rehearsal. He said something along the lines of 'You're very good. Did you get some training somewhere?' Apparently, in the response he got her full operatic credentials and more. Wind up merchant that man.

FINAL THOUGHTS

Stuart Hepburn's first script leans playfully into its Western influences. From the sheriff's badge in the title sequence to Hamish wielding his speed gun like a gunslinger, the episode walks a careful line between homage and originality. When Paul admits he writes cowboy novels under the pulpy pseudonym Chuck Sadler, the show's genre-blending crystallises.

At its heart, this is a story about the tension between tradition and change. The arrival of Paul and Vicky, with their urban aspirations and somewhat clumsy embrace of Highland culture, highlights the real-world dynamics of incomers reshaping rural communities. Thankfully, the episode avoids the typical 'outsider versus locals' narrative often seen in rural dramas (and taken to extremes in *The Wicker Man*), with Lochdubh's residents responding with mild irritation rather than outright antagonism.

With regards to Esme's Gaelic teaching, that viewers were hearing the language on BBC One in 1995 still feels remarkable. Thirty years later and despite the establishment of Gaelic-language channel BBC Alba in 2008, such moments remain rare on mainstream channels. Notably, Plockton was at one time home to Gaelic scholar Sorley MacLean, who introduced the teaching of Gaelic at the high school while headmaster between 1956 and 1972.

It's also worth noting the presence of Dolina Maclennan, one of Scotland's most respected Gaelic-speaking actors, whose role as Flora, Isobel's colleague at the newspaper, brought further authenticity to the series. Her inclusion reflected the show's engagement with Highland culture and the importance of Gaelic voices within it.

Amid these cultural clashes, the episode quietly plants seeds for future storylines. The introduction of Shirley Henderson as Isobel, a reporter for the *Lochdubh and District Listener*, might seem incidental: she's first glimpsed sitting beside Hamish in Vicky's kitchen, her gaze fixed on him while he remains oblivious. But in this small moment, we're watching the beginning of one of the show's central relationships.

The closing scene encapsulates everything that made *Hamish Macbeth* special. As Hamish slips away from the ceilidh to engage in some quiet poaching, we find him pausing beside the water with Wee Jock, looking up at the moon. 'Oh man, doesn't get much better than this,' he observes, and viewers may well agree. It's a moment that perfectly balances the show's appreciation for Highland tradition with its understanding that sometimes the best traditions are the ones that bend the rules a little.

3. THE BIG FREEZE

Writer: Dominic Minghella
Director: Patrick Lau
Original broadcast: 9th April 1995, 8pm

GUEST CAST

Stuart McQuarrie (DS Cronk), Bill Leadbitter (DI Willie Bruce), Anne Kristen (Miss Meiklejohn), Alasdair MacQuarrie (Danny MacLellan), Dolina MacLennan (Flora), Gilbert Martin (Markwell), Jake D'Arcy (Scott), Alan Tall (Young Crofter), Johnny Irving (Old Crofter).

SUMMARY

'The Big Freeze' opens with Rory observing TV John visiting Esme and telling her 'I love you', much to Rory's concern. DI Bruce arrives at Lochdubh police station to install a new computer system, highlighting Hamish's backlog of paperwork and administrative issues. This leads to tension between Hamish and TV John, who has been helping with station duties.

Meanwhile, Major Maclean stages a break-in at his own home to claim insurance money, with Hamish reluctantly helping cover it up. When Bruce believes the notorious 'Raspberry Ripple Mob' is responsible and the Major reports the 'theft' to Mr Markwell, a loss adjuster, Hamish must navigate an increasingly complex web of deception.

The heart of the episode emerges when we learn TV John has been taking secret reading lessons from Esme Murray, using money he took from the station's petty cash. When confronted by Hamish about the missing money, an ashamed John leaves town and his new friend, a young neighbour called Danny MacLellan, pulling his caravan behind him in his Lada.

John deliberately leads the police to catch a real criminal, Markwell, thereby redeeming himself. Hamish offers his friend his job back and promises to get rid of the computer, though he notes he still needs help feeding Wee Jock as the dog will only take food from TV John. The episode closes with Alex's prize-giving speech about the power of words and the importance of telling the truth, resonating with the episode's themes about secrets, shame and friendship.

COMMENTARY

Shirley Henderson: *Hamish* was nice and complex and fresh. It kept twisting; one week he'd be looking at me, the next Valerie would do something that took his attention. It was a kind of light-hearted Sunday night entertainment to keep you coming back for more.

Dominic Minghella: By the time we were thinking about me writing an episode, we were all so immersed in it that the tone was easy to write into. I don't recall the script changing much, but I expect I had plenty of help from Deirdre and Scott Meek.

David Ashton: That did quite an interesting thing, because when I read it at first I thought it was quite comedic and I was prepared to go into it from quite a comedic angle, and in fact the director Patrick Lau was very good and took me aside and told me, 'This man has done this, he's desperate, there's a great deal of shame connected to what he's done because he's failed in his own eyes and he's manufactured this insurance scam,' and he deepened by quite a long way my approach to the character.

Ralph Riach: The only episode that jarred with me was the one where TV John was learning to read and write, because I just didn't buy that at all. I could accept he might not be able to read and write, but I couldn't buy the notion that having been born and brought up in Lochdubh, they wouldn't have known. So in that respect, it was hard for me.

Anne Lacey: I was a bit shocked by that at the time.

Valerie Gogan: They maybe didn't plan that at the beginning, they just thought it might tug at the heartstrings a bit because he was such an integral part of everything.

Ralph Riach: The wee boy that lived next door, Danny, was a delight to work with. The scene we had in the caravan was lovely.

Alasdair MacQuarrie (Danny MacLellan): The caravan where they filmed was somewhere we used to go to play all the time, on the way down to Coral Beach. Ralph was absolutely brilliant. He took me under his wing and helped make sure that I looked at the right place at the right time and didn't make too much of a mess of it. The night filming was way past my bedtime, it all just felt like such a great adventure.

David Ashton: Although you've got the comedic quality of it, there was a lot of feeling in it as well. And working with Bobby in that particular episode was very good. He's such an understated actor, and yet when you see him on the screen, everything is there. I found working with him on that episode very interesting indeed.

Alasdair MacQuarrie: I didn't really see Robert Carlyle much. He was obviously the star of the show, so he was off in his own caravan. Even though he wasn't as famous as he became, there was still a kind of delineation between him and the rest of the cast. When you met them, it was like meeting a new friend and they'd all chat away to you.

Valerie Gogan: I remember standing on the stage. Everything had a sort of second meaning in that episode.

Alasdair MacQuarrie: Most of my primary school were in the hall for the presentation scene. That day was very kinetic and busy. I always had this impression that you'd be there for days trying to get a minute's worth of footage, but in actual fact it was pretty slick. When they announced that Danny had won the prize, I turned to my on-set mum, while sitting right behind me is my actual mum, as an extra. I've still got the book I was given, a copy of *Gulliver's Travels*.

John Lunn (Composer): There was one car chase in episode three where I actually used bagpipes in the way Lalo Schifrin might have used a brass section in the seventies. I used strange cluster chords on the accordion. I learnt to play the banjo, initially just to get a feel of how it would sound in the show, but ended up just recording it myself.

Alasdair MacQuarrie: I went on a school trip, I think it must have been the summer after the episode was shown. I was on a ride at Euro Disney and there was an elderly English couple who recognised me. I was amazed. I was absolutely sure that somebody had put them up to it.

Many years later I joined the Royal Marines and the troop got wind that I had been on TV and ordered a load of DVD copies of it. In the episode I say I have a laser phaser, so they made me do weapons presentations on the laser phaser. I had to make up a whole story behind the range of the laser phaser, reloading capacity, things like that, which they found hilarious, me not so much.

Final Thoughts

Episode three takes the controlled chaos of Lochdubh to new heights, juggling a variety of storylines with impressive ease. Within the first few minutes, we have Hamish solving a theft, TV John foreseeing doom and DI Bruce making his return, all while Isobel edges her way further into Hamish's world.

Somehow these various strands work, even if not everything rings entirely true. Quite how TV John convinced the entire village that he could read and write, particularly while helping Hamish with his paperwork for an unspecified amount of time, is unclear. Regardless, it's a welcome opportunity for more screen time for Ralph Riach, while the focus on his character allows for new information to be revealed, including the fact that he worked on oil tankers and, as he tells young Danny: 'I came back to life.'

Isobel arriving to help Hamish set up his new computer may seem quaint today, but while 1995 marked the year Windows 95 would make home computing more accessible than ever, only around 1% of British households had internet access, mostly through slow dial-up connections. Meanwhile, the arrival of Old Crofter and Young Crofter as dry-witted commentators adds some fresh humour, and new characters, to the mix.

The episode marks the first time we see all three points of the show's central love triangle share the screen, with Alex's return forcing a confrontation about Hamish's chronic inability to express his feelings. Meanwhile, Isobel's quiet attempts to grow closer to him show both her growing affection and her awareness that it may be hopeless.

The final image of Isobel walking alone through Lochdubh's empty streets highlights the programme's ability to find moments of genuine emotion amid the comedy and quirky crime plots.

4. WEST COAST STORY

Writer: Bryan Elsley
Director: Ian Knox
Original broadcast: 16th April 1995, 8pm

GUEST CAST

Muireann Kelly (Janice), Ken Drury (Cameron Dicks), Rab Christie (Jimmy Soutar), Alex Norton (Duncan Soutar), Laura Kellman (Phyllis Dicks), Hugh MacQuarrie (Kenneth Dicks), Ron Donachie (Zoot McPherrin).

Summary

When Hamish's bank account runs dry and his credit card is cancelled by bank manager Cameron Dicks, he finds himself turning to local shopkeeper Rory Campbell for help. In exchange for food, Hamish reluctantly agrees to join Rory's ambitious production of *West Side Story* in the village hall.

The amateur dramatic production serves as backdrop for a forbidden romance between Jimmy Soutar, a farmer's son, and Phyllis Dicks, the bank manager's daughter. Their relationship mirrors the musical's themes of star-crossed lovers, complicated by Jimmy's father Duncan facing financial ruin at the hands of Phyllis's father.

Religious tensions emerge when Phyllis's zealous brother Kenneth discovers her involvement in the 'sinful' production. Meanwhile, Hamish and the villagers uncover Cameron Dicks' hidden past through an old acquaintance named Zoot McPherrin, learning that Dicks' supposedly deceased wife is actually alive and running a shop in Wick, a secret he's kept from his children for years.

Phyllis threatens to leave home and tell her brother the truth about their mother if Cameron doesn't let the Soutars keep their farm. The situation comes to a head when Duncan Soutar has an emotional breakdown and attempts to commit suicide. Cameron Dicks manages to stop him, just as the Doc and Hamish catch up with the pair. As the musical gets underway, Duncan Soutar arrives to sit in the audience.

Commentary

Ian Knox (Director): The whistling at the beginning is mine.

Bryan Elsley: I didn't know Bobby Carlyle, but I really liked him when I met him and I kind of knew that he could be quite funny. The show is a galaxy of Scottish comedy. Some of the funniest people around were in that show.

Deirdre Keir: Bryan came back with 'West Coast Story'. With any series with multiple writers, you have some that just drop out because they can't get it, but Bryan absolutely got it.

Andrea Calderwood: When Bryan's script came in I thought, *Oh my God, he's doing West Side Story*. There was a real sense of 'Let's just go for it,' there was no self-censorship and no 'We better be careful.' The bolder, the better.

Bryan Elsley: I think I went to a couple of meetings and it wasn't quite the same in those days, it wasn't all about story rooms and all that kind of thing. It all happened on a sort of individual basis. I had a couple of meetings, possibly with Daniel and Deirdre, and just went from there. I think I'd literally been watching *West Side Story*, which is to this day one of my two or three favourite films of all time, and I guess I just came up with the idea. And no one seemed to think that was a bad idea.

Deirdre Keir: Bryan gave us the story. On reading it and seeing that there would be a need to clear the rights to use with Leonard Bernstein's estate, I immediately sent the script off to the BBC's legal department. That's what's great about working with the BBC, there are departments there staffed with people who will help you. As an independent producer we have to do so much of this work ourselves, but as this series was being made by Zenith for the BBC who would broadcast it in the UK and then sell it worldwide, everything we did needed to be in line with their rules, regulations and agreements as regards copyright and licences.

So I requested from their legal bods absolute guidance and I got it. The script came back from them and there it was, carved in stone, what we could and couldn't film while bringing Bryan's story to the screen. It was exactly what I needed. After all, there's no point producing a show that can't be shown.

Bryan Elsley: Nowadays I know much more about the difficulties of rights, copyright, intellectual property and all that kind of thing, but I had no idea about it in those days. So I just came up with the idea and handed it off to them to fix up. I think they might have rung [*West Side Story* director] Robert Wise or his wife or something like that to get some kind of permission. But permission was secured at quite a high level.

Deirdre Keir: Ian Knox came on to direct that. He'd directed my dad [actor Andrew Keir] in a film which I'd really liked, so I called him and said, 'Do you want to come and do some *Hamish*?' The directors came on to do them in pairs, they'd shoot two episodes back-to-back. We were chatting, and he told me he'd climbed all the Munros. I said, 'I've got the film for you, [episode six] 'A Bit of an Epic'.

Then Bryan Elsley's script came in and I said, 'Ian, I don't know if this is your bag, but I'll absolutely get you all the support you need, the choreographers, music, time to rehearse with the actors for the dancing, but it'll be back to back [with 'A Bit of an Epic'], so you'll be up a mountain which you can do standing on your head, then you'll do this.'

He phoned me up a few days before he was due to come up and prep two episodes back to back, which is really tough, and said, 'I *really* want to do 'West Coast Story', I'll do a lovely film. I don't like the mountain story.' So I was running around at very short notice to do the mountain film. Ian did have lots of time to do rehearsals and he did do a very nice film, but the irony is he's not had the residuals.

Ian Knox: I think there was a hold-up with the script on the mountain one. That seemed to be quite a difficult one for them to lock off script-wise. As the shooting day was approaching, post-production on 'West Coast Story' was going to overlap with pre-production on the mountain story, which needed quite a lot of work in terms of finding the right locations and so on. It was in the interest of doing the best I could with 'West Coast Story' and finishing it off properly. Bryan had written something incredibly charming, without being saccharine.

It was a gentle, fun story about this crazy life in the Highlands, which I was a bit familiar with as I'd shot a film up in the Orkney Islands and got involved with the local amdram group there. In fact, when I went to see them they were doing *West Side Story*, so I'd kind of seen it and I loved it. It was so funny but also charming, the energy and passion they put into it.

Scott Meek: I had a personal weakness for the episode that can never be seen. The reason I like that so much is largely because of the wicked amusement it gave me when I told all my chums who were in it that they were going to sing and dance. I was met with, 'Absolutely not, we're not going to sing and dance,' led by Bobby, who was really reluctant to do it. I thought the notion of them all doing *West Side Story* in the village hall was so funny.

Duncan Duff: I don't think that would have been in Bobby's comfort zone.

Deirdre Keir: Bobby was well out of his comfort zone, in fact he said to me when he read the script, 'I can't do singing and dancing,' and I said, 'But that's the gag, that's the schtick.'

Bryan Elsley: I did hear eventually that Bobby had been a bit nervous about it. But he was tremendous.

Ian Knox: I watched it again recently for the first time in 30 years and what struck me about it was that Bobby's clearly enjoying himself. He looks like he's having a ball. And he was. They were all really into it. It looks like a cast that's having fun. I knew a lot of the actors, I'd probably worked with half of them before. They were a real crème de la crème, some of the best of the bunch in Scotland. It felt like I was stepping into a familiar ensemble situation with a bunch of people that I thought were great and I really wanted to work with. They came up trumps.

Andrea Calderwood: Because Bobby has got such a range as an actor, you knew he could pull it off. I think that's what I said at the first commissioning meeting, 'Bobby can do anything, he can play the psycho but he can be charming,' and he is charming and handsome. If you have a strong and versatile actor in the lead, then you can be confident you can get them to sing and dance or kick in headlights. I think that was what was nice, being able to make Bobby a household name [as Hamish] rather than to put him in the 'Scottish psycho' pigeonhole.

Deirdre Keir: We had all these actors around Bobby who'd done pantomime and comedy, so they just picked him up and went for it.

Ian Knox: [Working with Bobby and Shirley was] pure joy. I met Shirley for the first time during rehearsals and Bobby took me aside and said, 'Just watch and listen,' so watch what Shirley has got to give here. These are his scenes that he's talking about and he's very generous in that way, kind of inviting me to throw the spotlight onto her. He liked and really respected her as an actor and he's smart because when she shines and is brilliant and inventive, then it ups everybody's game—it's good for him and it's good for the show. It was a very good piece of advice because she's an extraordinary and unusual actor. As soon as we got to work, I completely understood what he was getting at.

When actors come on set, they're inventing emotionally with their guts. It's not a thinking process, but a doing process. I like to watch actors and see where their instincts take them, what choices they're making instinctively, and then you just kind of take what's on offer and shape it. The director thinks in terms of story and shots, but actors invent in ways we can't because they're working on another level. If you leave them alone during rehearsals, they give you incredible things you wouldn't invent yourself. That's why it's crucial to watch what they're doing and see what they're offering before jumping in and locking it down.

Duncan Duff: We had to go to these rehearsals and, of course, life imitating art, because we had to rehearse to get to the level where we could realistically be rehearsing the numbers.

Ian Knox: What was so good about how that was set up, which I can't take any credit for, was just the kind of Scottish reluctance to let go and kind of be daft. It was great fun rehearsing because they just loved it. As soon as you got them moving, you got them into doing these daft routines, they just went for it. They weren't playing it for laughs, and neither was I. I think that gives it a certain charm and reality about it. It's difficult to get the tone right on a thing like that, because it would be so easy for it to tip into complete sentimentality. I hope we didn't do that, but I have heard from people that they just find it too soft. But that's kind of what it is, that's the genre. It's made for a kind of Sunday night audience who like that sort of thing.

Duncan Duff: We had our rehearsals in the village hall. That's where we ended up shooting it. It was very funny.

Ian Knox: I liked the way the whole thing choreographed. It came from the script which had a real kind of fluidity about it. Also, I'm quite musical and was really keen to do something musical. I enjoyed crafting the choreography to that score. It's such a great score, and it's a favourite film of mine. I think that the choreography gave us the best shots. The tracking shots take us on a journey around the three storylines and then back into the hall.

Ralph Riach: I was playing the accordion, Esme was on piano and the camera was on me. I had this accordion that I was told you didn't move your hands like a normal one. The camera was on a track and I didn't know where it would be watching. So I was standing still, moving my fingers, so when the camera goes by it just looks like I'm standing there doing f– all.

Ian Knox: He plays the first couple of notes in the closeup and then the camera's off him. I'll just take that as a legitimate editing note.

Bryan Elsley: I think I invented Zoot. I've always had an affection for the kind of utopian episodes of *Star Trek* [1966-69]. They've always got a charismatic leader, so I think I just dreamt him up.

Ian Knox: Ron Donachie needed broad shoulders for that, broad everything really. I'm not sure if I'd worked with him before, but he was someone that I really wanted to work with because I'd seen a lot of his work in theatre and on screen. I put him forward [for the role] but he was probably on everyone else's list as well, because he was just so right for it. He was a popular choice.

Ron Donachie (Zoot McPherrin): That just came out of the blue and it was a couple of days' work up in Plockton. It was brilliant fun, because Zoot is such a great character. Various people involved in the production of it, between the producer, the director and the writer, I'd worked with all of them before. There are two or three good scenes, but they're just wee bits. They needed someone to come up, learn his words, get the Kaftan on and go away again.

Deirdre Keir: So 'West Coast Story' was transmitted in the UK and I was happy as I could see it had good potential for sales overseas. After we had delivered the series, I got a call from the BBC asking me if I had completed all the necessary clearances. I said 'Yes. They are in the production file.' You have to produce a file at the end of every show with the paper trail, every agreement, every contract: it's all recorded there as part of the delivery. As far as I understand subsequent events (and I understand very little!), while we had stayed completely within the terms of the agreement to obtain the rights, the Bernstein estate were not happy and took issue with BBC, who decided not to sell 'West Coast Story' beyond the UK. Maybe the Estate thought we were filming a production of *West Side Story*, which of course we were not.

Not including this film as part of the series for other countries to enjoy was a huge sadness to me, to our cast and production team and to Zenith. It was a good film, which we had had such pleasure making, while keeping to the timing of what was allowed in the agreement, to the quarter second. It had been recognised by all parties from the outset of production that the series could have enormous appeal in say Australia, US, New Zealand and Canada because of its setting in the Highlands and Islands and in Wester Ross, with the stunning scenery everywhere you looked. And by filming the entire series there, we stood on our heads to capture that, despite the midges, the storms and no mobile reception!

Ian Knox: It's a great sadness because it's one of my babies. It's been behind me since completion. A repeat would have been quite nice. I do hope it gets out, eventually.

Nicholas Renton: It'll become a cult movie one day.

Deirdre Keir: It has been shown on ITV3. I was really surprised about that.

Stuart Davids: That was one of the strangest for all of us, but it is the lost episode because they couldn't release it. That was another dark episode as well, with Alex Norton's character about to kill himself.

Ian Knox: I've always tried to choose projects, particularly in TV, that I think are going to be fun to do, either because the material is really good or because the people that I'm working with are really good. I think at that time I was quite committed to doing shows in Scotland, I had a real sense of where I was coming from as a Scot. I'd done *Shoot for the Sun* [1986], *Down Where the Buffalo Go* [1988], I did a film called *The Privilege* [1982] and I think *Hamish* was the last of them. It just expressed something that I love about Scotland. I mean, it's a wee bit twee, but I think that's just part of that confection. It was great fun; I enjoyed it and I enjoyed working with all of that group. *Hamish* was quite cheeky and funny. It had a kind of sense of its own daftness in a way, and I like that about it.

Bryan Elsley: I was running a little community theatre company in the Lake District and didn't have much money, so the fee for writing *Hamish* sort of revolutionised our life. I think we might have bought a new car. It was a big deal for us.

Ron Donachie: The Sunday night slot that *Hamish* had is very conventional, very saccharine, and you can understand why: people have had their weekend, they're going back to work and just want to put their feet up and watch some nice scenery before they go back to work on Monday. *Hamish* did all that for them, with a great love story, a terrific leading man, all these mad characters and underneath it all there was a genuine air of uncertainty going on which gave it a terrific edge.

FINAL THOUGHTS

Establishing Hamish as a cash-strapped copper in the opening moments of 'West Coast Story', writer Bryan Elsley gleefully empties what's left of our hero's wallet, forcing him to trade dignity for dinner by joining Lochdubh's ambitious amateur production of *West Side Story*. But while Bernstein and Sondheim's musical explored gang warfare in 1950s Manhattan in its loose adaptation of Shakespeare's *Romeo & Juliet*, Elsley transplants those themes of forbidden love and social division into something uniquely Scottish.

As Isobel observes, *West Side Story* is all about 'forbidden star-crossed love', a comment that resonates beyond the romance between Phyllis Dicks and Jimmy Soutar, speaking to the series' own growing love triangle between Hamish, Alex and Isobel. Regarding said triangle, after watching Hamish and Isobel almost kiss on the couch, a 'karmic surge' according to TV John, there's now no doubt that Hamish knows how she feels about him.

Bryan Elsley uses the musical framework to explore themes central to both *West Side Story* and *Hamish Macbeth*, including the power of community versus authority and the sometimes destructive nature of parental control. Where *West Side Story* ended with tragic death, 'West Coast Story' cleverly inverts expectations during its tense standoff finale, finding resolution through revealed truths rather than violence.

There's also an undercurrent of Highland folklore. When Duncan Soutar speaks of hearing 'the seal folk' calling to his dead wife, wanting to claim their son Jimmy too, TV John's response is tellingly ambiguous: 'A thing doesn't actually need to happen for it to be real.'

The episode now occupies a curious place in TV history. It may be one of *Hamish Macbeth*'s most fondly remembered episodes —voted joint first with 'Wee Jock's Lament' by IMDb users— but the BBC has never repeated it, nor released it on VHS or DVD, and as of early 2025, it remains absent from BBC iPlayer because of rights issues. While fans can still track down 'West Coast Story' on rival streaming services, it's ironic that this story of forbidden love has become a forbidden piece of TV by its original broadcaster.

5. WEE JOCK'S LAMENT

Writer: Daniel Boyle
Director: Nicholas Renton
Original broadcast: 23rd April 1995, 7.30pm

GUEST CAST

Patricia Ross (Susan Graham/Rose Hart), Billy McColl (Francie McGilp), Ken Hutchison (Harry Dobbs), Rab Christie (Jimmy Soutar), Greig Guthrie (Wee Boy), Dolina MacLennan (Flora), Michael Marra (Jackie Dallas), Christine Primrose (Dale Dallas), Graham De Banzie (Robert Graham).

Summary

As the episode opens, Rose Hart, a mysterious woman with a broken-down van and a West Highland Terrier, accepts a lift from Hamish into Lochdubh. Back in the village, two escaped convicts—Harry Dobbs and Francie McGilp—accidentally run over Hamish's beloved Wee Jock. Despite Doc Brown's efforts to save him, the dog has to be put down, leaving Hamish devastated.

While the village tries to help—from TV John attempting to place Wee Jock in the newspaper's deaths column to a spectacularly ill-timed Country & Western performance at the pub—Hamish arms himself with his service revolver and heads into the hills after the killers.

He finds Harry and Francie living rough, with Harry suffering delusions about becoming a monk in the wilderness. Hamish poses as a hermit, teaching them survival skills while trying to understand what kind of men would kill a dog. The truth emerges during a nightmare-plagued night around the campfire. Years ago, the men accidentally killed a young boy in a hit-and-run and concealed both body and crime. Harry's guilt has driven him to the edge of sanity, while Francis carries the weight of their shared secret.

Meanwhile, TV John's second sight shows him Hamish about to commit murder. He leads Doc Brown and the McCraes on a desperate trek through the hills to prevent tragedy. Their pursuit culminates in a tense confrontation on a rope bridge where Hamish decides not to kill the men.

The episode takes an otherworldly turn when Hamish visits the dead boy's parents and discovers that Rose Hart, the woman he met earlier, was actually the ghost of Mrs Graham's sister who died years ago, while her dog was the ghost of Wee Jock. The Grahams give Hamish a new puppy, Wee Jock II, while TV John plays a lament on the bagpipes.

Commentary

Andrea Calderwood: Episodes like 'Wee Jock's Lament' stay in people's minds and I think that's why *Hamish* was such a success.

Stuart McGugan: *Hamish* was a cut above the Sunday night scripts. Danny Boyle scripts were the best, there were others that were more traditional, but his were different. He killed the dug!

Nicholas Renton: [Daniel's scripts are] like an onion, you keep going in and in and you find another layer and it's all explained.

Deirdre Keir: It's what he loves, and that's why his plotting and characterisation is brilliant. He's very good at the dark past, sins of omission and redemption.

Nicholas Renton: [We met a woman who] was a psychic from Skye and had second sight, we had some interesting conversations. If you have the second sight, you don't really talk about it. I asked her, 'If you're aware something is going to happen to someone, how do you cope with it?' She wouldn't talk about that side of it, but she said, 'I had a dream once about rocks falling, then there was an earthquake a few days later.' So they're in touch with something. There's absolutely something there, but maybe she has dreams of rocks falling three times a month.

Deirdre Keir: My dad was living on the Clyde and just down from him on this wee lane was a farm and the farmer's wife had second sight. He explained he'd known her for years and her husband died and he went up to offer his condolences. They sat talking, and she said, 'Well, I knew it was going to happen,' but he was explaining her reluctance to talk about it because it's not a gift, it's a curse. I never asked Daniel if he knew someone with second sight. I wouldn't be at all surprised if his granny had it.

Filming outside Rory's store. Photo by Kay Herbert

Ralph Riach: Being a bit of a prophet, having the second sight, the wisdom, it was a great period of my life for the three years we did it. I lived in London for a few years and had a friend called John Geddes. I moved back to Elgin, but kept in touch with John. I had a dream one night that John had died of food poisoning and I thought that doesn't sound like John Geddes, it's not nearly dramatic enough. I hadn't spoken to him for a while, so I rang and he wasn't there. He'd been to the doctor's and had a brain tumour that he died from.

Duncan Duff: The first time I met Danny [Boyle] was when he came up to Plockton and I think we filmed at the Doc's house when Hamish brought me Wee Jock to see if I could save him. The entire village wove their way to the Doc's house, a great property in Plockton that was a little bit remote. Like the character of the Doc, it was slightly apart.

Having shot that, we were all walking back towards the village and it was low tide, so we cut across the beach and somebody said, 'Oh, Duncan, by the way, this is Danny Boyle.' We fell in step and chatted a wee bit and he made this lovely comment, he said, 'You've got the right eyes for the Doc.' He was implying I had that slightly dreamy look in the eyes and that was definitely what I think I was principally called upon to do, partly the dope smoking, but partly he was on another plane of existence.

'Wee Jock's Lament' was the first episode we did, which involved the principal characters in the village going off and looking for Hamish, I think because we were worried he was going to kill the convicts who had run over Wee Jock. We were out in the middle of nowhere and in nice weather as well, because I think we started in late August or September that first series. They brought the beginning of production forward each year.

That first year we didn't finish till December, by which point it wasn't light till nine in the morning and dark by four, which wasn't terribly practical. We got some glorious weather and if it wasn't for the midges, it would have been absolutely fantastic. It's like the Western, it was the posse getting ready to go off.

Jimmy Yuill: I have memories of Kenneth Branagh coming up for a long weekend with another friend, [the actor] Nicholas Farrell. It must have been after we'd done *Mary Shelley's Frankenstein* [1994], I think they had the use of

113

Francis Ford Coppola's [the film's producer] plane. They flew into Inverness and hired a car to go to Plockton for the weekend. I went out filming and they went off for a walk. Kenny was wearing a distinctive orange anorak. We were filming a scene with Bobby on a hill while myself, Brian and Ralph were in a valley, and the assistant director started shouting that there are people walking in the background, one of them in an orange anorak. He was trying desperately to get them out of the shot. So they're in the back of the shot and I'm thinking; *I know who that is. What're the odds of that?* I couldn't tell anyone who it was. I couldn't say, 'Oh, that's my mate.'

James Fraser (ex-Kyle of Lochalsh resident): When I lived in Kyle I was on the Gala committee and we had two big marquee tents that were hired out to the film crew for use on remote locations for changing, storing equipment and catering. There was a donation of a couple of hundred quid each time we had to put them up and take them down and move to the next shoot. The most remote one was on the crags above Duncraig. We got up to the tower by vehicle, but took a fair effort to get to where they had the shoot. Luckily, we were young back then.

Deirdre Keir: The unit could just about support you going [into the hills] and getting those shots. There was a lot of schlepping up hills.

Nicholas Renton: Even carting just one camera around was very, very heavy. You have to have a lot of support.

Deirdre Keir: Our four-wheel drives came from Sharp's Reliable Wrecks in Inverness. We didn't have a deal with Land Rover or Mitsubishi or Honda or any of that crowd. I thought, *What's local? Inverness.* [We called] Mr Sharp and said we'd be coming up and could we get some 4x4s which we'd be hiring for around 18 weeks, so I had a very old Nissan truck and there were knackered old 4x4s all over the place.

Nicholas Renton: We were taking heavy gear. When we went to Skye, it all had to be carried up by Sherpas.

Deirdre Keir: I'm really glad we shot it on 16mm film. We couldn't afford 35mm. Fred [Tammes] and our directors of photography could really work with exteriors, and if you were in the police station, they knew how to set that up so you could see the water outside and also see inside. My production manager wanted to go home because the director of photography was faxing in lists of stuff. Fred was in New Mexico with Antonia Bird making a movie, so there were lots of phone calls and this huge list of kit and there was no way we could afford to get that up from London. There was a lot of haggling and everyone was worried he wouldn't come.

Nicholas Renton: We picked him up from Inverness and it was almost two hours and he didn't say a word. Fred is Dutch, so Dutch paintings, Dutch landscapes are kind of built into him. He'd lived in England for 20 years, but he'd never been to the Highlands.

Deirdre Keir: He got out of the car and was completely overcome by the crags, the sea and the light. He'd just come from the desert and the light was exactly the same every day.

Nicholas Renton: There was a lovely lady called Annie Rees, who was the production manager, tough as nails but with a big heart. She was old school, did it by the book. There was a lot of night written into the script because writers write night then we get up and it's September so there is no light really, so what do we do? We said, 'Look, the Scots have this term called gloaming, so we create gloaming.' I remember being in a conversation with Annie and Fred and she said, 'Right Fred, when does gloaming start?' and he said, 'It depends on the day Annie, it could start at midday,' so we invented early gloaming and late gloaming.

Deirdre Keir: We segued into shooting day for night and I said to Fred, 'You remember those old John Wayne films where they shot day for night all the time, is that what we're going to do?' He nodded and so we started shooting day for night.

Nicholas Renton: We had lots of gloaming and Fred was very clear about that. It was all done in camera really.

Deirdre Keir: It wasn't done in grading afterwards.

Nicholas Renton: On a Sunday you could start gloaming at four in the afternoon and finish at 10 at night.

Duncan Duff: We were shooting one scene right up on top of a hill beside the campfire. There was a panning shot that lingered on each one of us. I remember being up there with the crew and, of course, one other thing that was very special about *Hamish* was there wasn't just a camaraderie amongst actors. It was very much the entire crew, because everybody was away from home. Everybody who would otherwise have just got in their cars and buggered off back to their home life and away from work couldn't do that. That was wonderful. I have a clear memory of looking around and thinking, *To be out here on a nice evening, the sun's just going down, we're doing something that's real quality. Having a laugh with a really nice bunch of people, it's just magical.*

Nicholas Renton: The real 'Wee Jock' moment was the piping at the end. That was almost the only day I think in the fortnight when the sun was out and you could see Skye beyond. If the weather had been bad, I'm not sure we would have gone back.

Deirdre Keir: I got to choose the lament. I got to sit in my office and listen to pipe laments for days. We had a local piper come from Inverness.

Alasdair MacQuarrie: There were three white stones made [for the cairn], maybe in case they broke one. We had one in our house and another couple of families in Plockton managed to get them as well. I remember that sitting in one of the rooms for a long, long time.

Stuart McGugan: Ron [Donachie] was telling me that after Wee Jock was killed, there was a pretend cairn built and coach loads of pensioners would turn up and cry beside it. The second year saw coach loads of Australians turn up because it was sold over there.

Ralph Riach: I was in Australia, I was looking for the other terminal at Sydney airport, and this bloke came up to me and said, 'You're a film star aren't you?' I said, 'No I'm hardly a film star,' and he said, 'It's *Hamish Macbeth*, isn't it? You sometimes find people looking at you and you think, 'Why are they looking at me?' For me, I'm still Ralphie Riach fae Elgin and I just think it's weird.

Charlie MacRae: One Australian lady asked me about Wee Jock. I told her where he was killed and that they had to do six retakes. She said, 'Was the dog killed six times?!'

JUST AS THE episode saw the departure of Wee Jock, it also meant the exit of the canine performer who portrayed him, Zippy, who was replaced by eight-month-old Zack from Dingwall. According to one newspaper report, Zippy had suffered from flatulence so bad that Robert Carlyle had demanded a replacement.

Final Thoughts

'Wee Jock's Lament' marks a pivotal moment for *Hamish Macbeth*, firmly establishing the supernatural as a key element of the series. From TV John's vision of impending tragedy to the ghostly presence of Rose Hart, the episode weaves these otherworldly elements into the fabric of the story, creating an unsettling atmosphere throughout.

Writing for *CST Online*, Dr Melissa Beattie noted that because *Hamish Macbeth* and *The Wicker Man* were both filmed in Plockton, they function as 'paratextual' companions, with *Hamish* subverting the earlier film's representation of Highland spirituality. While *The Wicker Man* portrayed the Highlands as a place of dangerous pagan rituals, *Hamish Macbeth* transformed similar elements into something 'intelligible, progressive and "cosy"'. The supernatural elements here—TV John's second sight and Rose Hart's ghost—are protective rather than threatening.

Instead of presenting rural Scottish mysticism as sinister, the show grounds these elements in 'the intelligence and compassion of its eccentric characters' while remaining authentically Scottish. Beattie suggests this may explain why, years later, Plockton's Tourist Information Centre prominently displayed *Hamish Macbeth* memorabilia while *The Wicker Man* items were notably absent.

Hamish's pursuit of the escaped convicts responsible for Wee Jock's death takes him deep into the Highland wilderness, where the physical landscape mirrors his internal struggle. Robert Carlyle's performance here is a standout, capturing Hamish's barely contained fury and the realisation that his role is not to punish but to heal.

6. A BIT OF AN EPIC

Writer: Julian Spilsbury
Director: Sid Roberson
Original broadcast: 30th April 1995, 8pm

GUEST CAST

James Faulkner (Colonel Don Maxwell), Iain Lauchlan (Jimmy McCormack), Jake D'Arcy (Scott), Robert Willox (Walker), Philip McGough (George Standish), Susannah Hitching (Jenny Carpenter), John Warnaby (Mike Beardsall), Leda Hodgson (Helen Wadlow), Graeme Alexander Young (Mark Glasson), Jon Croft (Malkie Clunie), Will Morgan (Gregor).

SUMMARY

Outside the Stag Bar, Colonel Maxwell's Executive Expeditions group faces early tensions when Paul, one of the guides, is fired after a drunken incident. The next morning, Isobel joins Maxwell's corporate team-building expedition up Ben Drach, with Hamish initially declining to participate.

The group includes marketing manager Jenny Carpenter, her admirer Mike Beardsall, the asthmatic George Standish and other office workers pushed far outside their comfort zones. After Hamish spots concerning signs about Maxwell's judgment, he joins the hike. Meanwhile, Alex returns to Lochdubh hoping to speak with Hamish, only to learn he's up in the mountains.

When the group reaches Ben Drach's summit, Maxwell pushes them to attempt the more dangerous McKenzie's Point despite obvious exhaustion and injuries. After Hamish suggests a safer route down, the group splits, with George, Helen and Mark following Hamish's path while Isobel stays with Maxwell's team, spurning Hamish's concerns.

Unable to shake his worries, Hamish returns to find Maxwell increasingly unstable, quoting Shakespeare as his behaviour becomes more erratic. The situation turns deadly when Jenny becomes trapped on a dangerous ledge. As Hamish attempts a rescue, Maxwell, whose judgment is impaired by health issues, cuts the rope in a misguided attempt to save the group, plunging to his death.

The episode reaches a climax with a mountain rescue and Isobel telling Hamish she loves him as he hangs over a cliff. With the group finally saved, the final scenes show the weary survivors returning to Lochdubh, where a delighted Alex asks Hamish to marry her in front of the villagers, leaving Hamish speechless.

COMMENTARY

Jon Older (First Assistant Director): I knew Deirdre Keir from when I started my telly career at Granada and she was one of the assistant directors there. Deirdre was ADing a show called *The Mallens* [1979-80], and when I went out on my very first day on a set, she was the one in charge. So I got *Hamish* through knowing her. I only did [director] Sid Roberson's episode in year one. I liked him a lot. He was quite a scary bloke to look at because he used to be a bodybuilder before he became a commercials director. How he made that transition, I'm not sure, but he had a great directing technique. He wasn't really an actor's director: he'd look at a page and say, 'All right, you stay there, you say that, you go there and then you speak...'

There's a sequence when they're halfway up the hill, when Hamish comes back to persuade them to change their mind and go back. He falls out with Isobel and they have a row and to me, although Shirley's a brilliant actress, that was over the top. It was way more than it should have been, but that's the sort of thing Sid wouldn't have picked up on. He was more concerned about where the Steadicam was going to go. It was all Steadicam once we got going up the mountain, which is how we could get around. We knew early on that there was going to be only minimal lighting outside, so [director of photography] Peter Jackson, a lovely old school guy, took a couple of sparks up with reflector boards for close-ups but otherwise we didn't carry loads of kit around from one place to other because we just would never have made it.

Stuart Davids: You had to get all that hardware up there, cranes and everything and I really don't think they'd have the budgets to do that now. Everyone set the bar very high, and that's not there anymore.

Jon Older: That was a tough shoot, but it probably wasn't as tough as it looks because we were quite lucky with the weather. It was late in the year so it was always a bit miserable, but I don't think we were badly weathered off at any time on *Hamish*, which is quite remarkable because the whole weather system around Plockton is unique, it changes from one day to the next. Most of the locations were carefully picked to be about 20 yards from a road, I think we sold that well. Regarding the sinking into the bog, the art department dug a big hole in the marsh and stuck a wheelie bin in it so that we could put in the actor and then pull him out. So he was actually standing in a wheelie bin.

Valerie Gogan: I was quite excited that there was going to be a helicopter. I was really excited about *going up* in the helicopter, but I didn't get to. They said, 'No, only the people insured for going up in the helicopter are going up in the helicopter.' We were all back in the pub for hours, waiting to find out what happened in the mountain rescue.

Jon Older: We had the helicopter for one or two days. The main unit only had it for one day. Just near the end, when the helicopter comes to rescue them, there's a shot that we did with the cast and the helicopter. But all of those long sweeping helicopter shots, there weren't any drones in those days, were all done by a second unit and a team of seven stand-ins. There's one cheeky shot of the stand-ins, when they almost get to where they stop and start to fall off the ledge. The helicopter tracks around them and they're all carefully not looking at the camera because it's not the actors.

When Colonel Maxwell is hanging suspended off the edge, we did that for real. Obviously, he was on the safety line, anchored so he couldn't have gone anywhere, but he was literally hanging over a drop and it would've hurt him if he'd fallen off. Then we cut to the wide shot of the dummy falling, which looks a bit pants. We did a terrible process shot of the moment he's falling through the air [mimes arms flailing]. We shot that in the castle in Plockton, which was our production base. We set up a green screen, I think we did it flat on the floor. It just looks awful and why they bothered to include it, I don't know. Overall, I thought it looked amazing for the resources that we had.

Deirdre Keir: When we started, we didn't have the Isobel/Alex strand. We had Hamish's tortured past and part of his history in the first episode is Alex. We had that group of characters and started putting together a couple of lines about who the characters might be. I said to Daniel [Boyle], 'I'd quite like to do a strand about these two through the series.' Daniel looked at me and said, 'Well you'll just have to say what you want to happen, I'm not very good at that stuff.' I said, 'No, these have got to be standalone stories, but let's weave it in a little bit.' So we worked quietly at that.

Shirley Henderson: The love thing just developed into something deeper from us doing it. It started to build and became maybe more than they thought. It became more than I could imagine from how it started.

Dominic Minghella: I think that was something I was most passionate about, so I probably did the needlework. I was always concerned for Hamish to have flaws, and the principal element of that for me was his inability to see that Isobel admired him.

Andrea Calderwood: Hamish was a bit of a fish out of water. He was very much his own person, maybe slightly reluctantly doing what he was doing, which is where the relationship with Shirley and Val came in. He didn't necessarily want to be there in that job, but he was. So there was always a bit of an edge to it. And despite himself, he loves the place. He loves the people. He falls in love with the girls.

Shirley Henderson: That was a great episode because we really did go up there on the rocks. Then in the car coming back, will we, won't we get together, and it almost was and then Valerie is in the pub and they get together and it changes everything.

Valerie Gogan: I was heartbroken, it was like real life. The helicopter had gone up the mountain, and it was like that thing where you know it's too late and you're grasping at straws, like asking somebody to marry you when it's far too late. You know it's too late, but you try to claw back something that's gone.

As filming often does, you wait for a long time. It did actually feel like waiting, waiting, waiting and then you just know it's gone, you've lost. You feel for your character, you feel like, *OK, I lost, I've made a mistake, I've fucked it up. He's already checked out.* We've all been there in that situation. When somebody's checked out, you can't do anything. You try harder and harder, and it's just a lost cause. It's quite sad.

I suppose he ended up with the right girl, Alex. Maybe it was one of those situations where she wanted it when it was gone. We never really discussed that. Shirley's quite quiet, and I am too. We always got on well, but we never went and discussed it. We just came at it from two poles apart, and that's how we did it. I think that probably is the best way to deal with that situation.

We were told not to say anything [about the resolution], but I think we wouldn't have anyway, because you don't want to spoil it for people. I can't remember necessarily signing anything, but I definitely wouldn't have said. It would have ruined it.

ROBERT CARLYLE ALSO kept quiet about how the cliffhanger might be resolved when pushed by *TV Week Australia* in 1996: 'On the one hand Hamish is caring, loving and generous. But when it comes to his love-life, he's completely useless. So, who will he choose? That's the terrible dilemma. People will have to tune into the next series to find out!'

Final Thoughts

'A Bit of an Epic' lives up to its title by delivering one of series one's most ambitious episodes, blending high-stakes mountain rescue with romantic revelations. What begins as a routine corporate team-building exercise becomes a taut drama that would leave viewers on tenterhooks until the series' return.

Julian Spilsbury's script builds tension through Colonel Maxwell's increasingly dangerous decision-making. His insistence on pushing his inexperienced climbers toward Mackenzie's Point sets up a confrontation between Hamish's practical concern for safety and Maxwell's philosophical obsession with pushing human limits.

Back in Lochdubh, life continues in its own eccentric way. The McCraes announce plans to expand their lobster business into Europe, local trade not being what it was (presumably after the events of episode one), with Lachie Jr earnestly studying Spanish, while TV John steps up in Hamish's absence. Esme and Rory make their first public appearance as a couple, marked by an awkward champagne order at the bar. These lighter moments provide welcome relief from the tension on the mountain.

What makes the episode particularly memorable is how it interweaves personal drama with physical peril. Isobel's declaration of love for Hamish comes at the height of danger—'If you go, I'm coming with you!'—while Alex's unexpected return to Lochdubh creates a second cliffhanger.

It's a fitting season finale that leaves viewers eager to see what lies ahead for Hamish and the residents of Lochdubh.

EIGHT
AN ARRESTING OPENING

For Andrea Calderwood, the success of *Hamish Macbeth* came as both validation and revelation. The series wasted no time captivating audiences, settling into its Sunday night BBC One slot in spring 1995 with viewing figures that quickly averaged around 10 million per week. Such was its immediate impact that a second series was commissioned before the first had even concluded.

Calderwood remembers the moment she learned just how successful the show had become. During a script read-through for *Small Faces*, Gillies MacKinnon's 1995 film that would mark BBC Scotland's first feature production, someone slipped her a Post-it note with the overnight ratings: 9.9 million viewers. With adjusted figures, they'd broken the coveted 10 million mark, the traditional benchmark for a genuine hit.

'It felt like such a brilliant achievement,' says Calderwood, 'to have a show that was so true to itself, that had all that creative originality to it and that reached a big audience. It gave me a lot of confidence as an exec and then as a producer, it showed me that what you need to do is go for your gut instinct on things.'

For the young executive, *Hamish*'s success challenged conventional wisdom about what audiences would accept. 'I think it signalled a new era and a new approach to making Scottish drama,' she explains. 'For me, there was a feeling that you can do something that's distinctive and the audience will find it, rather than feeling that you have to hit a formula and dumb down.'

This lesson would shape her entire approach to her production career. 'I've said it repeatedly through the years: the things I've done that have worked well have been the ones that are original. Any time I've tried to do something that's formulaic, it hasn't worked so well. So either I just don't know how those formulas work or I'm much better at doing things that are distinctive and original.'

The experience also highlighted the value of having seasoned professionals at the helm. 'For me as a young exec, that was what was so good about having such an experienced team with Scott and Deirdre on it, that combination of boldness and experience,' she says. 'Scott's obviously got very original tastes as a producer. He wouldn't have done a formulaic mainstream series, because he's got a distinct original taste and is a big backer of talent. So I think for all those reasons, I think it was a pretty perfect combination.'

For BBC Scotland, *Hamish Macbeth* marked a turning point, proof that regional drama could be both distinctively Scottish and universally appealing. The series had found that rare sweet spot between artistic integrity and commercial success, setting a new standard for what was possible in the Sunday night drama slot.

A HIGHLAND HIT

Reviewing 'The Great Lochdubh Salt Robbery' in the *Daily Record*, John Millar likened *Hamish Macbeth* to *Heartbeat*, noting parallels in their protagonists' disdain for authority and rapport with locals. However, he felt the 'heilan' copper' offered greater depth as a character and the McCraes 'could become the Arfur Daleys of the glens'—a reference to the wheeler-dealer character from the ITV comedy-drama *Minder* (1979–94)—even if the real police might not be impressed by 'Hashish Hamish'.

The first episode was also well-received in Plockton. Charlie MacRae told the *Press & Journal* that 'It started a bit slow, but the scenery was lovely and local people enjoyed seeing themselves as the extras.' Douglas Hamilton of Plockton Stores revealed that 'Some of the older people were not so keen on it, but on the whole it went down well.'

The Scottish Tourist Board reported a tourism surge, with hotels at their fullest in five years. The series was part of a wider screen-led tourism boom, with *Rob Roy* and *Braveheart* set for release later in 1995, though *Hamish* had beaten them to showcasing the Highland landscape to millions of potential visitors.

Some businesses were quick to capitalise on the show's popularity. In Caithness, Lochdhu Lodge began advertising holiday rentals, its name resembling the fictional Lochdubh. Co-owner Jim Dale acknowledged the connection was advantageous: 'The fame of the fictional place will do us no harm.'

Ratings remained relatively steady across the six weeks of series one, with the finale attracting 8.5 million viewers, competing respectably against ITV's flagship drama *Prime Suspect* (1991–2006), which boasted nearly 13 million.

On the eve of series one's final episode, the *Herald*'s George Hume reflected on how *Hamish Macbeth* had transformed Plockton, noting local businesses' enthusiasm and the challenges posed by filming during peak tourist season. The 12-week shoot for series two was scheduled to begin in late July 1995.

While Northern Constabulary maintained their professional distance—'A very firm line has been drawn under *Hamish Macbeth*'—shopkeeper Douglas Hamilton candidly remarked on the strain filming of the second series would place on accommodation availability. 'They will occupy the cottages and take the hotel rooms that ordinary visitors would have taken... they will not be able to get into the hotels and cottages they used the last time because they are already let.'

One four-legged Plocktonion, Heather the Highland cow, a familiar sight lumbering through Harbour Street during filming, became a safety concern because of her horns. As a surge of tourists posed for photos with Heather, owner Dolan MacKenzie reluctantly decided to sell her, stating, 'I could never have it on my conscience if a child or someone lost an eye.'

Beyond tourism and wildlife, *Hamish Macbeth* spurred a mini property boom in Plockton. Inquiries poured in for village flats, including those in a newly converted church hall.

The series also sparked controversy as demand for West Highland Terriers like Wee Jock surged. Unscrupulous breeders were 'churning out' Westies in puppy farms for £300 per animal, with breeders receiving up to 100 enquiries a day. This prompted the Scottish Kennel Club to warn buyers against poorly bred puppies that hadn't been screened for hereditary diseases.

FACT VS FICTION

BBC One's *Points of View* revisited the first series with residents in Inverness. While some police officers enjoyed the show as a parody of Highland life, others, like Inspector John MacDonald, felt certain situations were exaggerated. Community councillor Kay MacLennan explained that she 'did not think it showed the police in a very good light', while community education worker Pablo Mascarenhas joked that most viewers might think the show was 10% fact and 90% fiction—though he believed the reverse was closer to the truth.

At the 1995 BAFTA Scotland awards, Robert Carlyle won Best Television Actor for *Hamish Macbeth* and *Cracker*. The series itself was nominated for Best Drama, while Daniel Boyle earned a nod for Best Writer. Though neither won, Carlyle's victory underscored the success of casting him as Hamish.

Around this time, Carlyle's reaction to press coverage of his personal life soured, in the main thanks to the *Sunday Mirror*'s decision to track down his estranged mother and publish an interview with her. 'I opened up the paper and there was my mother, whom I hadn't seen for thirty-two years,' the actor told *HQ* magazine. 'It makes you feel lousy.'

As the buzz around the series continued to build, expectations for series two rose significantly. The warm reception to *Hamish*'s debut series had not only changed Plockton, but had firmly established the series as a Sunday night fixture. What lay ahead would test both the production team's creativity and the audience's loyalty.

NINE
FIRE GODS AND NEW FACES

SPRING 1995

THE HELICOPTER BANKED SHARPLY over the Hebridean coastline as Ming Ho and the location team scanned the beaches below. Somewhere down there was the perfect spot for a plane to land, if they could find it. Bryan Elsley's ambitious new script, featuring nods to *The Wicker Man*, had sent them island-hopping across Scotland's West Coast, searching for locations that could bring his vision to life.

Back at Zenith's production office, a gnawing concern was growing. Elsley's script had somehow become too much for a 50-minute episode and the summer shooting schedule was approaching fast.

Ming Ho's desk was already covered with script drafts and story outlines. After working as the company's in-house development executive across dozens of projects, she was now focusing her attention on *Hamish* full-time as script editor. The transition made sense as she'd worked with producer Deirdre Keir before and had been involved in *Hamish*'s early development before other projects pulled her away.

The foundation was solid. Daniel Boyle would continue as lead writer, his distinctive vision having defined the show's tone from the start. Stuart Hepburn was set to return, having proven himself adept at balancing the series' mix of comedy and darkness. Dominic Minghella, who'd served as script editor and writer of one episode on the first series, would continue to contribute as a writer.

As for Bryan Elsley's new script, tough decisions would need to be made.

Deirdre Keir: On the second series I asked Bryan Elsley to do one and he just couldn't get it down to 50 minutes.

Bryan Elsley: I'm not sure what that idea was. No doubt it was absolutely ridiculous.

Nicholas Renton: It was about the island of Eigg. There was a German millionaire who had bought it and he believed in sun and fire gods and there were aircraft landing on it.

Ming Ho: It was an ambitious story, which involved a plane landing on a beach as the regular BA/Loganair scheduled flight did every day on the Isle of Barra, where the beach is the island's airport. I think there were also elements of smuggling, inspired by *Whisky Galore!*, which was filmed on Barra. We went on a recce to the Western Isles for this, flying by helicopter from Inverness to Castlebay on Barra and over potential beaches on the beautiful Harris, Lewis, and Benbecula en route. We spent a couple of days scouting locations around the island, including Kisimul Castle in the bay.

Nicholas Renton: There were about 40 pages that were absolutely brilliant, except we could only do 45 pages max, and it all came to grief.

Bryan Elsley: I didn't perform and Deirdre unceremoniously fired me. I was summoned to Plockton and Deirdre said, 'Well, it's not really working out with this episode, is it?' I said, 'Just give me another few days and I'm sure I'll be able to finish it.' She said, 'Well, no, I don't think so Bryan, I think we'll probably get Danny to fix it up.' I said, 'Maybe I could speak to Danny about it?' And she said, 'Actually, he's already done it.'

Nicholas Renton: Then Daniel came in and wrote two episodes, just like that.

Ming Ho: The plot proved too complex and the script went through a number of drafts. I felt there was a lot of promising material in it and was keen to persevere, but we ran out of time in the production schedule. A decision had to be made of whether to keep on for another draft or two or bail out and commission a different story.

It may seem a bigger task to start again, but sometimes a script loses clarity and momentum if the storyline fundamentally isn't working and the writer feels bogged down by too many notes; everyone gets tired and confused, and the spark dies on the page. It can be cleaner to take a completely different tack. It was a shame to lose Bryan's script. I think it was replaced by 'Isobel Pulls it Off' by Dom Minghella.

Bryan Elsley: I probably just didn't have the craft. Like a lot of emerging writers, I was pretty pleased with myself in general and I thought I could do anything, but I was actually struggling to do anything. So I got fired from the show in the second year and was very upset about it at the time. But it's the kind of thing that does happen in television; I don't really think you are a television writer until you've been fired. You learn a lot from it. You learn that you probably weren't working hard enough, and you weren't deep enough in it.

It's a long time ago now and, in fact, getting fired from that show was one of the best things that ever happened to me. I vowed that would never happen again and I would work harder and try to be a better writer. I richly deserved that firing.

A NEW LACHLAN SR

Series two also saw the loss of original cast member Jimmy Yuill, who left Lochdubh and the character of Lachlan Sr behind, deciding instead to remain on the Cornwall-set ITV detective series *Wycliffe* until 1998. Billy Riddoch would play Lachlan Sr for the rest of the series.

Today, memories differ as to the exact reason for Yuill's departure.

Scott Meek: We tried to establish a principle with salaries that was very straightforward. Enormous problems happen in film and television when actors talk about how much they're paid and no matter what you say, when they're sitting around, they talk about how much they're paid. So we established a very open tier system. If you were in the top six or eight, you'd be paid this. There's a band A and a band B and C, so everyone knows that they're on the same pay and that's how we structured it. As we went into the second series, Jimmy was less enthusiastic about that structure and we failed to reach an agreement. So we either had to change the structure or we had to change the casting.

Deirdre Keir: Jimmy was fantastic in that part, so when we knew we'd got a recommission there was frantic phoning everyone, asking if they'd do it again. His agent called to say it was a question of billing. I said, 'If we change billing for one person, we'd need to do it for everyone.' She said, 'Well he's not going to do it,' and I said, 'Well, I'm really sorry about that.' My dad used to tell me about billing and it really mattered to actors. I wasn't being disrespectful to him, but it meant the opening title sequence would have gone on forever. Andrea was really surprised and asked what we'd do. I said we were going to recast. Looking at the first series, he was fantastic, and it was a hard old gig for Billy to follow that.

Jimmy Yuill: First of all, it was 30 years ago. I can't remember exactly what I was thinking at the time, but I was on a roll. I'd just been on a set with a hero of mine, [Robert] De Niro on *Mary Shelley's Frankenstein*, I was number two in *Wycliffe* and I had two young kids. If it had been just about money, I would have done it.

I remember being slightly disappointed when they sent me a script from the second series ['The Lochdubh Deluxe']. The locals think a spaceship has arrived and at one point we're all naked on the hill, beating ourselves with branches. I said to Nick [Renton], 'Do you know what I would do? I would get the *Northern Times* [newspaper covering the north of Scotland], read the 'Seen and Heard' section and look at the court cases—the reality is infinitely more crazy than UFOs.' There was a guy in our village; he robbed the one-armed bandit at the golf club. Because there was a hole in the bag, the police caught him when they found a trail of sixpences leading to his front door.

Duncan Duff: Because I had family in Dingwall I used to pop over there and they loved *Hamish*. I think people from that part of the world did because it was like, 'We're not a bunch of teuchters [a sometimes derogatory Scottish Lowlands term for those living in the Highlands].' I think it represented something much more interesting. It wasn't patronising to anybody and, as Scottish people, we're all aware of the 'shortbread and tartan' thing. We all have a complicated relationship with that. Scottishness is complicated.

Jimmy Yuill: Maybe I was too close to it? Maybe that was a bigger issue for me than I realised at the time. I loved every bit of it, but there were a lot of things all happening at one time that must have merged together to say, 'This isn't going to work out.'

Scott Meek: As everyone else was happy, and it seemed to work, we decided that as Jimmy had other things to do and through the brilliance of Julia Duff or the intervention of God, Billy Riddoch appeared and effortlessly took over.

Jimmy Yuill: Billy fitted perfectly into my costume. They didn't even pretend it wasn't me—you think they might have said, 'Oh, it's his twin brother' or something. Billy phoned me up and said, 'Jimmy, I feel terrible' and I said, 'Billy, don't worry one second.' He said, 'No, they've put me in the costume.' I said, 'Is it my costume?' and he said, 'Yeah'. I said, 'It doesn't matter, Billy, it's a business and I'm taking a risk not doing it.' I also wasn't sure how long Bobby would be doing it. Ralph wasn't happy, but I said, 'I can't do it, Ralph.'

Ralph Riach: I missed Jimmy, he had that something. Maybe he had that mentality? Billy Riddoch was fantastic too, though.

Stuart Davids: Billy became my father, which was great. They were both great to work with.

Valerie Gogan: I think Jimmy kind of felt ownership because he was from near there. It was a shame that he didn't come back because he's such a character. You get a bit shocked by it, you think everybody's replaceable. You thought you wouldn't be able to do that, but they just brought in lovely Billy Riddoch.

Anne Lacey: Billy did a great job taking over from Jimmy, who was a hard act to follow and some people didn't even notice.

Scott Meek: I showed an episode from the second series to someone senior at the BBC who actually said, 'Jimmy Yuill was particularly great in that episode,' and I said, 'Even more remarkably great when you consider it's not him.'"

Duncan Duff: I was very fond of Jimmy and I was very sad that he didn't come back. I think Billy did a fantastic job of coming into a very difficult situation. But I loved Jimmy because I felt a connection with my father coming from that part of the world and knowing that part of the world. He was brilliant in it and we had a lot in common and got on really well. He was a little bit older than me, but that made him interesting. He was a father figure and a great character.

Stuart McGugan: I knew that when we came back Jimmy wouldn't be there but Billy would—different actor, different dynamic. There weren't many cast changes.

THE OTHER CAST change occurred with the departure of series one's Zippy, after his role as Wee Jock came to a dramatic end, and replacement puppy, Zack, who played Wee Jock II.

For the second series, Fraoch (the Gaelic word for heather) joined the production in Plockton as a recast Wee Jock II.

Owner Irene Anderson described Fraoch as a 'canny dog with a sweet nature', revealing he got to know his way around Plockton 'after lamp-posts were daubed with his favourite liver gravy' and that fame hadn't gone to his head: 'He still fetches me my slippers when I arrive home!'

TEN
RETURN TO PLOCKTON

SUMMER 1995

THE WARM EVENING air drifted across Plockton's harbour as Robert Carlyle lit a cigarette outside his caravan in the village car park. A year ago, he'd been just another promising actor in an offbeat Scottish police drama. Now tourist coaches lined the waterfront, their passengers clutching cameras and newly purchased Wee Jock merchandise.

Just weeks ago, he'd been in Glasgow hurling pint glasses as the psychotic Begbie for *Trainspotting* (1996). Now back in his police uniform, he watched as the village changed around him.

Plockton's craft shop had started selling 'Souvenirs from Hamish Macbeth Country' to eager tourists. The Balmacara Hotel's public bar proudly displayed a poster declaring it the location of the first series' cliffhanger ending.

The locals had developed a protective formation in the pub, closing ranks around their temporary policeman with a wall of fisherman's jerseys designed to wear down over-enthusiastic fans. But the tide of visitors was becoming harder to stem. 'No Vacancy' signs appeared everywhere.

Plockton's Craft and Gift Shop, which doubled as Rory's store

Blue-rinsed ladies from the home counties ambled along the seafront. Amateur artists set up easels to capture the morning light on the harbour.

The BBC wanted 12 episodes for the next series. Carlyle had refused, revealing to *Time Out* that it was 'a constant struggle to keep quality rather than commerciality the primary force'. But as his reputation grew with each new role, maintaining that balance was becoming increasingly difficult. Fan mail arrived by the sackful now, mostly focused on the pressing question that seemed to obsess viewers: who would Hamish choose?

Other offers were starting to come his way, and if *Trainspotting* did well he couldn't commit to more than a third series of

Hamish Macbeth. The big screen was where he really wanted to be.

WELCOME TO LOCHDUBH

Alongside *Hamish*'s returning cast and crew were fresh faces like Toby Hefferman, who joined as third assistant director. Having worked with first AD Jon Older on *The Famous Five* (1995–97), he was thrilled to be on the production. 'I was immensely proud to finally work on something that was being aired on TV on a Sunday evening, and that my mum liked,' he says today.

Arriving in Plockton was an adventure in itself. Without Sat Nav, he'd relied on a map to navigate his way from London, assuming that reaching Glasgow meant he was close. 'I thought it'd be a quick hit from there,' he laughs, 'but it took another six hours on winding B roads to get to the middle of nowhere. By the time I reached the pub in Kyle, I thought, *Where are we?* But once I got into it, it was brilliant.'

Local talent also bolstered the team, including 19-year-old Plockton native, Sarah Bruce. A media student home from university, Sarah seized the chance to gain hands-on experience. 'Filming went on until October and I figured experience was more important.' She quickly became indispensable, standing in for cast members like Valerie Gogan and Shirley Henderson, while also taking on the less glamorous tasks of stopping traffic, fetching items and making tea.

The second series of *Hamish Macbeth* was bringing changes to Bruce's home.

Nicholas Renton: Year two the coaches arrived, the boat trips, the tea towels... I said in the very first meeting with the local councillors, 'Plockton is very well known, it's on every calendar, but if this show does well people will want to see it because it's the Old Country. You'll get a lot of visitors.' And that's what happened. Nobody was making eye contact with me.

SPEAKING TO *RADIO TIMES* during a 1994 set visit, community councillor Charlie MacRae touched on the changes he'd witnessed in Plockton through the years. 'My father was a fisherman and when he was a young man there would've been boats as far as you could see across the water. Then the trawlers came and the haddock disappeared. All we've got left here now is tourism.'

Duncan Duff: The first series was broadcast in Australia and it was huge. My brother's a dentist in Australia and it was the number two show after *The X-Files* [1993–2002], which in the mid-90s was a massive phenomenon. When we were shooting series two, people from Canada, New Zealand and Australia would turn up. They would make a detour to see the village where *Hamish Macbeth* was shot; they couldn't believe their luck when they would turn up and we were in the middle of shooting.

Anne Lacey: By series two and three the fans started to turn up. The locals were great and used to keep tables for us at the pub. They didn't bat an eyelid and took it in their stride.

Charlie MacRae: It certainly increased the tourists from all over the world, with Australians top of the list. We needed the tourists as the village had many old people and they kept the three hotels and our shop open.

Calum Mackenzie: After the first series, the next year everybody who had a West Highland Terrier in Britain took them to Plockton—there were hundreds of them.

SETTLING BACK IN

Valerie Gogan: By the second year there'd be tourists coming along to try and watch the filming because it was a bit of a hit. You'd have to have a bit of space where people could go, like a kind of caravan. There weren't any big American-type Winnebago things. Bobby had to do a lot of interviews and I was really impressed how cool he was with it. He's quite laid back and not nervous. He's very good at all that sort of thing.

Shirley Henderson: Filming was hard sometimes, but we had a laugh. We were all just in one little caravan when we came off set. They plonked this little caravan in the car park, and we all walked to work. We all used to sit in there, me, Brian Pettifer and Ralph Riach, and they used to tell stories and make us giggle and giggle, and it was just lovely. It was a nice atmosphere.

Duncan Duff: It's a magical place. We had some brilliant weather in series two or three, because we were starting a bit earlier, more like July. I remember experiencing those long evenings where it was light until two in the morning and you could still see by moonlight. You've got the hills opposite and when the weather's nice, with the rocky outcrops, it's a bit like the south of France.

Scott Meek: I would arrive regularly to tell them the rushes or the cut was looking great and sometimes to tell them about storylines that were coming up.

Toby Hefferman: We were all of an age where nothing really mattered, it was a new experience. I lived above a pub in Kyle of Lochalsh, and a lot of other people lived in Plockton because they got first dibs there. You'd wake up, and you were literally on the set. The fact it was a real-life place was extraordinary and

146

everyone embraced it. The ceilidhs, the drams, all those things that you don't experience unless you're immersed into that world.

Ming Ho: Happy memories of the shoot in Plockton: hospitality in the many B&Bs we frequented. Those of us who visited on a casual basis—writers and execs travelling up and down—would spend a night or two in different B&Bs, often moving several times in a week. We therefore became breakfast connoisseurs, sampling not only the full Scottish, which included black pudding and sometimes haggis, but smoked haddock, kippers, porridge, yoghurt, stewed fruit, croissants, eggs all ways, mushrooms on toast with fresh garden herbs...

At one point, Dominic and I only half-jokingly contemplated an episode called 'The Great Lochdubh Breakfast Competition', in which landladies pitted against each other would succumb to dastardly doings! Happy days.

Duncan Duff: The first series was the first time I'd been a regular on a TV show and I'd been married for about five years at that point. My wife came up to visit, and I said to her, 'We've been thinking about when we should start a family. I've got this series, and it looks like it's pretty good, we may get more out of it. So we could start thinking about having a family now.'

Cut to series two and my wife is heavily pregnant. I'm up in Plockton, and I go out with Stuart Hepburn, who's up for a few days, and we get wellied as I'm not working the next day. Stuart is putting me right on fatherhood and parenting and what to expect and all that.

So we have this long night. I was staying in a B&B in the village. I staggered home, crashed out on top of my bed, didn't even get out of my clothes and at about 7 o'clock in the morning the landlord knocks on the door: 'Duncan, I've just had a call from your wife and her waters have broken.' I thought, *Oh my God, what the hell am I going to do?* I phoned production and said, 'My wife has gone into labour, help!' They swung into action, a flight was booked and a car was sent to pick me up. I was rushing down to London, thinking, *Will I make it?* Because I'd never been a father before, I imagined you go into labour and an hour and a half later the baby arrived. Of course, it took 24 hours, but I arrived in plenty of time.

Stuart McGugan: The location was beautiful. Sometimes I thought the audience wanted to move the actors out of the way to look at the scenery. One year, I think it was 1996, there was a heatwave. I flew from the south of France up there and the weather didn't change. It was so hot the midges didn't come out. After a while work got in the way. There's a fabulous mushroom season up there.

Valerie Gogan: I got into picking mushrooms when I was there. Initially I thought I'd go looking for magic mushrooms, I thought it would be the right time of year. That was the plan, but I didn't really know enough about it so I was worried I was going to poison myself. I was in the cottage at this point with Anne. I asked Nick Renton round for dinner and I'd collected loads. There's chanterelles obviously, you can always tell because they're bright yellow, them and the boletus. Nick looked questioningly at the table with loads of mushrooms and said, 'What are we having for dinner?' as if I was going to poison him, but I was very careful about what I actually ate.

I came a cropper a bit. I would go out walking for hours and hours if I wasn't filming, because you're there and there's nothing else to do. Some of the guys in the truck passed me and I was freezing, I was like, 'I wouldn't mind a lift back into the village,' and they went, 'Don't pick her up, she likes to go walking,' and I was shouting, 'Come back!' There were a lot of Highland cattle. Anne and I had some literally sticking their heads in the kitchen window of the cottage we were staying in. All nice memories.

Morag Mackenzie's cattle are given directions by one of the crew. Photo by Morag Mackenzie

Ralph Riach: I generally enjoyed myself, being driven to work every day. Although you might go along the same road every day, because of the weather and the climate it was always different. I remember thinking how lucky I was to be doing this job. There was one particular road we took and there had been a mist and all the cobwebs among the grass and the wild flowers were hung like wee jewels, just beautiful. Driving along the side of Loch Carron I thought, *God ma, you'd love this.* Standing up on the hills, I wondered, *How many millions of years has this looked like this?*

Nicholas Renton: There was a rather striking extra who had a baby on the hip and another little child. In year two, we went back and she had another baby on her hip and looked at me and said, 'It's all your fault.' I know who the dad was! We were like a gentle army, we didn't shoot, we did other things.

Toby Hefferman: The only thing that was really disappointing was the fact that the interior of the pub wasn't actually in Plockton, it was in Balmacara. That always threw me. I was like, how come the interior pub's not there? It was credit to them that they pulled it off.

Mike Shucksmith (Chairman, Balmacara Community Trust): The community of Balmacara got a donation for the disturbances. We still have the letter.

Excerpt of letter from Casper Mill, Location Manager (21st October 1996): I am pleased to enclose a cheque for £250. This is to thank the Balmacara Community for putting up with any disruption caused by ourselves, and our vehicles, during our filming this summer.

THIS MODEST COMPENSATION was part of the production's strategy to maintain local goodwill, though not all interactions went so smoothly.

The *Daily Record* reported that 'angry villagers' in Kyle of Lochalsh wanted 'to book telly bobby Hamish Macbeth... for obstruction' after series two's filming. Complaints included the crew ordering the Co-op to quieten its tills, insisting another shop remove its trolleys and asking ladies fresh from the hair salon to stay indoors. Bank manager Rob Anderson remarked: 'I couldn't get home for my tea because the whole Main Street was blocked off. It was most upsetting.'

ELEVEN
PRESCRIPTION FOR SUCCESS

AHEAD OF *HAMISH MACBETH*'S return to BBC One on 24th March 1996, ITV, the broadcaster's chief rival, announced it would move the fourth series of its own rural Scottish drama, *Doctor Finlay* (1993–96), from Friday nights to Sunday, directly opposite *Hamish*.

Finlay would start its run on 31st March 1996, with BBC Scotland's Head of Television Colin Cameron telling the *Daily Record*, 'I think it's daft if people are forced to choose between two excellent programmes from Scotland. But we've no worries over audience figures.'

The *Daily Record*'s John Millar criticised the decision. Explaining that simply setting the video recorder for one while watching the other wasn't an option for everyone, he added he had heard that even if the BBC moved *Hamish*, ITV would move *Finlay* directly opposite it: 'It's so daft, it makes you wonder if the folk in charge of the schedules aren't suffering from the telly equivalent of mad cow disease.'

Kind courtesy of Radio Times Archives

The 30th March 1996 issue of *Radio Times* provided further proof that *Hamish Macbeth* had captured the nation's imagination. Published a few days after the second series began on BBC One, the magazine awarded the series a much-coveted front cover. Shirley Henderson and Valerie Gogan flanked Robert Carlyle, with Wee Jock II completing the family portrait. The bold red headline 'OUR HERO!' and tagline 'Why everyone loves Hamish Macbeth' spoke volumes about how the drama had won over viewers across the UK.

'It's one of those iconic things to be on the cover of *Radio Times*,' says Valerie Gogan. 'As an actor, you think that's quite exciting, and I think even more back then it felt like quite a big thing.'

Behind that carefully composed cover shot lay a story of growing national obsession. *Radio Times* journalist Alison Graham had ventured to Plockton the previous summer to uncover what made the series so captivating.

She succumbed to the village's charms, describing the 'warm, sweet air' as 'some kind of narcotic that leads hardened city dwellers to totter into the realms of Highland cliche'. Between 'juggernaut breakfasts' and 'singing along to undecipherable folk songs in the village's two pubs', Graham discovered a production facing both practical challenges and unexpected levels of public interest.

Producer Deirdre Keir confided to Graham about the logistical hurdles: 'It's like being on a foreign shoot that is extremely problematic and expensive, and we don't have a huge budget.' But it was the public's investment in the series one cliffhanger that surprised everyone. The production had required cast and crew to sign secrecy clauses, with Keir revealing, 'My children were offered bribes at school to reveal the outcome and families who liked the first series have been coming to Plockton and asking me, "Who did he choose?"'

At the March 1996 BBC Scotland press preview, journalists were sworn to secrecy regarding whether Alex or Isobel would win Hamish's heart.

TOURISM AND TRAINSPOTTING

Not everyone welcomed *Hamish Macbeth*'s return, with *The Herald*'s Julie Davidson warning that TV tourism could spell disaster for Plockton. She compared it to Venice's transformation into a 'sterile Renaissance theme park' and argued the village risked becoming 'Hamish Macbeth Country'. While acknowledging the show's popularity, she suggested Plockton might regret trading its authentic character for 'the buzz of the shoot and a donation to the community coffers'.

Reader W.R. Anderson of Findhorn dismissed Davidson's view as 'distinctly elitist', pointing out the irony of her concerns about the railway line, which might close without tourist traffic. They argued the Highlands needed economic self-sufficiency, adding it was curious Davidson had no issue with places like 'Bronte Country' or 'Shakespeare Country'.

Some publicity ahead of *Hamish*'s second series focused on a supposed 'feud' between Robert Carlyle and author M.C. Beaton over the show's creative direction. Carlyle revealed to *The Mirror* in early 1996 that he had been prepared to quit following the cutting of a drug use scene from series one: 'If that had happened again or if the scripts had showed signs of being watered down, I would have been off.' Beaton strongly disagreed with that direction, telling the paper she would 'never forgive the BBC for making Hamish a drug taker'.

Shortly before filming began on the second series, Robert Carlyle and Shirley Henderson had found themselves in Glasgow on the set of *Trainspotting*, the film adaptation of Irvine Welsh's 1993 novel, under the direction of Danny Boyle.

Carlyle's scene-stealing portrayal of the psychopathic Francis 'Franco' Begbie—a volatile, glass-throwing thug who terrorises both friends and strangers alike—would stand in stark contrast to the policeman he'd soon be returning to in Plockton. The role would help cement Carlyle's reputation for completely inhabiting wildly different characters.

'Bobby shouted to me when we were there, "Isobel, what are you doing here?" I shouted, "Be serious, this is a proper film!", just nonsense,' says Shirley Henderson. 'I was only in for a couple of days on *Trainspotting* then we went back up [to Plockton] for the next year, but that was nice. Different things started to come along at that point.'

The pair were now working with two very different Danny Boyles, both of whom continue to deal with cases of mistaken identity decades later.

'I get invites to school reunions, letters from actresses...,' says *Hamish Macbeth*'s Daniel Boyle. 'I got nominated for a BAFTA and they sent the invitation to the other Danny. I once got a letter telling me how good my Olympic opening ceremony was. While Bobby was filming *Trainspotting,* the *Daily Record* published a photo of me alongside photos of Bruce Willis and Sharon Stone [to accompany an article about the other Danny Boyle's decision to focus on *Trainspotting* and not a Hollywood production with those two actors]. Apparently I'd turned down Hollywood for junkies in Edinburgh. Everyone thought I was a millionaire.'

TWELVE

SERIES TWO OVERVIEW

REGULAR CAST

Robert Carlyle (Hamish Macbeth), Shirley Henderson (Isobel Sutherland), Valerie Gogan (Alex Maclean), Ralph Riach (TV John McIver), Billy Riddoch (Lachlan McCrae Sr), Stuart Davids (Lachie McCrae Jr), Duncan Duff (Doc Brown), Brian Pettifer (Rory Campbell), Anne Lacey (Esme Murray), Barbara Rafferty (Agnes Meldrum), Stuart McGugan (Barney Meldrum), David Ashton (Major Roddy Maclean). With Fraoch as Wee Jock II.

1. A PERFECTLY SIMPLE EXPLANATION

Writer: Daniel Boyle
Director: Nicholas Renton
Original broadcast: 24th March 1996, 7.15pm

Guest Cast

Philip Jackson (Malachi McBean), Juliet Cadzow (Bethsheba McBean), Brian Alexander (Jubel McBean), Ron Donachie (Zoot McPherrin), Laurie Ventry (Rev. Alan Snow), Rab Christie (Jimmy Soutar), Dolina MacLennan (Flora), Ronnie Letham (Peter the Fireman), Iain McColl (Neil the Bus).

Summary

Series two opens with religious zealot Malachi McBean, leader of the Church of the Stony Path, painting over road signs to rename Lochdubh as 'Gomorrah', before cutting to an almost bacchanalian barbecue outside Hamish and Alex's home, where the entire village is enjoying themselves.

The situation escalates when local free spirit Zoot McPherrin—who appears to walk on water thanks to a clever camera angle—arrives with his followers, adding a touch of hippie mysticism to the village's already complicated dynamics. Tensions arise when Malachi denounces Hamish and Alex's unmarried living arrangements outside the police house.

When Isobel attempts to investigate the Church for a story, she's injured in an accident with McBean's tractor, prompting a furious response from Hamish that raises questions about his feelings for her.

After McBean claims to have encountered Satan himself (who resembles Hamish, only with green eyes) in his barn before it mysteriously burns down, the village descends into paranoid speculation. TV John encourages this by teaching Barney and Lachlan Sr an 'ancient Aztec ritual' for protection, while the local pub becomes festooned with garlic.

The truth, when it finally emerges, is more complex than anyone imagined. Rather than the supernatural encounter McBean described, the barn incident involves an elaborate scheme where McBean himself was attempting to appear unstable to push his wife, Bethsheba, into leaving him for Rev. Alan Snow. The final twist reveals that McBean and Zoot have been secret lovers, meeting at Zoot's villa in the Algarve, while the religious mania was all an act to help Bethsheba and Snow overcome their guilt about their own relationship.

While Hamish solves the mystery to prove he wasn't the 'devil' in the barn, his efforts to reassure Alex about his feelings for Isobel only create more uncertainty in their relationship.

Commentary

Stuart Hepburn: Second series are often the best series you'll get of anything, you can say, 'That worked, that worked, that didn't.' I think the second series became supercharged. Zoot for instance, you bring him back. British TV is often so short you don't get the chance. I think the second series was much more relaxed, simply because you knew it was good and it would work.

As the second series was in development, *The List* had reported that writer Daniel Boyle had initially proposed a rather daring resolution to the first season's love triangle cliffhanger. His suggestion to have Alex, Isobel and Hamish all living together and the latter looking 'like the luckiest man in the world', was promptly rejected by BBC executives. 'There are kids watching,' said Boyle, 'and whether you like it or not you have to take on board there are things you can't get away with.'

Nicholas Renton: It was a very weird episode. It crossed several lines, it trod over different barriers.

THE STAGE PRAISED the episode, noting that 'Whether at the centre of a love triangle or accusations that he is Beelzebub, Carlyle is utterly compelling and Danny Boyle's writing is as dry and satisfying as a malt whisky. As long as director Nicholas Renton makes sure his Highland hero continues to have his flings, the Scottish Tourist Board can rest easy.'

Philip Jackson (Malachi McBean): I'd worked with Nick Renton before and he sent the script out of the blue. There was something very quirky about that programme—it didn't run along conventional lines at all. It was the first time you'd seen Robert Carlyle and he set the tone of it. Shirley Henderson is amazing. That area of Scotland has an atmosphere to it. Plockton is quite a strange place. You look along this very placid lagoon, and then all these seals pop up. We went to Skye and Kyle of Lochalsh, and I did the train journey from Inverness.

Deirdre Keir: It was a very busy episode. It was a different unit; some of the guys came back, but they weren't all available, so it was hit the ground running, let's get on with it. We needed the weather to get the barbecue. [Watching the scene again] the hair was standing up on the back of my neck and I was think-ing, *I don't believe we did this.*

Nicholas Renton: Zoot walking on the water.

Deirdre Keir: Ron Donachie, the big old heavy who plays [Ian Rankin's detective] Rebus on the radio and is always 'The Mob', to get him to do that...

Ron Donachie: I like to think that because I made a bit more of [Zoot's first episode] than was maybe there, they wrote a whole episode around me for the next series where I end up as the local bisexual love god. Not many of those come up in your life! Walking on water in Plockton and standing on the top of a hill doing druid stuff, it was just fantastic fun. It's a great shot that, pulling up and seeing everybody doing this mini-Woodstock up in the Highlands, which was of course Zoot's big thing—everyone should have these big love fests and get blasted.

Filming the barbecue scene. Photo by Sarah Bruce

Sarah Bruce (Runner and Stand-In): There was a celebration scene outside the police house with bunting, stalls and lots of people. They were doing an aerial shot above the causeway. It was a hot day, and one of the extras fell ill. An ambulance had to be called, but filming couldn't be halted as aerial shots were really aerial back then. There were no drones, and it was a pricey helicopter. They filmed with the ambulance in the shot and removed it during post-production. I waited to see how that had turned out—no ambulance!

Philip Jackson: The night I arrived, I hadn't met anyone yet, and I was staying in someone's bungalow where they rented out a room. I went to the pub and met Bobby and Ron Donachie. The local pub had about 60 or 70 single malt whiskies. Bobby said, 'Have you heard of this one?' and I hadn't heard of any of them. 'Try that... Bowmore! You like that? Now we'll go for something peatier... Lagavulin!' It went on for ages. I reckon we had about 20 whiskies, and I'm not used to drinking it. My wife will tell you it makes me go a bit crazy. But I think it put me in the zone for Malachi.

Ron Donachie: That was a good script. I play a lot of policemen, soldiers and prison warders, that's the way TV works. So, when you get something like that, you think, *What a gas.* Over the years, I've done a lot of Danny's [Boyle] stuff, and whenever something comes through the door with his name on it, you think, *We'll be alright here.*

Philip Jackson: It was quite an over-the-top performance, a lot of shouting. I asked the vicar where I lived about speaking in tongues as I wanted to take it seriously. He explained it was originally about being inhabited by the Holy Spirit or a devil, a supernatural influence that makes you express things in a language unknown to mankind.

Anne Lacey: It was all behind closed doors with Esme and Rory. There was a scene where we played strip Scrabble. All I took off was an earring, and Brian was in his vest. The owner of the house was absolutely disgusted with that sort of thing taking place in her house.

Philip Jackson: There were serious midges, they got in your ears. Somebody said myrtle leaves were a remedy. It was a labour of love. We were there for a bit more than a week, rehearsing on the day and shooting the scene.

Nicholas Renton: We sent Bobby off to do his driving licence at the end of series one for series two, and he failed. Then he sat it again in Fort William.

Deirdre Keir: When he was taking his test in Fort William, somebody leaked it to the press. They were waiting with a photographer. He arrived very nervous, and Fort William is a High Street with little streets running off it. The mother of all storms came down. The tester came out, and they set off with the wipers going at double speed. At one point, the tester said, 'Turn right here, Mr Carlyle,' and he turned onto a ginnel off the High Street. This car came towards him, and Bobby thought, 'Oh, fuck.' The instructor said, 'Drive on.' There was no passing place. She reversed, and Bobby thought he'd failed again. When they got back, he stopped in the rain, and the photographers were there. The tester came out and said, 'He's passed. Get out of the way.'

Brian Pettifer: I sold Bobby his first car, it was a BMW. First time I saw him after he bought it he'd run it into a tree or a fence. But he's a good driver now, I think.

FINAL THOUGHTS

'A Perfectly Simple Explanation' subverts expectations by transforming what appears to be a tale of small-town prejudice into an unexpected love story, setting up series two's more ambitious storytelling. The episode challenges the usual clash between strict religion and free-spirited beliefs often seen in Highland-set stories.

Comparing 'paratextual' partners *Hamish Macbeth* and *The Wicker Man* for *CST Online*, Dr Melissa Beattie pointed out that while the latter shows Christianity and pagan practices as dangerous enemies, *Hamish Macbeth* takes a much friendlier approach. Instead of portraying either McBean's religious devotion or Zoot's New Age commune as threatening, the episode reveals that love matters more than spiritual differences.

The surprise that Malachi and Zoot, seemingly complete opposites, are actually in love shows what Beattie calls the series' message that 'with love as its foundation, multiple different iterations of spirituality can live in harmony'. Beattie also highlights how the episode avoids the easy trope of portraying the zealous preacher as purely villainous. Though Malachi is shown putting stones in his shoes and speaking in tongues, he's ultimately revealed to be acting out of compassion, wanting his wife to find happiness with Rev. Snow.

This complexity reflects what Beattie sees as the show's commitment to depicting Highland communities as intelligent and compassionate rather than backward or threatening. Daniel Boyle's exploration of same-sex relationships in Lochdubh sets the tone for a second series that would continue to surprise.

2. IN SEARCH OF A ROSE

Writer: Stuart Hepburn
Director: Mandie Fletcher
Original broadcast: 31st March 1996, 7.15pm

Guest Cast

Alastair Mackenzie (Gavin Robb), Anne Kristen (Miss Deidre Meiklejohn), Sarah Collier (Mrs. Lucinda McLorg), Craig Ferguson (Torquil McLorg).

Summary

'In Search of a Rose' opens with Hamish and Wee Jock investigating a washed-up life belt from Rose, a boat belonging to local fisherman Murdo Meiklejohn, whose sister Deidre seems oddly unconcerned about his three-week absence.

Meanwhile, a mysterious visitor named Gavin Robb shows interest in Agnes at the pub.

Barney Meldrum launches an ambitious new tourist venture: guaranteed whale-watching trips aboard his boat, the Fat Chance. It soon transpires that Barney has joined forces with Lachie Jr to use a winch to pull a fake killer whale through the water.

The scheme works until the whale 'breaks' in front of a boatful of tourists, including Torquil, the son of a QC, and the scam is exposed, but not before a package is retrieved from the water by Lachie Jr. He promptly feeds the 'cattle cake' to his cows. When they reacted badly, Hamish realises that it's actually Moroccan hash, leading him to suspect drug smuggling.

The episode climaxes with Hamish and friends taking Barney's boat out to investigate the location of the drug drop, with Hamish diving under the water where he finds Murdo Meiklejohn's boat and sees an arm inside the hull.

Back on the surface, Barney sees Gavin and Agnes talking on the beach and changes direction to confront them. Arriving on dry land, the truth emerges: Gavin is actually Agnes' son, given up for adoption when she was 16. She had kept this secret from Barney to protect his dignity, knowing all along their infertility issues were his. Back on the boat, Alex jumps into the water to find Hamish, who emerges safely from his underwater expedition.

The other mystery is solved when Murdo's body is recovered. To prevent his boat from being repossessed, the fisherman had attempted drug smuggling, only to sink off the coast of his home village. His sister gives him a burial at sea.

COMMENTARY

Long before Barney Meldrum's mechanical whale surfaced in Lochdubh bay, a real-life local entrepreneur was making waves of his own. Calum Mackenzie, owner of Calum's Seal Trips in Plockton, had built a reputation for his guaranteed seal-spotting tours around the village's sheltered waters. His confidence in delivering on this promise was so absolute that he offered customers their money back if they failed to spot any seals.

'I was once investigated by the Office of Fair Trading,' Mackenzie recalls. 'Somebody told them I had plastic seals on the rocks.' The accusation was serious enough that officials dispatched two officers to investigate the alleged deception. Though the inquiry quickly confirmed everything was legitimate, the incident made its way into the local papers, creating a ripple of interest well beyond the Highland coast.

'I've no need to plant plastic seals,' Mackenzie told *Hamish*

Macbeth's publicist for the episode's press notes. 'I know where the real ones are, and on a good day we can see 200.'

One newspaper article, framed and displayed in Calum's shop window, caught the attention of *Hamish Macbeth* writer Stuart Hepburn, who immediately recognised its potential.

Down by the water

Stuart Hepburn: I'm interested in female characters. Men have had a good innings; there's not much more you can say about the male menopause, though I was aware Barney was maybe in the middle of one of those things.

Stuart McGugan: I loved the episode with the whale. There was a lovely scene with myself and Bobby when I tell him I'm infertile. It was a smashing moment, just the two of us staring into the middle distance and talking to each other.

Mandie Fletcher: The film I'd done [1994's *Deadly Advice*] was with Zenith. Scott and Deirdre asked me to come and do the whole series, but I had my own commercial company and I said I couldn't make that commitment, but I could come up and do two episodes. I went to meet Stuart Hepburn in Dunblane, where we talked through the script. There was no time for rehearsals because there were episodes before and after mine, so you're doing it on the hoof, which I quite enjoy. They know what they're doing, they know their characters. I was very fond of the women. I thought Barbara was remarkable, a lovely woman, and Anne Lacey, a gorgeous woman.

Barbara Rafferty: Danny is a great writer, but some writers don't really write well for women. There were other writers and occasionally the women got more to do.

Mandie Fletcher: It's such an ensemble piece—you're with everyone in a group all the time, all in the pub. Then, to have these moments where you have some time with Barbara or Shirley or Alastair, was lovely. It's always great in ensemble shows to have a moment to work one-on-one and give someone a bit of time and attention.

Stuart Hepburn: My stuff always comes out from one wee thing, but then it's got to be about something else. You've got to find out what it's really all about, lost love, longing, death and that sort of stuff. The story of the son, that's from talking to women of a certain age. Things happen to them in their teens, that's where that came from. I'm really interested in how things look from the outside but aren't what they seem. So, if you've got an older lady getting dressed up and meeting a young man, the husband's obviously going to think one thing, and so is the audience. All I'll say is that I come from a complex family, and maybe there was something like that in my past.

Mandie Fletcher: I was absolutely livid that there was the episode with the old lady on the beach ['No Man is an Island'], and I got the same amount of time to tit about with boats. I did

54 slates before lunch one day and we had to go all the way out onto the water. Of course, when I thought the whole thing through, I made one schoolboy error: boats don't stop. They just keep floating. I had dramatic bits with the boat stopping and them getting out, but the boats just float around. By the end, I could've killed someone—I've never worked so hard in my life. But it was amazing to be out on that loch. I remember looking down and seeing the bottom 40 feet below.

Jon Older (First Assistant Director): I had one of the best days I've ever had on a shoot when they went down to find the wreck. We did that on location in the bay because the water was remarkably clear, and somehow the day I scheduled us to do it was absolutely gorgeous. Mandie and I just sat on the deck of the support boat, drinking tea and having cucumber sandwiches, watching monitors while they got on with it below. It was one of the easiest days I've ever had.

Calum Mackenzie: I remember one of my best paydays. Casper [Mill, Location Manager] was the man with all the money. He had a pocket full of cash. I was using the main pier daily [for running my seal watching trips], and Casper came to me and said, 'Calum, we're filming at the main pier in a couple of days. Would you mind not doing any trips?' I said, 'Well, you'll have to pay me for all my full trips.' So he took out the equivalent of about six fares and paid me cash. I went away sailing, and in the background of that episode I could see my boat.

Toby Hefferman (Third Assistant Director): Credit to Casper, he kept everyone happy. These days it would have to be a contract. Back then there'd be cash, the brown envelopes that would go out. Depending on where you needed to film and how tricky people were, the weight of that envelope would differ. You're not allowed to do that anymore.

Stuart Hepburn: Barney's boat... that came from something that happened to me in Ardfern. A friend of mine had this boat called Summer Wine and we'd take visitors out. He said, 'Stuart, can you come and do a bit of mackerel fishing with them, we'll see an eagle.' I said, 'Ronnie, you'll be lucky if you see an eagle,' and he said, 'You'll see an eagle, don't you worry.' He pointed and said, 'Look, there's the majestic eagle!' and I said, 'Yes, it's the eagle,' while seeing a buzzard. This kid turned to me and said, 'My daddy's a QC' and I said, 'Aye, I bet he is.' That's where that came from. Ronnie made them catch the mackerel then sold it to them!

Jon Older: My principal concern with that kind of thing is losing someone over the side, someone falling in the water, which fortunately never happened. A friend of mine, Stuart Brisdon, built the whale. He's a special effects guy and designed it to be towed through the water. God, it was a pain, it was really heavy. There's a shot where they tip it over to show Hamish underneath, and I don't know how we managed it because it weighed a tonne. The top was fibreglass, but he'd built a big steel rig underneath to keep it stable in the water.

We were on land doing a run-by of Barney's boat with everyone on it, and we had to keep going back and doing it again. Meanwhile, I was watching the tide creeping in behind us. Mandie kept saying, 'No, one more, just one more!' The water got closer and closer until I finally had to call it: 'OK, that's it. Everybody out,' or we'd have drowned.

Stuart Hepburn: I almost wanted to destroy someone at the BBC because the whole thing was predicated on this whale that they'd made and did they not put the whale turning upside down in the trailer? That's the second act crisis.

Toby Hefferman: *Hamish* was super ambitious for its time. We had a really good crew. Maurice Cain, the production designer, was brilliant at what he did. There were some strong heads of department who embraced the ambition and could make it a reality. It's a massive shout out to the crew, because they were so ready for the challenge. They embraced it and pulled it off. There were some big logistics and things that you wouldn't do now with health and safety. We didn't have a tribe of safety divers standing by, we just used the local boat charter. Robert was the fisherman who'd take us out. It was a brilliant time because you had to be really resourceful. The actors had to be super patient as well.

Barbara Rafferty: One day a lot of us were off and we used to go around the Kyles on a boat. I jumped in the crystal clear water and I nearly died of the cold.

Valerie Gogan: I went into the sea and they gave me what was meant to be a dry suit, but it was far too big for me and it filled with water. I was in there for ages and it was late October or November, it was bloody freezing. There were two boats, the one that we were on and the one that they're filming from, and the nurse said, 'I think we'd better get Valerie out, she's gone blue.' They got me out and they were saying, 'Just pee into your suit,' because that's supposedly one of the things they do, and I was saying, 'I can't, I just can't do it,' so they got the tea urn and they put a cup of tea down each arm. I put my arms down and all the tea went right down through the whole thing. It was the best cup of tea I ever had.

ROBERT CARLYLE ADMITTED at the time that the scuba diving sequence was 'a bit hairy', telling the *Irish Independent* that 'After going down about 20 metres my ears really began to hurt with the pressure. It was scary.'

Toby Hefferman: When I came in, I was thrust straight into it. On my first day, I didn't know who Robert Carlyle was, I didn't recognise him from anything. We were shooting with him on a boat, and I put Bobby in a minibus with the crew to get to the location. I thought nothing of it. It was just like, 'Come on, load up the bus.' He was the only one with a car. His driver pulled me aside and said, 'He doesn't travel in a minibus, he travels with me.' Bobby was sussing me out. Then suddenly you bond and everything is good.

FINAL THOUGHTS

Inspired by a news story about plastic seals in Plockton's harbour, 'In Search of a Rose' begins as a comedy about tourist deception but develops into something far more poignant. Barney Meldrum's guaranteed whale-watching enterprise, with its bagpipe soundtrack and carefully rehearsed patter about 'the world-famous Lochdubh light', initially suggests pure farce.

The episode's central relationship—Barney and Agnes—has been building since the series began. Here, Stuart Hepburn's script delves deeper, using Barney's desperate tourism scheme to explore a marriage under strain. Barbara Rafferty and Stuart McGugan deliver some of their best performances, especially in their final scene, where Agnes explains she kept her secret to protect Barney's dignity.

While it's a pity Agnes' son is never mentioned again, Alastair Mackenzie would later become better known as Archie MacDonald in another BBC Sunday night drama, *Monarch of the Glen* (2000–05).

3. ISOBEL PULLS IT OFF

Writer: Dominic Minghella
Director: Mandie Fletcher
Original broadcast: 7th April 1996, 7.30pm

GUEST CAST

Robert Cavanah (Gary Ross), Robert McIntosh (Editor), Iain McColl (Neil the Bus), Libby McArthur (Gloria), Sheila Keith (Aunt Ella), Dolina MacLennan (Flora), Gary Lewis (Dave the House-Seller), Alan Tall (Young Crofter), Johnny Irving (Old Crofter).

SUMMARY

When a job interview at a bigger paper falters due to her 'having too many scruples', Isobel decides it's time for a change, triggering a transformative makeover set to Cyndi Lauper's *Girls Just Want to Have Fun*, complete with references to the era's popular Renault Clio 'Papa! Nicole!' adverts.

Meeting Neil soon after his bus has been forced off the road by a stranger in a black car, Isobel later spots a group of men test driving what could be the culprit. After photographing the car, she takes the pictures to be developed before going to the gym and meeting Gary Ross, an ex-journalist now working in PR.

Lottery fever grips Lochdubh as TV John predicts a win for the village syndicate. Lachie Jr pursues his dream of becoming a DJ, while the villagers debate what they'd do with potential winnings. Hamish dreams of buying a boat.

As Isobel's budding romance with Gary develops, he offers to help trace the licence plate of a car in her photos. Hamish, clearly jealous, warns Isobel about Gary's criminal record (possession of cannabis in 1986), but she dismisses his concerns.

The plot thickens when Gary is revealed to be working for a car company trying to retrieve Isobel's photos of a prototype vehicle. Hamish locks Gary in a cell overnight after suspecting he's over the legal alcohol limit, prompting a confrontation with Alex over his jealousy-driven actions.

The episode reaches its climax when the village lottery syndicate believes they've won, only for Lachlan to confess he's lost the winning ticket. In exchange for Isobel's photos, Gary's company agrees to buy Lochdubh a new bus to replace Neil's damaged one, a solution that allows Isobel to help her community while maintaining her journalistic integrity.

COMMENTARY

Dominic Minghella: I can't remember how I came up with the Isobel story. I felt proprietorial about that character and wanted her to be more than just a lovelorn girl on the sidelines, so that was probably my starting-point.

Shirley Henderson: You go quiet for an episode, then something interesting happens to you in the next one, but you're still in the background and connected with everybody. That was what was nice about it, you never quite knew whose story was going to come to the front next. My first kiss on screen was on *Hamish*; first with Robert Cavanah, then with Bobby.

Mandie Fletcher: I enjoyed spending time with Shirley Henderson. She's an extraordinary actor, but also a rather extraordinary person. Off-screen she has self containment; she's this quiet, sweet person, but she's very much her own woman and I thought she brought that to the character. That whole episode was about her, and I remember sitting in the kitchen with her thinking, *Isn't this nice? It's just the two of us and we're having such fun.*

Jon Older: Shirley was a sweetheart, never any trouble. She was always on the money and up for doing it again. I think we all knew that she had good things ahead of her. Some leading ladies can be quite difficult, but she wasn't. Those more intimate scenes, with just two people instead of eight principal cast and a dozen extras, were always a joy.

Shirley Henderson: We were always very excited to get the scripts. They were very emotional sometimes and sad—the human condition in an accessible television way. Bobby's character was very confused a lot of the time; he had to be there for everybody and be a policeman. I had to be a journalist, but I also had feelings. I wanted to run sometimes, but also to be there. Everyone had a reality, even though there was a fun layer on top. Underneath, there was complexity. You felt for everybody, but within that, there was comedy. All the writers brought something great.

Mandie Fletcher: I always said to Robbie Carlyle that *Hamish Macbeth* was a Western. You've got your lady bartender, the law, the bad guys: it's a Western. That's how I shot everything and thought everything through. I had one scene where Hamish walked out of the shadows to confront Gary. I wanted Gary to look into the shadows before Hamish appeared. He was like a magical avenging angel, you don't see him until he's there. That was me having fun. I was never sure if it came across on screen.

Stuart McGugan: Barbara and I got a good little double act going. She's very passionate and fiery and I was always trying to annoy her. During that one, she kneed me in the groin behind the bar and I subsided behind it, out of camera view. It was all our idea, we came up with it on the hoof. The crew would let us play around with ideas, see what it looked like. The relationship was terrific.

Toby Hefferman: We tried to shoot [the Renault scenes] like a commercial.

Sarah Bruce: I was paid an extra £50 that day to teach the cast Highland dancing for the celebration scene. I'm actually sitting at the bar in that scene and trying to yell the moves without moving my lips.

FINAL THOUGHTS

Stuart Hepburn's script carefully seeds future developments, including Lachie Jr's DJ aspirations and Alex's wistful talk with Hamish about escaping to 'our' island. Even a passing mention of Zoot builds on the show's expanding mythology.

The most powerful moment comes not from the main plot but from a quiet scene where Alex confronts Isobel at the police house. 'This is my home,' Alex asserts, while Isobel counters, 'It used to be the police station', a perfect encapsulation of the territory both women are trying to claim. Their battle for Hamish's attention remains unstated but drives everything that follows.

Look out for an appearance by Scottish actress Sheila Keith as one of the old ladies using Hamish's Land Rover as a taxi. Once referred to as 'the female Boris Karloff', Keith's work in several British horror films ensured she had cult status in 1996. Keith would return as Aunt Ella in the last episode of the second series.

Actor Gary Lewis also pops up in a small role as Dave the House-Seller—he'd go on to gain greater fame as Jamie Bell's dad in *Billy Elliot* (2000).

4. RADIO LOCHDUBH

Writer: Daniel Boyle
Director: Nicholas Renton
Original broadcast: 14ᵗʰ April 1996, 7.30pm

GUEST CAST

Peter Wight (Sidney Braithwaite), Dinah Stabb (Magda Milligan), Brian Alexander (Jubel McBean), Margery Withers (Jean McNeil), Hugh Munro (Hector McNeil), Ronnie Letham (Peter the Fireman), Iain McColl (Neil the Bus).

SUMMARY

Alex Maclean's melodramatic readings from *Far From the Madding Crowd* have transformed Lochdubh into a literary haven, with silent book-lovers filling the Stag Bar instead of drinkers.

Behind this cultural renaissance is Radio Lochdubh, an illegal station run from a barn by Lachie Jr and his friend Jubel, featuring the 'gorgeously gorgeable News Queen' (Isobel), sheep advice from Professor Merino, and star attraction 'Book Lady' (Alex). When Hamish learns that detector vans will be coming to shut down the operation, he finds himself caught between enforcing the law and disappointing Alex.

His dilemma deepens after a chance nighttime encounter with Isobel beside the water, where he confesses he's tired of 'living a lie' and the pair kiss. The next morning, Hamish attempts to tell Alex about his feelings for Isobel but delivers such a convoluted speech about never wanting to hurt her that she misunderstands his meaning.

The station goes mobile when detector agents Sidney and Magda arrive, with broadcasts coming from various locations around Lochdubh. Sidney's pursuit of the pirates is complicated by his equally unsuccessful romantic pursuit of Magda, who claims 'terrible foreboding' about physical intimacy.

The village's literary awakening takes an unexpected turn as villagers debate existentialism versus innate morality in the pub. The philosophical discussions transform Barney, who starts smoking Gitanes, before declaring 'Everything's free!' to delighted patrons.

As Sidney finally tracks the broadcast location during Rory's poetic turn as 'Big Grocer', Magda's visions intensify. Alex confronts Hamish about Isobel and quietly announces her plan to leave, but promises to finish her reading series first.

While driving the mobile radio station in bad weather, Alex takes a wrong turn and finds herself hanging over the edge of a ravine, as Magda 'shares' her vision with TV John of Alex falling to her death. The episode ends with the village grieving for Alex, while Hamish sobs alone at home and Isobel watches the police house from a distance.

COMMENTARY

Valerie Gogan: Going into season two, they said to me, 'OK, you're going to get shot.' I said, 'Oh, that's amazing,' then I went, 'Wait a minute, shot dead?!' There was going to be a clan battle, and something would go wrong. I really wasn't happy about that, so there were a lot of discussions. I felt very strongly that it would do an injustice to the situation with either girl unless you gave them both a proper chance. Because you'd root more for Hamish, there would be no kind of struggle there. I wrote a long letter to Scott Meek and Nick Renton. So there was no clan battle, and I didn't die until I fell off the cliff.

Scott Meek: I was the one that went up to break the news to somebody if they were going to die. Somebody had to go and tell an actor that their character is going to be killed, and they're not always thrilled about it.

Shirley Henderson: That was a shock when Alex was killed. We all hated it. It just wasn't what we imagined at all. We'd get stuff when it was necessary, and I don't know the workings of it.

Ming Ho: I recall discussion about the point of killing off Alex: to place an emotional obstacle—guilt—in the way of Hamish and Isobel getting together too easily. Hamish and Alex could never really have settled together. They were an attraction of opposites whose relationship would have crumbled without that fundamental transience of her coming and going from the village.

At the start of series two, we find them living together in the police house and hosting a barbecue, but this comes as something of a surprise, given that series one has ended with Hamish having to make a choice between Alex and Isobel. I don't think we believe it's going to be happy ever after. It's just a question of how and when they break up. Hamish and Isobel were intended as soulmates, but if they had got together with no problem, there would be no dramatic tension.

Nicholas Renton: That was the shock, when Deirdre [Keir] came in at the start of the second series and said, 'We're going to kill one of them off, the fair-haired one, 'cos nobody likes the fair-haired one, they're all rooting for the dark-haired one.' When the fair-haired one was killed off, the whole country turned against us because they really liked her after all!

Scott Meek: Valerie took it very well, she's a trouper. All you can do is promise them they'll get a good dramatic death. We'd built up the thing with Valerie and Shirley, and there's a limit to how long you can extend those. We wanted to make a decision about it rather than not. Honestly, when we started, we probably imagined Valerie's character would go on longer than Shirley's. But it became clear that there was something between Bobby and Shirley on screen, they just worked so well together. It became more interesting to take them as the couple.

Stuart Hepburn: That was really quite difficult, both actresses were friends of mine.

Nicholas Renton: The book club in 'Radio Lochdubh' came from Daniel Boyle's background. He'd gone to sea as a young man and was a valet. I don't think he'd had much formal education, but when people left the ship, they'd leave books behind, so he'd pick them up and read them. Someone would leave *War and Peace*, so he'd read it. Then it'd be Barbara Cartland. He viewed everything he read with equal importance. Those scenes are about his background, when they pick up Camus and quote the first line of the play without knowing it's a Frenchman. It's the most autobiographical bit he ever put in.

Deirdre Keir: Daniel phoned me up to discuss what book Alex would be reading, and I said, 'What do you think?', knowing about all the tremendous reading he'd done. 'Should we have a bit of Hardy? Do I have to read Hardy?' I said I'd do it, so I looked at *The Mayor of Casterbridge* and *The Native* and faxed it through. He said, 'That'll be fine, I don't have to read it, just put it into the script!'

Valerie Gogan: I wanted it to be *Far From the Madding Crowd* specifically because I love Thomas Hardy, little things like that are very important to me. The props guys gave me a book that I would read, and I said, 'But it's not *Far From the Madding Crowd*' and they went, 'What?' I said, 'I asked for *Far From the Madding Crowd*, it's got to be that one,' and off they went. Then they came back with a copy.

Shirley Henderson: All that stuff down at the water was really beautiful, late at night and in my head, whether it's true or not, there were all these giant red and white mushrooms. I think now, *Is that real? Did that really happen, or is it just me imagining it happening?* With us down by the lake and Hamish kissing Isobel for the first time. So that's a nice memory, but I don't know if it's completely real or if I made it up because they finally get a little moment together.

Valerie Gogan: Shirley was always fantastic at doing close-ups. You could see everything in her face. Ian Knox always said that about Shirley, and about her stillness. I tend to move about and talk a lot, that's probably nerves. If you've only got a very few lines, you end up going over and over them in your head, but when you've got more, you can sit back on it. You've got to know what you're doing, but you've got to know it so well that you just throw it away.

Shirley Henderson: It was all very romantic. It wasn't over the top, it was probably quite real in the sense of it's hard to get what you want, and do you want that anyway? What is it that you want? You've got this other person that still loves you and do you love them? It took its time and never went over the top with it. It was quite subtly done, and then they hold hands and walk into the distance. The audience thinks they're seeing more than they really are.

Valerie Gogan: Although it's not bad weather there because it's in the Gulf Stream, you are a victim of the weather. So for instance, the scene where I said, 'Do you love me, Hamish?' and he's in the bath and I'm sitting on the loo. It was meant to be outside, but the weather was bad so we brought it inside. I think it worked so much better. It was such a low key domestic setting.

Stuart Davids: They weren't afraid to push the envelope. I think the whole thing of him being in the middle of this love triangle and Valerie dying on the side of a cliff, that was all mad.

Valerie Gogan: We'd had the wrap party the night before we shot all that, so I couldn't really enjoy it. Everybody else was going home apart from the crew and me. We had to do all the foot slipping, hanging off the door and falling down. We'd done the lying down bit, the rescue, earlier because they got Mountain Rescue out to go down the mountain with me. I think that was quite early in the morning.

Sarah Bruce: I had to stand in for Valerie for the death scene. It involved me hanging off the door of that van over the edge of a quarry road. Thankfully (or weirdly?) they provided a crew member to support my feet, so I wasn't truly hanging. It was my first involvement in a night shoot and, of course, they had to try out the storm effects while I was hanging. I was pretty exhausted and cold when they came to actually shoot it with Valerie. As I sat down, one of the lovely caterers brought me a hot chocolate and gave me a wink. It was hot chocolate with a heavy dash of rum! I crave that whenever I'm cold now. Weirdly, I didn't even know at the time that it *was* her death scene.

Deirdre Keir: You'd feel sorry for Valerie or anyone who has to play Alex because she was kind of the rich bitch and always arguing, all they did was row and knock sparks off each other.

Valerie Gogan: I knew I was meant to be the more bitchy one, the one that had gone down to England and been a bit more cutthroat and ambitious, so maybe she didn't deserve him, all that sort of stuff. It was nice to have the local girl get the guy, I think that probably was the way it was meant to be. But I believe that Alex really loved him, so in that way she wasn't all bad.

Donald Murdoch (Accordion, The Incredible Fling Band): When the 'Radio Lochdubh' episode was filmed I was studying in Nautical College, South Shields, and my band mate Wilfar Matheson was on holiday in America, so our stand-ins were a local character called Alec 'The Bomber' MacLean and Alistair Rob, both sadly no longer with us. Then, at a later date, we were flown down to London to overdub the music in a recording studio. Quite a bizarre experience.

FINAL THOUGHTS

What begins as a lighthearted tale about pirate radio turns into one of *Hamish Macbeth*'s most devastating hours.

Through Alex's bookish radio slot, reading passages from *Far From the Madding Crowd*, the episode foreshadows its own tragic ending. When Alex speaks of characters who 'felt like one who had sinned a great sin' or reads, 'how very well you knew that your new freak was my misery', the parallels to Hamish's growing attraction to Isobel become impossible to ignore.

Valerie Gogan gets some of her best moments as Alex, particularly in her final confrontation with Hamish. Her line, 'You should have told me and not had me hanging around here like too much excess baggage' carries the weight of every unspoken truth between them.

Robert Carlyle matches her intensity with Hamish's stunned grief in the closing scenes, a man who wanted to avoid hurting someone only to cause deeper pain through his indecision.

By the time TV John delivers the news—'She's dead, son. She's dead'—*Hamish Macbeth* has changed forever. What began as an exploration of community through shared stories ends with the community sharing a different kind of story, one of loss and guilt.

5. NO MAN IS AN ISLAND

Writer: Daniel Boyle
Director: Nicholas Renton
Original broadcast: 21st April 1996, 7.30pm

GUEST CAST

Edith MacArthur (Belle Carter), Gerard Kelly (PC Duggan), Michael Mackenzie (Ferdinand McLopez), Iain Andrew (Mr Stevens).

SUMMARY

Following the tragic events of the previous episode, Hamish leaves Lochdubh and sets sail for a remote island where he spent time with Alex. After setting fire to his boat, he has a brief vision of Alex, before he takes out his revolver and almost places it on his lips, just as he hears someone singing *I Do Like to Be Beside the Seaside*.

He meets Belle Carter, who is standing with her foot on what she believes is an unexploded WWII landmine. Rather than maintaining a safe distance, Hamish sits beside her all night.

Overeager Constable Douglas Duggan arrives as Hamish's temporary replacement back in Lochdubh, determined to find crime where Hamish seemingly found none. TV John, protecting Hamish's position and keen to keep Duggan busy, orchestrates an elaborate ruse involving the village's 'five families' of illicit alcohol producers—the Camerons, the McGurks, the McFees, the McGraws and the McLopez's—that has Duggan arresting the entire village.

John frequently reminds the locals about 'the man before the man before Macbeth', a cryptic line that guarantees their assistance. Duggan is soon overwhelmed with prisoner processing, cooking meals and TV John's suggestion to release daytime offenders to make room for 'night people', creating an endless cycle that drives the constable to the brink.

On the island, Hamish reveals his truth: he had brought Alex to this very island where their romance blossomed, but when she later returned to Lochdubh, his feelings had shifted to Isobel. His guilt over never telling Alex before her death has driven him to contemplate ending his life.

The return of Wee Jock to TV John by a boatman alerts him to Hamish's intentions. John arranges for Major Maclean and Isobel to take Barney's boat to the island, where they find Hamish refusing to leave Belle despite her worsening condition.

In a dramatic rescue, the Major bluffs about mine-defusing expertise, drilling a hole in the casing before telling Belle she can safely step off. When nothing happens, they prepare to leave—until Hamish realises the Major had no expertise and had risked his life solely to save him. Seconds later, the mine explodes, confirming the danger was real all along.

As they return to Lochdubh, an exhausted Duggan prepares paella for his Spanish prisoners while TV John reveals that the legendary 'man before the man before Macbeth' is now a renowned police commissioner.

COMMENTARY

Scott Meek: When we got that script, I called up and said, 'There's a woman standing on a landmine that's going to go off and our hero's going to kill himself—so is this kind of like the Beckett episode we're doing?' I loved it because it breaks all the rules. It's completely insane. The stuff with Gerard Kelly is pure farce, and the stuff on the island is serious drama.

Deirdre Keir: I was watching the last two episodes last night. I thought Daniel worked well with the whole guilt thing over Alex, going to the island. My husband watched it with me, and at the end, he said, 'That's the best one.'

Nicholas Renton: If someone has an idea like that today, by the time it's been through the mill of six or seven executives, it doesn't exist anymore.

Michael Mackenzie (Ferdinand McLopez): Daniel Boyle had written this character called Ferdinand McLopez. I got this whole backstory about the fact the Spanish Armada had to make its escape around the north coast of Scotland and his ancestors had been shipwrecked. The art department ran with that and I got a crest for the McLopez's, a Spanish galleon sinking into a sea of grapes. The motto was *Nihil Nisi Caledonius*, which is the Latin for 'Nothing but a true Scotsman'. The other thing is they were one of five families who lived up in the hills.

Daniel Boyle: Kelly was brilliant. Nick Renton really grasped it. It could have been too knowing.

Calum Mackenzie: My wife made the paella for the McLopez clan. She had a restaurant at the time, and they asked her to make it. I had to go down to the shore at night in the dark to find some mussels.

Michael Mackenzie: Gerry Kelly comes in to take over Hamish's office, and everybody decides the only thing we could do is get arrested. Bobby and Edith MacArthur are on a beach with a bomb, the serious side. We were the silly side. We marched into town shouting our family war cry, which is *Pòg mo thòin*, which in Gaelic means 'Kiss my arse'. I was surrounded by my four sons: Jesus, Manuel, Jose and Trini, the wee one being Trini McLopez [a play on Trini Lopez, singer of *If I Had a Hammer*]. There were always jokes a lot of people might never quite get.

Deirdre Keir: I worried about the balance in tone there very much. It wasn't the performance from [Bobby and Edith MacArthur], because they were fantastic, but to cut back and forward to the replacement policeman was a hard one to get the balance right. I don't how they did it, but it worked, seesawing from something that was grotesque; the whole village was arrested, all that with Michael [Mackenzie]. It was bold to cut from that absolutely black farce in the village to something that was about guilt, but Daniel pulled it off. People had invested in the show and him betraying Alex and Alex dying.

ROBERT CARLYLE HAD always found particular satisfaction in episodes like 'No Man Is an Island', where the emotional and psychological stakes were elevated. In a 1997 interview with *The Box*, he reflected on the episode's unusually sombre content: 'After Alex died and, when he went off to kill himself, that's dark stuff for Sunday night.'

Despite initial scepticism about taking on a rural police drama, territory far removed from the edgier roles he was known for, Carlyle found himself persuaded by Daniel Boyle's willingness to explore deeper emotional terrain.

Speaking to the *Sydney Morning Herald* that same year, Carlyle elaborated on what it was about Boyle's writing that had ultimately convinced him to take the role: 'The hash smoking, the difficulty in communication—the more we spoke the darker the character became... you see a really dark side of the guy, particularly with the death of the girlfriend... I think some of that was as good telly as you'll see.'

David Ashton: If you just think of the nerve of the writer there, a whole episode based around a woman with her foot stuck on a mine and we've got to get her off the damned thing. It was absolutely believable, but when you read it you thought, *How is this going to work? How are we going to keep this going for a whole episode?* And when we came to do it, it was terrific.

Valerie Gogan: I think [Hamish's vision of Alex] was our last scene together. I actually filmed other scenes after that, but I think that was the last scene with me and Hamish.

Edith MacArthur: I watched it when it was going out. You didn't miss an episode of *Hamish Macbeth*. That was a wonderful episode. It was a long shoot. The first thing you heard of me was when you hear this woman's voice from far away and she's singing *I Do Like to Be Beside the Seaside*. There was a tremendous amount of preparation of course, because she's got to have her foot on the landmine all the time or it's 'Boom!', the end of everything, including Belle Carter. That would have killed off Hamish Macbeth. I did get a bit stiff.

Nicholas Renton: We helicoptered out to an island almost off Barra and Bobby was put down for an aerial shot and [first assistant director] Tim Lewis doubled for him in the boat. The wind was so high we almost didn't get the shot. Bobby wanted to come home, but we put him in the back of the helicopter, flew up the Sound of Sleat with the sun going down and came out of a cloud and in front of us was a perfect rainbow which was a ring. I never knew rainbows were rings at about 1000 feet. That's the kind of experience you get up there, that's part of the *Hamish* experience. Trying to get the bloody seagulls to stay up there long enough... once they'd had their chips they all went away.

Toby Hefferman: We did a helicopter shot of Hamish with a gun. I was the comms guy and the prop guy had the gun. I remember thinking, 'Oh my God, this place is desolate.' We would do a weather call every day at 10 o'clock and it was too cloudy or the weather conditions weren't right. So we'd cancel it for the day and think, *Well, what should we do? It's 10am, we'll start drinking*. I thought, *Oh, that's what they do here*. Because there's nothing else to do.

Edith MacArthur: It was very bright all the time and I don't think it rained. The sand on that beach looked like something from a Hollywood film, it was absolutely beautiful. The visuals were God's gift to the Scottish Tourist Board. Every shot was a postcard.

Deirdre Keir: To find somewhere that looked like an island we left Plockton and went down to Morar, a good way down the coast. The whole unit moved there to shoot the day and night on the beach. Charles Denton became Head of Drama in London and had been head of Zenith. My luck was out because he knew a lot about production and he came to Morar.

We were doing day and night on the beach and we'd received the weather forecast and it wasn't good. There was nothing we could do indoors, and it was logistically very difficult with these huge dunes and getting out there for a night shoot. He came up and we went out for dinner and he said, 'That wind and rain isn't looking very good tonight, are they actually shooting? What's your weather cover?' I said we didn't have any. 'You haven't got any weather cover?' I said, 'Do you want a pudding or shall we just go out?'

Nicholas Renton: We went out and the whole unit was in little tents with rain bouncing off like pebbles. Being the good leader, I was going from tent to tent, sticking my head in. Bobby was one for feeling the cold.

Deirdre Keir: We trudged through the wet sand and Nick's trudging up and down. The forecast from the coastguard was 'Bad, worse, worst.' There was no way we could shoot a foot. We sat in the coach absolutely soaked and I said, 'I think we're going to wrap it.' It was pitch black and to get all those huge lights, the tracks and everything back, we had 4x4s on the dunes. We were all soaked to buggery and Charles said, 'Can I do anything to help?' I said, 'Yes Charles you can. Can you get some of the artistes back up to the hotel as they're absolutely soaked?' So he helped out.

We hadn't got a shot that night, it was ghastly, but we talked and decided to pull back to Plockton. Then Charles came out and said, 'That's the best visit I've ever had to a location. What are you going to do now?' I said, 'We're going back to Plockton to find a location to mug up as a night shoot,' and Charles said, 'Great, can I come?'

Nicholas Renton: I got back to the hotel and looked at the sky and could see the moon. The rain had stopped, but it was three in the morning.

Edith MacArthur: Then we had a change of beach. I can't remember why that was, but we suddenly were being whisked off to a different beach. I was put up in a different hotel. It was like a wonderful holiday for me. It was such a good time up there, I enjoyed doing it all from start to finish.

Deirdre Keir: So we went round to Loch Carron with Fred Tammes and we looked at this rocky beach and Fred said, 'There's no sand, I can't shoot this.' I said, 'We can get the sand, we can't not do this.' And he walked up and down and said, 'Well, if I have to, I have to.' Nothing fazed lovely Fred, but he was a bit huffy that day. We were all tired and tearful. So I got on to the production manager to ask for sand and the nearest sand was north of Inverness.

The people of Lochcarron were a bit sniffy because we hadn't done any filming there. I said, 'You see that bit of beach? Do you mind if I bring some sand there?' It belonged to the golf course and the National Trust. We phoned a contractor on the east coast and he thought it was Christmas. He sent six lorries back and forth with sand and we put the sand on the beach and everyone came and stared.

Nicholas Renton: Fred had spotted a big promontory and thought it was much better.

Toby Hefferman: That was a really fun episode. It was a night shoot; we were working late at night and it was cold. My memory is that might've been Robert Carlyle's favourite episode because it was real drama and there was some real acting. Then we'd go to the ceilidh every night. Our unit nurse broke her leg because she was involved in a ceilidh accident, dancing wildly.

Nicholas Renton: The second problem we had with the BBC [after the drugs] was the gun in the mouth. That went on forever. 'Could we see him put the gun in his mouth?' Of course you had to. If he was just waving the gun around, it looked like he was going to shoot the seagulls. The gun has to go in the mouth. 'Will it go in for eight frames or 20 frames?'

Deirdre Keir: Because people will see it and want to shoot themselves. Which is why you can't show someone jumping off a railway bridge, because it'll make them want to do it...

Nicholas Renton: But you can show them on the bridge and splattered on the track.

Deirdre Keir: But British Rail won't let you shoot on the track.

Scott Meek: I had to go to a huge BBC meeting to justify that. It was pre-9 o'clock, and he puts a gun in his mouth. It caused a huge panic at the BBC because you can't do that. I argued that if it's good enough, then sometimes you have to break the rules.

Ralph Riach: Gerry Kelly was terrific in that one. It's such a great concept, fun, the fact that they're all in cahoots. TV John just had to say to McLopez, 'Does he no' remind you of the man before the man before Macbeth?' and he goes, 'Oh I see what you're up to...' Those boys were local boys but they were such romantic, handsome looking buggers with their black curly hair.

Duncan Duff: That was a superb episode and Gerry absolutely revelled in it. He was full-on, and that was his style, to go for it with characters and he could do that in *Hamish Macbeth*: it was appropriate, it was brilliant, and he absolutely took full advantage of it.

Michael Mackenzie: Gerard Kelly was one of the good guys. He was a lovely, kind, decent, honest, sweet man. And very talented. Audiences absolutely loved him and he loved them. He worked with and for his audience all the time. I always thought he was a bit over the top on television, certainly in *City Lights* [1984–91], which he did with dear Andy Gray. The Scots audiences loved it because they come from that Music Hall tradition and they enjoy that kind of broad, slapstick sort of acting. All the greats did variety theatre.

I'm working with Una McLean at the moment, and Una was brought up in the *Five Past Eight* [summer revues], working with Rikki [Fulton] and Jack [Milroy], Johnny Beattie and Jimmy Logan, all these people who could go across genres. That's what we do in Scotland, the actors can cross genres all over the place. Rikki Fulton was a very good serious actor.

Gerard Kelly was a very good serious actor and a very, very funny comic actor. He was a very good actor, first and foremost. We all loved being with him. He was a lovely, lovely man and [his death in 2010] was a tragic premature ending. We lost a great talent there.

David Ashton: The good ship *Hamish Macbeth* took in all-comers. We'd just bring 'em in, sort 'em out and spit 'em out again. We had a lot of fun.

Deirdre Keir: One production manager couldn't stand it up there and drove just about everyone off the road. Gerard Kelly, if he was off at three in the afternoon and wasn't needed the next day, he'd go back to Glasgow. I asked him why he was travelling down and he said, 'I need a curry.' The place completely freaked him out. He was completely magic in that show. Mad eyes.

Nicholas Renton: I'd been up there when I was a child and I wasn't frightened by the place. Some people went up and couldn't take the awayness.

Edith MacArthur: I would never have dreamt of calling [Robert Carlyle] Bobby. I don't think I even called him Robert. I didn't talk to him much, he didn't invite conversation. He was the local copper with the wee white dog. I had a feeling Robert didn't care for it all that much. It probably stopped a lot of shooting with the dog doing things it shouldn't be doing. Shirley was approachable, you could chat to her. She's so unusual, a brilliant actress.

Toby Hefferman: Wee Jock was alright. He wasn't really trained very well. Sometimes the dog was interested in being in the shot, sometimes it wasn't. He was a bit yappy. Bobby wasn't a fan, I don't think he liked dogs at all.

FINAL THOUGHTS

'No Man is an Island' sees *Hamish Macbeth* deliver one of its most ambitious episodes, playing out like two shows happening at once.

On the wind-battered beach, Robert Carlyle and Edith MacArthur create powerful drama as Hamish confronts his guilt over Alex's death. Back in Lochdubh, chaos reigns as Gerard Kelly's PC Duggan attempts to impose order on the unruly villagers.

Kelly's contribution can't be overstated. Known for his versatility, he brings both ridiculousness and earnestness to Duggan, elevating what could have been simple comedy into something far more compelling.

At the heart of the episode is Hamish's confession about his relationship with Alex. Robert Carlyle delivers perhaps his finest performance in the series, as Hamish admits he began deceiving Alex the moment she returned to Lochdubh, leaving her 'surplus to requirements'. His self-loathing feels viscerally real, the tears genuine. It's a brutal and moving scene that needs the lighter moments, like the entire village bickering about Duggan's cooking skills in the police cell, to balance it.

6. THE LOCHDUBH DELUXE

Writer: Daniel Boyle
Director: Nicholas Renton
Original broadcast: 28th April 1996, 7.15pm

GUEST CAST

Andrew Keir (Murray McMurray), Jimmy Chisholm (Christie McMurray), Daniel Boyle (Mr Fergusson), Ida Schuster (Mrs Lewis), Robert Carr (Harry Macleish), Laurie Ventry (Reverend Snow), Sheila Keith (Auntie Ella), Jake D'Arcy (Sawney Weir), Robert Ellis (Tam Duff), Joseph Greig (Dugal Finlay).

SUMMARY

Opening with Cnothan funeral director Murray McMurray and his nephew Christie preparing the deceased Bella Campbell —one of Rory's aunts—ahead of her funeral, the two men soon begin debating what is clearly an ongoing issue. Christie demands cost-cutting measures while Murray insists on dignity.

As Murray reminisces about his time in school with Bella, Christie menacingly dons latex gloves and looms over his uncle, seemingly about to strangle him, only to be interrupted by housekeeper Mrs Lewis arriving with tea—'You're a lifesaver, Mrs Lewis' becoming Murray's (unknowingly accurate) refrain throughout the episode.

At the funeral, the minister repeatedly confuses Bella with her very-much-alive sister Ella during the service. At the wake, Christie nearly triggers a fight by suggesting Barney Meldrum is charging for the refreshments. Hamish then prevents Christie from handing Rory his bill, promising to leave him at the mercy of Barney.

Murray talks to Lachlan Sr about hiring Lachie Jr for £3 an hour, hoping to groom a successor. Murray reveals that he's desperate to prevent Christie from taking over the family business, horrified by his nephew's modern ideas for renaming burial grounds as 'slumber lawns' and coffins as 'astral barges'.

When Lachie Jr discovers his father has effectively 'sold' him to the undertaker, he's horrified. Hamish suggests a clever strategy: if Lachie pretends to love the work, his father will quickly remove him to preserve the McCrae family business.

Meanwhile, cemetery caretaker Harry Macleish claims aliens abducted Bella Campbell's body. Though sceptical, Hamish plays along, organising a volunteer UFO watch while privately suspecting Macleish has been selling cadavers.

After Christie complains to Murray that Lachie is being paid too much while the latter is repairing the hearse, he once again attempts to kill his uncle by dropping the vehicle on him, only for Mrs Lewis to appear with more tea. He tries again later on with a heavy object, but Mrs Lewis is 'a lifesaver' once more.

The alien story unravels when TV John witnesses Macleish accepting money from Sawney Weir, the Cnothan crematorium supervisor, initially suggesting a personal vendetta related to an old affair between Bella and Weir's father (though it turns out it was actually Ella who had the affair).

Investigating further, Hamish discovers Christie and Sawney have been running a scam, selling the same luxury Lochdubh Deluxe coffin repeatedly and secretly cremating bodies. Aware he's about to be arrested, Christie takes his illicit earnings and hides in a coffin headed for cremation, only to end up trapped inside. Despite a frantic race to save him from incineration, both Christie and the money are cremated.

In the aftermath, Murray offers a more permanent job to Lachie Jr, who accepts, though Lachlan suggests they could one day merge and become McCrae & McCrae. The episode ends with father and son both claiming to be positive about the future, before tearfully going their own way.

COMMENTARY

Jimmy Chisholm (Christie McMurray): I came back for 'The Lochdubh Deluxe'. I would have had to audition for that one, it was quite a big part. Deirdre was at my audition and very hands on.

Deirdre Keir: When Jimmy came back, he said to me, 'Do you think anyone will notice?'

Jimmy Chisholm: I was delighted to get the part. Christie was one of the greatest characters I'd played at that point, such a nut job. The whole idea of digging up coffins and using them again was genius. And I got to work with Andrew Keir.

Deirdre Keir: My mum was in the first episode of the first series and my dad was in my last episode of the second series. Daniel kept writing these 80-year-old characters and we kept saying, 'Why does he write them so old, they're all dying and can't remember their lines.'

Nicholas Renton: We spoke to Iain Cuthbertson, but he'd had a stroke and couldn't remember his lines.

Deirdre Keir: By the time we got to 'The Lochdubh Deluxe' we'd been through all the older actors. My dad was absolutely adamant he wouldn't act in anything of mine because all the other actors would think he got the gig because I was his daughter. Nepotism! I'd been a production manager on a show in Italy and the director had cast him not knowing he was my father. Then I did one called *The One Game* [1988] and had to get someone really quickly. I phoned and said, 'Dad, please come and do this.' 'No.' So I said, 'If you don't do this I'll never speak to you again.' He said, 'That's emotional blackmail! Don't come on set, don't get in my eyeline.' We got to this one and he wouldn't do it, he held out for three weeks.

Julia Duff: I'm sure there was someone we were going to get to do it, but they died.

Deirdre Keir: I went and spoke to his wife, my step mother, and said, 'We've run out of people in their 70s and 80s, there isn't anyone else left, please get him to come and do this.' He wasn't well. He was in his 70s and he looked very ill.

Jimmy Chisholm: I was quite starstruck because he was world famous, but he was a darling man. He was very quiet, didn't say much, but when he did it was always worth listening to.

Nicholas Renton: I recall Billy Riddoch having fascinating conversations with Andrew. Billy would prepare himself meticulously, so if a director then says, 'We're not going to do it like this, we're going to do it like that,' that becomes really difficult. Then there was Andrew, veteran of umpteen theatre productions, sitting on horses waiting for charges with Richard Burton sitting beside him, and we were doing a long scene in the pub...

Deirdre Keir: During that two-hander at the beginning, when dad asks him if he can have his son?

Nicholas Renton: Yes, and Billy was having difficulty, I'd asked him to drink at one point or something, and Andrew said, 'You know you need to be prepared, if a director asks you to do it with a somersault, you do it with a somersault.' This extraordinary tutorial was going on.

Jimmy Chisholm: I had to show the audience who Christie was and what he was up to. It was quite complicated to pull off, but I think we got it right in the end. You also had to go deeper because Andrew brought this granite-like influence to the middle of it all. Meanwhile, you had this weird nephew jumping around, trying not to be seen as he got up to all sorts. Suddenly, I'd appear at the back, and you'd think, *Is he going to kill the old guy?* Then Ida Schuster came in, and Christie says, 'Oh, you're a lifesaver!' It was all very theatrical.

Nick Renton would direct me in front of the camera, saying, 'Right, when this happens, I want you to do that,' always asking me to keep it subtle. But then the cameraman behind him was going, 'No, more, more—make it huge, do it big, it's brilliant!' We had all sorts of fights, me, Nick, and the cameraman. I said, 'Look, I don't know who I'm supposed to listen to!' I think it did need to be played in that arch way.

David Ashton: Andrew played it totally seriously, and that's what made it funny.

Jimmy Chisholm: The cameraman made up a lot of the character. I think it was him who said, 'Wouldn't it be great if he disappears from shot and the camera doesn't move? He slinks out and then appears when the camera gets to the other side of the room.' Just little gimmicks that happened as we were doing it.

Deirdre Keir: Actors need good directors.

Nicholas Renton: They also need directors who like actors, and not all directors do. I was lucky, I came from theatre so I had 10 years or so of working with actors in that situation and there you have to like an actor, you have to love an actor, otherwise you don't get the show on. I'm just fascinated by the differences between actors. If you put Andrew there in the same room as Jimmy Chisholm, they're completely different in technique yet they can play a scene together.

Stuart Davids: Nick Renton is tremendous and from a theatre background. He's one of the best directors I've worked with. He was obsessed with the show and he pushed you to think about your character.

Nicholas Renton: The sight of Stuart and Andrew together, with the same sort of physicality, it's unbelievable. That's the thing Eastern European films are made of. They began to walk the same.

Deirdre Keir: Being around that area and being respectful, you have to understand the values there. We needed a graveyard where Ella/Bella is being laid down and none of the cemeteries would let us in.

Nicholas Renton: There was a beautiful kirk on Skye and I asked if I could dig a grave and they said, 'You must be joking.' But it had a wall around it and if you put the camera in a certain place, the wall disappeared into a kind of gulley, so we could do our bit outside the graveyard and by using the right lens it looked as though it was all the same thing.

Deirdre Keir: That was unusual because I've shot in graveyards all over the UK and I've never had a problem as long as you're respectful, but not there.

Nicholas Renton: There are no crematoriums on the west coast. It's a primary school with a chimney stuck on it. I went over to Inverness to look at the real thing, but we couldn't take the crew all the way over there. But it wasn't right, it felt completely wrong.

Deirdre Keir: My kids watched the show every week as it went out and they'd been up to Plockton a few times. My son has a phobia about death and when we got to the bit with Christie going in the coffin to be incinerated with his money, my 9-year-old shot out of the room.

Jimmy Chisholm: Being in that coffin was quite horrible. They set up the coffin so they could take bits off to stick a camera up my nose, or whatever. It wasn't comfortable because we had to put smoke in it as well. It's quite scary, but that's the thing about what we do. You have to imagine how you would feel in that situation. We spent a couple of hours just doing that wee bit. No one had done it before, so they'd ask, 'Can you breathe if we do this?' I'd say, 'Well yeah, I can hold my breath for a while.' They'd reply, 'No, we don't want you holding your breath.' They were trying to learn how to do it and how not to kill the actor at the same time. Very cutting edge.

Nicholas Renton: I thought that was worse than putting the dog in the fridge, but nobody agreed. It's so strange it's not on [the BBC's] radar.

THE EPISODE'S DARK humour, specifically Christie being locked in a coffin and struggling to get out, led to complaints to the Broadcasting Standards Council about the scene being shown before the 9pm watershed. A spokesman said: 'The sequence was likely to have engendered fear and concern among members of the audience.' A BBC spokesperson claimed 'the tone of the episode had been surreal throughout, with allegations of grave-robbing and alien abduction, and believed it a fitting climax for a series whose comic approach was already well established.'

Jimmy Chisholm: I didn't know anything about that. You wonder how they could say that if they'd watched it. But you just wouldn't see stuff like that nowadays. It was such an experimental piece. By the time the first series had been on, people had gone, 'Oh, I think we know what this is now.' By the second series there was so much interest in it, but at no point did anyone say, 'They won't let us show it.' *Hamish Macbeth* was from another world. It was very funny. You either got it or you didn't, but you had to find out what it was first.

ONE OF THE critics who got it was the *Daily Record*'s John Millar, who wrote on 4th May 1996 that 'Other programmes would have been content to let [Christie's] suit get slightly singed and had him rescued at the last minute. But the wonderfully quirky series went the whole way, and the underhand undertaker was reduced to ashes. Terrific stuff.'

Deirdre Keir: There's that wonderful gag that Lachie Jr was just going to do the job for a little while. He was just going to kid his dad on, and then at the end he's really interested in it. He actually leaves his dad at the end, he cries as he goes and his dad cries.

Stuart Davids: I'll never forget when I had to cry and leave. Nick made me go away and psych up for it for about an hour. He basically had me walking around a field, so that when he shouted turnover I could do the crying. It's one of the hardest things I've ever done, because he's so serious about it. It was never treated flippantly, it was like we were doing Shakespeare.

David Ashton: *Hamish Macbeth* was never overtly funny, nobody played it for laughs, or if they did they got sorted out very quickly, either by the cast or by the director.

Anne Lacey: At the end [of series two] I didn't know it was going to finish and I'd planned that I'd do one more series and then come out. But when I look back I think I was mad, that I should have been delighted to stay. I remember thinking it was fine to leave after three years.

Final Thoughts

While earlier episodes built toward romantic resolution, 'The Lochdubh Deluxe' shifts focus to broader themes, dismantling Hamish's world and shining a light on secondary characters. The McCraes take centre stage in this episode, their relationship developing into something far more poignant than a comedy double act.

The main plot is quintessential Daniel Boyle: a pitch-black comedy involving recycled coffins and crematorium fraud, with a touch of UFO-themed absurdity. Boyle also cameos as the deceased 'Mr Fergusson' in the opening moments of the episode, lying on a slab behind Christie as the latter contemplates strangling his uncle. Andrew Keir anchors the episode with his gravitas as Murray, balancing Jimmy Chisholm's delightfully unhinged performance as Christie.

But as always, *Hamish Macbeth* blends the absurd with moments of emotion. Lachlan Sr's attempts to spin his son's departure as a 'merger' opportunity fail to disguise his heartbreak. The scene where Lachie Jr drives away from his father, leaving both men in tears, carries a surprising weight for characters initially played for laughs. There's also a passing reference to Isobel's absence from the episode, as we learn that she's moved to Glasgow.

By pushing the boundaries of what was acceptable in pre-watershed TV, 'The Lochdubh Deluxe' solidified the show's reputation for daring storytelling. The episode feels less like a series finale and more like the end of an era for Lochdubh.

THIRTEEN
CHOOSE LOCHDUBH, CHOOSE STARDOM

By EARLY 1996, *Hamish Macbeth* had become the standard-bearer for a dramatic transformation at BBC Scotland. At the corporation's spring season launch, BBC One Controller Alan Yentob celebrated Scotland's role in reviving network drama, while BBC Two's Michael Jackson described the region as being 'at the forefront of network production'. With its annual budget set to rise to £40 million, BBC Scotland had evolved from regional outpost to major player.

For Andrea Calderwood, this success represented a broader shift in British TV's power dynamics. 'At that point, you could almost choose to do things through BBC Scotland or London,' she explains. Her strategy of aggressive expansion had paid off; in her first year alone, she had tripled the division's output by embracing independent productions alongside traditional in-house projects.

The timing had been perfect. The BBC's Hatch Report had set an ambitious target for 25% of productions to be produced outside London, though as Calderwood notes with a hint of irony, executives were careful to insist 'it's a target, not a quota'. This push for regional production, combined with the BBC's new openness to working with independent production companies, created unprecedented opportunities for creative collaboration.

'There's such talent in Scotland,' Calderwood says, reflecting on her guiding principle that Scottish talent could create programming with both national and international appeal. But she was equally pragmatic about bringing in expertise from elsewhere when needed, as demonstrated by 1997's historical drama film *Mrs. Brown* (released as *Her Majesty Mrs. Brown* in the US), where Scottish producer Douglas Rae's story about Queen Victoria and John Brown was enhanced by the talents of English writer Jeremy Brock and director John Madden.

This blend of local talent and wider collaboration was already proving successful with *Hamish Macbeth*. The series exemplified everything Calderwood had been fighting for: distinctively Scottish storytelling that could capture a national audience.

Sunday evenings, described by *The Stage* as a 'battleground' for British broadcasters, saw *Hamish Macbeth*'s second series thriving as part of BBC One's ratings-topping triple bill: *Antiques Roadshow* (1979–), *Hamish* and *Birds of a Feather* (1989–2020). *Antiques Roadshow* hit a high of 14 million viewers early in its run and, by April, maintained a strong 9.27 million. *Hamish* closely followed with around 9 million viewers each week.

ITV's decision to pit *Doctor Finlay* against *Hamish* backfired. A few weeks after *Finlay*'s fourth series ended, the *Daily Record* reported its cancellation due to falling ratings. An insider called the scheduling 'stupid... splitting the audience'. Even actor David Rintoul, who played Doctor Finlay, admitted: 'We were always going to have problems once *Hamish Macbeth* became part of the equation.'

Author M.C. Beaton's stance towards *Hamish Macbeth* seemed to have mellowed by April 1996, when the BBC's *Points of View* visited her at home in Gloucestershire. Explaining that she had originally likened the decision to cast Robert Carlyle to 'expecting Robert Redford and getting Danny DeVito', she then admitted, 'I think Bobby Carlyle does a splendid job'.

Beaton also praised Zippy, the original Wee Jock. 'I thought that dog was a marvellous actor, and I was very disappointed when they killed him off,' she said. 'Although the series isn't like the books, it's captured the spirit of the books. I'm sure a lot of people will go there now thanks to the series, so I'm pleased.'

Fresh from the success of *Trainspotting*, which topped the UK box office and became the highest-grossing British film of 1996, Robert Carlyle spent spring 1996 filming a low-budget film about male strippers in Sheffield to be released in 1997: *The Full Monty*.

In May 1996, Carlyle won Best Actor at the Royal Television Society Awards, with critics hailing his standout portrayal of Begbie in *Trainspotting*, one that was at odds with his small screen persona in *Hamish Macbeth*, the role he would be returning to in a few months' time.

FOURTEEN
SMELLING THE POMADE

SUMMER 1996

THE VAST ROOM in Duncraig Castle had likely hosted grand Victorian dinners in its heyday, where lords and ladies once gathered around gleaming mahogany tables. Charles Salmon stood in the doorway surveying what would become his office upon taking over as producer on *Hamish Macbeth*'s third series, a far cry from coordinating the globe-trotting adventures of *The Young Indiana Jones Chronicles* (1992–1996).

After three years racing between international film sets, juggling time zones and location permits from Tunisia to Prague, there was something appealing about settling into one place, even if that place was a slightly dilapidated castle with buckets placed in corridors to catch leaking rainwater.

His desk, positioned by a window overlooking Loch Carron, stood at the far end of what might have once been a ballroom. The long walk across bare floorboards to reach it reminded him of a Soviet general's headquarters, though he had rather different plans for the space. Within days, he'd moved in more furniture, set up a large table for impromptu meetings and started encouraging the kind of creative cross-pollination that had worked so well on *Young Indiana Jones*.

The contrast between productions couldn't have been starker. Where *Indiana Jones* had required coordinating hundreds of crew members across multiple continents, *Hamish Macbeth*'s vital signs could be taken daily in Plockton's two pubs. His predecessor Deirdre Keir had crafted something special here, a close-knit creative family that had found its rhythm over two successful series.

But TV shows, like families, need room to grow. As Salmon thumbed through the scripts for series three, he could see both the challenges and opportunities ahead. The show needed to reach 20 episodes to help foreign sales, meaning a big budget two-part finale was on the cards.

Meanwhile, his lead actor had just wrapped a low-budget film about male strippers in Sheffield that no one, least of all Robert Carlyle, expected to amount to much.

Change was coming to Lochdubh, whether anyone was ready or not.

Deirdre Keir: I worked on the development of series three. I had two kids while I was doing one and two and I'd been away for so long that I said I couldn't do series three because they'll have forgotten who I am, I'm going home.

Ming Ho: Each series was a long shoot in Plockton over the summer, from June to September/October; you either have to leave your family for that time or take them with you.

Deirdre Keir: Scott [Meek] said, 'Well just work on some script development for series three.'

Ming Ho: Deirdre was involved in development of the scripts for series three, but when it went into production Charles Salmon took over. His style of working was different to Deirdre's, with more focus on the practical side of filming than on the storylines and script process.

Charles Salmon (Producer): We had a meeting, and I said I was going to follow what she had set up. But she encouraged me to do what I wanted, or what I felt could add to the series. When you're in that sort of position, you've got to respect the past and the family traditions, but also you're hoping you can inject a bit of new life. During your period as a producer, you try and make everything a little bit bigger and better. It was getting that balance.

Ming Ho: Series always open out the longer they go on, because you have to find more story material.

Charles Salmon: You've got to keep things fresh. You're always looking for ways of doing that with fantastic directors. I knew Mandie Fletcher already. Nicholas Renton was very much the lead director. I took his advice about many things because he knew the series so well. But then we had the lovely Jonas [Grimås], who was a real breath of fresh air.

Jonas Grimås (Director): By the time I got to direct *Hamish*, I had made twelve films in the UK. Mostly documentaries, of which three were for Channel 4, and a couple of short films for television. In 1993 I directed *Marooned*, a short film set in Glasgow produced by Andrea Calderwood, it was her second film as a producer. She suggested Robert Carlyle as the lead. We all met up in London and talked about everything under the sun except the script. By the time we all had to leave, Robert stopped at the door on his way out, turned around and asked if he had got the part. 'Of course you have,' was the answer. The film went on tour in cinemas around the country as the opening film in Habitat's travelling anniversary film festival celebrating design in film and was eventually nominated for a BAFTA. So that's how I got to know Bobby. I'm sure this is the primary reason I was considered to work on *Hamish Macbeth.*

Another reason might be that I went back to Sweden in 1995 to direct a drama series called *Radio Shadow* [*Radioskugga*, 1995–97]. This was a fairly untypical Swedish production with a dark sense of humour where a very successful Stockholm radio DJ gets the sack and ends up running a radio station in a very small village called Backwaters [Bakvattnet]. There's an obvious kinship between the two, and for some reason Scott Meek saw two of my subtitled episodes and decided to give me a chance.

Charles Salmon: I got the directors to meet and discuss how to broaden the season and make it bigger. Bobby gave me a hug and said, 'I know what you're trying to do, and that's fantastic.' The show had a great atmosphere, and everyone was happy to be part of it, always helping each other.

Nicholas Renton: There was a huge pressure by series two to do more than six episodes. Season three went up to eight, and [we were still being asked] 'Why aren't you giving us 12?'

Scott Meek: We did eight episodes in season three to reach 20 overall, unlocking more international sales opportunities.

Ming Ho: During series three I was also script editing a Zenith/ITV/Carlton series, *Bodyguards* [1996], starring Louise Lombard and Sean Pertwee, which was shooting in London. It was the days before email, and even mobile phone coverage on location in Plockton was patchy at best; quite a challenge to keep on top of both shows simultaneously! I remember long hours standing by the fax machine, feeding in pages and pages of scripts.

I guess the pragmatic answer [to the question of why Daniel Boyle was writing six out of eight scripts for series three] is that we didn't do that many drafts of each. Having since worked as a writer myself on series such as *EastEnders* [1985–] and *Casualty*, where you might write 10 drafts of each script, the way we worked on *Hamish* was remarkably respectful and sympathetic to the writers.

Charles Salmon: It was in the air that [Bobby leaving] was a possibility. I think that was the reason for the special two-parter. It was a way of rounding things off. His career was really taking off at the time.

'THERE ARE JUST not enough likely crimes in Lochdubh to keep on going indefinitely, it's ridiculous,' Robert Carlyle told *Time Out* in 1996, highlighting a major issue facing the production team of any crime drama set in a small town that needs to generate plots for multiple series.

Duncan Duff: Between series, we'd all go off and do other work, but Bobby's career was on a different trajectory. Between series one and two, he did *Trainspotting*, and by series three, everything had taken off. I remember him mentioning a film about male strippers in Sheffield while we were travelling in a car together. We all looked at each other, thinking, *What? Sounds interesting*, and he said, 'Straight to video.' Then it came out and was massive. Each time he came back, his profile grew, and his projects became more outrageous.

Charles Salmon: He wasn't convinced it was going to be a great film. I remember him being a little bit negative about it, but it's very hard; it's the experience that you had, how you got on with everybody. He had just finished filming, so he hadn't seen any assemblies and wasn't really in a position to know what the final look was going to be.

Ming Ho: As I recall, we always knew he wouldn't sign up for more than three series. He was never the kind of actor to tie himself into a long-running Sunday night show, and we didn't consider trying to carry on without him.

Deirdre Keir: Most production companies will continue a successful series as long as possible, but Scott was the opposite. He said, 'Let's do it well, and if we sense people are getting tired or the quality might drop, we'll stop before that happens.' It was a brave approach for an independent company that needed money. The writers worked hard to avoid formula, and Scott discussed it with Bobby, who was balancing *The Full Monty* and *Trainspotting*. Given his professionalism and drive, it was bloody exhausting.

AS THE THIRD series entered production under the shadow of Carlyle's possible departure, questions loomed about the future of *Hamish Macbeth*.

FIFTEEN

THE BEGINNING OF THE END

SUMMER 1996

ON A BRIGHT SUMMER morning in 1996, Plockton presented two faces to the world. To casual visitors, it appeared as a perfect crescent of whitewashed houses curved around a sparkling harbour, with fishing boats bobbing on the water and rhododendron-filled gardens tumbling down to the shore.

The twisted spine of the Cuillin Hills on Skye provided a dramatic backdrop, while the turrets of Duncraig Castle peeked above thick woods on the nearest promontory. It was a scene that wouldn't have looked out of place in *Brigadoon* (1954).

But there was another Plockton too. In the village's only car park, the cast and crew of *Hamish Macbeth* gathered around their catering van, eating lunch off paper plates. Robert Carlyle, still in his police uniform, moved through the crowd speaking barely above a murmur.

Outside the Lochdubh Hotel looking towards Rory's store

The series had helped bring more money to local businesses. The craft shop now stocked toy police nightsticks alongside its usual wares, though the real Hamish would have had more use for a cattle prod, given the four-legged traffic that regularly strolled past.

Plockton operated on an entirely different rhythm from the urban world the TV crew had left behind, a fact captured in the locals' favourite tale about a Spaniard boasting of his country's word *mañana*, meaning tomorrow; 'Och,' replies the Highlander, 'we don't have anything as urgent as that'.

Even justice worked differently here. When local boys overturned bins after a big night in Kyle of Lochalsh, one was made to post a public apology on the town notice board and clean up the mess. He never named his drinking partners: in Plockton, you didn't tell tales.

This gentler way of life even seemed to influence the cast. Ralph Riach could be found gently chiding young autograph hunters about their manners. 'Did you say please?' he would ask with a firm smile, only signing after receiving the magic word.

The community had not just adapted to its dual identity; it had embraced it completely.

* * *

It was on 25th June 1996, just a few weeks into filming, that the *Daily Record* reported that *Hamish Macbeth*'s lead writer was stepping away from the series. 'After the new series it will be the end of *Macbeth* for me,' said Daniel Boyle. 'I don't know if the show will carry on, but I have just about exhausted all my possibilities for *Hamish*. Other writers with fresh ideas can come along and keep the show going.'

One month later, the paper announced Robert Carlyle's departure from the show. It was described as a 'shock decision' and 'a bombshell for BBC chiefs who hoped the ratings winner would run for years'. A BBC insider lamented: 'It's a real shame because we thought the series could go on and on. It was a groundbreaking programme.'

Scott Meek: Danny felt he'd done all he could, and Bobby was ready to move on. We thought it best to end on a high and be remembered fondly.

Valerie Gogan: Bobby became so famous during that time from when we started even to the end of the first series, he just went stratospheric. He's such a good actor. All the regulars were great actors, but he became hugely famous. It's good that they got him for a third series because I guess he was getting offers left, right and centre.

Ralph Riach: I think Bobby had to do two years because he was contracted. We had to sign a contract for the first with an option of a second. But to his credit he gave us a third series, even though he didn't have to.

Stuart Davids: Although Bobby loved doing the show, he wanted to do other things. There was a feeling it wouldn't survive without him, whereas now you see programmes like *Heartbeat* and *Taggart* [where departed lead actors were replaced] and it's amazing what audiences will accept.

Lochdubh's police station and Hamish's home

Duncan Duff: I think he had a soft spot for *Hamish Macbeth*. I'm not going to speak on behalf of Bobby, but I think it was a show that he did care a lot about. He honoured the commitment to do three series, but there was no way on Earth that they would have been able to persuade him to do a fourth series. Fair dos, he did exactly what he promised he would do. There's a lot of Bobby in that character as well. I think he was excellent in it; it was perfectly fitted to him.

Mandie Fletcher: I think Bobby had had enough. I can remember coming up for that third series and thinking there was an atmosphere around the place. It wasn't like the series before where we seemed to be having fun and were sort of clinging together, but I think he wanted to be taken more seriously and thought it was all a bit light, which it is if you want to be taken as a serious actor. It was after *Trainspotting* and he'd played Albie [in *Cracker*] and I think [those roles] defined him.

Daniel Boyle: You could see he was doing it but wanted to be somewhere else. I sensed it.

Forbes Masson [Tam Flood, 'The Lochdubh Assassin']: Bobby didn't seem bored with it, and I noticed the producers really listened to him. He had quite an influence, which was good, as he clearly wanted more control over things to do with the production, which is what we all want. Everyone was really sad that it was going to end. It reminded me of *The High Life* [1994–95, the short-lived show Masson co-wrote and co-starred in with Alan Cumming]—at the time it felt terribly sad not to do more, but looking back, you think, 'Thank God we did.' It's better to leave people wanting more than to keep going until they say, 'Oh God, not this again.'

Toby Hefferman: After *Trainspotting* came out, because we'd all forged relationships, things didn't really change. But there was definitely a difference for newcomers coming in. Oasis were playing [at Loch Lomond], and we got free tickets. Bobby helicoptered there with his mate Jon White, the gaffer. We drove down, but he got us tickets.

Charles Salmon: Bobby was totally professional, great to work with. He tended to have his own circuit of friends on the unit. He wasn't quite as social as the likes of Ralph and Brian. If you went to the local pub, you'd often meet up with all the cast, but Bobby probably not so much. He was at that period already planning ahead. You sort of got the feeling that he was going to go and do other things.

Shirley Henderson: It did slightly change. There was a slightly different feel, but that's probably to do with the writing. Things develop and they get ideas from what's gone before.

Sarah Bruce: Series three was a slightly different vibe. Bobby had signed on for series three before *Trainspotting* came along and he came back, having filmed that and fresh from *Carla's Song* [1996] in Nicaragua. His career was taking off, so I think he naturally felt he was taking a step back coming to do one last series of *Hamish*. He was still professional and lovely and I think on many levels he wanted to see it through, but many of us felt for him when we were sure he'd had to turn down some great offers to fulfil his commitment. Series three was known to be the last when we started filming it. I'm not actually sure if the village knew that beforehand, but they would have before long. News has always travelled fast here!

Charles Salmon: I grew up in a small town in North Devon, so I understood the sense of community and the wacky things that can happen in such places. When I arrived in Plockton during early prep, I stayed in the Captain's House by the loch. After the long drive, I threw my bags in, grabbed a drink at the local pub, and sat in the empty garden across the road to enjoy the sunset. Suddenly, a dark cloud of midges descended on me—I'd never encountered them before. Running back, I saw everyone at the pub window laughing; they'd known what would happen and said nothing. It wasn't mean-spirited, just part of the welcome. That moment reminded me of Devon: When the newcomer arrived, you didn't tell them about everything at the beginning, you just allowed them to find out about them.

Jonas Grimås: When I first came to Scotland to shoot *Marooned*, it only took the steward on the flight to open the door and I felt as if I was coming home. Scotland is like a second home to me. If I didn't live in London I would live in Glasgow. Arriving in Plockton was a seamless experience; I felt welcome the moment I arrived. During my 12-week stay, I got to know a great number of people since many of the locals were involved in the project. It was hard to leave at the end of production.

Forbes Masson: It was a particularly lovely summer, and being in Plockton was gorgeous. Joining an established cast can be daunting—you have to hit the ground running—but everyone was so lovely, and I already knew some of them, like Ralph from drama school. Staying at the hotel was great but a bit dangerous. We'd go out for meals with our per diems and sit in the bar at night. You had to be careful not to get carried away, especially with filming the next morning and the whisky was a-flowing.

Duncan Duff: By series three I was up in Plockton and I had a small child and a pregnant wife. A daughter of somebody in the village, I think the postman, was acting as a baby minder because my wife worked and we were splitting it sometimes. She was up there and sometimes I had the baby up with me. For me, it was kind of like conception, birth and actually having a child [across three series].

Stuart McGugan: When *Hamish* began, they'd fly you up and down as needed, but once it became successful, the bean counters stepped in. In America, success means more investment; in Britain, it means restrictions. If you weren't called for four days, they'd fly you home, but not for three. By the third season, it was almost impossible to leave Plockton because they wouldn't pay. The accountants took over. The pleasure and freedom of it went, as we had other lives to live.

Valerie Gogan: I think initially it was meant to be two series of *Hamish* and then they went to a third and I was really sad not to be there. They invited me to the wrap party of the third one but I genuinely got a real proper flu, like you almost never get. I had such a bad throat. But it might have been a bit weird to go anyway. So I said I was coming, then I ended up bowing out at the last minute.

Michael Mackenzie: I was supposed to be in the very last episode that was filmed, which was the famous shinty match, but I couldn't do it because I was filming something else. I was very upset because I would have loved to have been in that. Everybody came back for that episode except for Ferdie McLopez, which was a shame.

Stuart Davids: [Lachie] was a really enjoyable character and very much so in the first series. I think Danny watched what we were doing and started to really write for us in series two and three. The whole undertaker thing was really enjoyable.

Scott Meek: *Hamish* was enormously, irrationally popular in Australia. By the time we go to series three, Australian tourists would come to Plockton when we were filming and walk into the pub and say, 'This is just like Hamish, it's as if you could almost see him,' and they'd turn around and see Bobby eating his tea and almost faint as if they'd walked into the show.

Villagers had become almost adept at becoming a visibly assembled wall between Bobby and gawkers, they'd kind of look after him. By series three Bobby was a bona fide TV star and some people behave strangely when confronted by that.

Toby Hefferman: Lots of people visited Plockton, and we often had to fend them off while filming. It was probably a mix of the show's success or because it was such an individual place to visit. Filming at Brian Pettifer's shop was the toughest, as it was a busy spot near a car park. The High Street was also a challenge, but everyone was incredibly cooperative. Tourists embraced the filming and, without smartphones or selfies, it was a more polite era. You were lucky if you had a camera on you. Fans weren't Timothée Chalamet types, they were there for Robert Carlyle or Brian Pettifer, a different tribe entirely.

Michael Mackenzie: We'd all gather at the pub. There were two pubs, and we all met and had a great time there. Often we'd then go to people's flats to have a drink, because when we were filming in the summer, the pubs would be just full of punters wanting to see the cast. So we tended to sort of sneak out and go elsewhere. But it wasn't outrageous, you'd be careful. If you were in early, you had to try not to be too hungover. At least not let it show.

MIDWAY THROUGH FILMING series three, another canine cast change took place when Fraoch was replaced as Wee Jock II. Charles Salmon explained to *Radio Times* that Fraoch had initially been hired for his perkiness but was swapped for 15-month-old Dex, who better met the demands of episode four. The new Wee Jock II had just a week to learn his predecessor's tricks.

20

Cattle Roaming
Free in this Area
Proceed with Care

SIXTEEN

SERIES THREE OVERVIEW

REGULAR CAST

Robert Carlyle (Hamish Macbeth), Shirley Henderson (Isobel Sutherland), Ralph Riach (TV John McIver), Billy Riddoch (Lachlan McCrae Sr), Stuart Davids (Lachie McCrae Jr), Duncan Duff (Doc Brown), Brian Pettifer (Rory Campbell), Anne Lacey (Esme Murray), Barbara Rafferty (Agnes Meldrum), Stuart McGugan (Barney Meldrum), David Ashton (Major Roddy Maclean). With Fraoch and Dex as Wee Jock II.

1. THE HONOURABLE POLICEMAN

Writers: Daniel Boyle & Dominic Minghella
Director: Jonas Grimås
Original broadcast: 16th March 1997, 7.30pm

GUEST CAST

Sally Dexter (Serena St. Claire), Sharon Small (WPC Anne Patterson), Mona Bruce (Edie), John Malcolm (Professor Svensson), Sheila Donald (Magistrate).

SUMMARY

Opening with a montage set to Ravel's *Bolero*, Major Maclean and his new companion arrive in Lochdubh while TV John helps Hamish prepare his uniform—and pipe—to impress WPC Anne Patterson, who is visiting for a week of training. Anne quickly falls for Hamish's new persona.

The Major has startling news: he's engaged to the glamorous Serena St. Clair, leaving his longtime housekeeper Edie devastated at the prospect of losing her position.

As Hamish struggles to maintain a professional relationship with the smitten Anne, the villagers form an impromptu conspiracy to present him as the model officer. At the Stag Bar, Barney is keen to let the regulars know that his latest guest is Professor Svensson, Professor of Erotic Studies at the Institute of Human Behaviour in Stockholm.

When Anne's pursuit becomes too intense, Hamish fabricates an assignment to send her away to Inverness, claiming she's researching a series of murders committed by women who poison wealthy husbands—a story inspired by Professor Svensson's recognition of Serena as 'Lottie La Rue', the star of a 1970s Swedish film with precisely that plot.

As the Major's wedding approaches, Hamish's made-up murder theory begins to seem disturbingly plausible. The Major had experienced a mysterious blackout in Tenerife that

Serena claimed to have called a doctor for, and Anne discovers a newspaper photo of someone resembling Serena connected to a husband's 'accidental' electrocution.

When the newlyweds return home from their ceremony, Hamish and the villagers burst in to prevent the Major from drinking what they believe to be poisoned champagne.

In the ensuing chaos, they discover Serena collapsed in the kitchen with her face in the wedding cake. The truth emerges: in revenge for her dismissal, Edie switched the champagne labels, exploiting Serena's allergy. Unwittingly, Serena had consumed her own poison intended for the Major.

As the episode concludes, Hamish reveals to Anne why he let her take credit for solving the case; he needs to maintain a low profile to remain in Lochdubh, the place he truly wants to be.

COMMENTARY

Jonas Grimås: Dominic Minghella is a very good writer. For some reason, on a first reading, the script didn't feel right. Our script editor, Ming Ho, who is an excellent writer in her own right, agreed with me and we tried to put our finger on what it was. In the end, it came down to the tone; in music, some pianists play Liszt and others play Mozart. They are both equally good, but demand different temperaments. That's all.

Dominic Minghella: I think I had a movie project and was by that point very disconnected from the show. The team wanted changes and asked Danny to enact them.

Jonas Grimås: Daniel was writing for Fox at the time, so at first he was not available. A week later, he had completed that work and we convinced him to travel up to Plockton for a meeting. He arrived late in the evening, was wined and dined and put up in a B&B for the night. The next morning we all met up at the production office where Ming and I briefed him on the problem. This lasted for about an hour, during which time Daniel said nothing but kept walking up and down the room, jerking his knees every now and then. When Ming had rounded off her briefing, Daniel looked at her and asked for a car to take him back to Greenock straight away, which is a four-hour drive.

Daniel Boyle: I wrote one episode in four days. There was a bit of a stand-off between the writer and producer. I listened to the story verbally and was able to get to the heart of it.

Jonas Grimås: A few days later the fax machine started spitting out script pages. I read them as they popped out, and I laughed from page one all the way to the end of the script. Daniel had taken the same plot, the characters and the locations and, as the original creator, turned it into something that was the same but very different. I still think he's one of the most amazing writers I ever worked with and I'm full of admiration for both his work and the man himself.

David Ashton: Danny [Boyle] often wrote scenes with elements of broad comic farce, which fits the Scots psyche— we're not afraid to lack taste and go for it. We're not vulgar, but we can be very broad and comic. Brian Cox and I often discuss how Scots can move seamlessly from high drama to utter ridiculousness without missing a beat, which is quite rare. English actors, by contrast, are more constrained by taste. We Scots don't have any—we just do it.

Jonas Grimås: On the day we were casting for my episodes, there was a tube strike. No-one knew when anyone was going to arrive, so me and the producer Charles Salmon decided to sit outside the offices at a trattoria and drink coffee while waiting for the actors to turn up. Sally [Dexter] turned up 10 minutes after Charles had to go off for a short meeting, so we started without him. She oozed charisma and had an extraordinary presence, so I knew immediately that she was right for the part and, later, that this was the role she'd been waiting for. As we were chatting away, we suddenly heard a strange sound coming from across the road, as if someone had just walked into a lamppost. Someone had, and it was Charles. Having left his glasses behind, walking down the road, he could sense Sally's qualities and got so distracted he forgot to look where he was walking. Needless to say, he too thought she was perfect for the part.

David Ashton: Jonas Grimås was good, he had that instinct for keeping things true that was incredibly important. Sally Dexter was wonderful, such a gas. Now she could sing, she was a great singer. There were actors who just came in and took to it like a duck to water, she was one of them.

Jonas Grimås: When shooting, Sally's part was a bit tricky because she is playing a character pretending to be someone else, and this took some nurturing to find the right balance in her performance. Having said that, her charms were blistering, and the camera loved her, so my work was made easy. Sharon Small's part, on the other hand, was so clear and self explanatory in the script that, most of the time, I could just stand back and enjoy the show. A director should always aspire to do as little as possible as to not stand in the way of the actor and the character and they both impressed me greatly.

Calum Mackenzie: We were out at the Plockton Hotel for my son's birthday and the crew came in after filming. TV John and some others sat down at the same table as us and the girl [Sally

Dexter] said, 'I've just spent the whole day with my face in a cake.' That was the episode where they tried to poison the Major. I always remember her saying, 'I've just spent the whole day with my face in a cake.'

Jonas Grimås: Handling tone is surprisingly never that difficult. When you work on a series, everything is anchored in the characters and the universe they inhabit, and this in combination with the scripts 'tells you how to do it'. Directors are just a glorified storyteller with an expensive habit. All good comedy springs from a genuine and truthful representation of the characters.

Nicholas Renton: Bobby's life story is interesting, he came from a really difficult background and turned that into something wonderful. *Hamish* is part of that journey he made as an actor. There was a side of him I never quite saw because I didn't quite have the script for it, it was a scene where he becomes rather *Some Like it Hot* [1959], Tony Curtis with the pipe.

Deirdre Keir: He's a chameleon.

Nicholas Renton: He really is, and the way he works on scenes is just beautiful, it comes as you talk about it and he finds it. The scenes he had with Shirley were always magic to work on.

'COMEDY ISN'T SOMETHING that I'm known for, or have even done a lot of,' admitted Robert Carlyle to the *Daily Record* in 1997, 'so this might even be the first time that some people have seen me crack a smile. This is the broadest comedy that I have ever done on television and it is difficult. I had to be careful not to look like an idiot. I thought it was time to have a laugh and just enjoy myself.

'I tried very much to create the look of the stiff upper-lipped hero of the 1950s movies. It helped give the character that old-style hero appearance. But the pipe was a tricky prop. I tried to let it drop as I reacted in mock surprise. But of course it burned me and my costume as it fell. So I stopped that.'

Charles Salmon: My main memory is the fun of working on varied storylines with different directors, each with their own priorities. As a producer, you're the guardian of creativity—supporting the team to do their best while managing costs and logistics. It's really about giving great creators the freedom to bring their vision to life.

David Ashton: Danny had a knack for picking things up. At one of our pub karaoke nights, someone said, 'C'mon David, gie us a song.' I was one of the quieter cast members—I read a lot, did crosswords, and was maybe a bit older—so nobody had ever heard a dickie bird out of me. But I used to sing blues and spotted *The House of the Rising Sun* on the list. Without further ado, I launched into it, much to everyone's astonishment. Later, Danny wrote a scene where I sang in the pub, this time Sinatra, with Ralph Riach playing piano. We did a very good version of it.

Toby Hefferman: The worst part was when we were filming in the pub, because we had to lock the street off. There was only one way in, one way out. In my naivety I locked the street off for 45 minutes at times. People would ask, 'Do you need to release the traffic?' and I'd say, 'No, everyone seems really happy.' I'm not sure if they were, but that was my memory of it. Then you'd get the Highland cows that would go through and we'd be like, 'Just film it, roll. We may have some continuity issues, but let's embrace it.'

FINAL THOUGHTS

Hamish Macbeth's third series opens in classic Lochdubh fashion; with romance, deception and a bicycle built for two. When Major Maclean returns from Tenerife with the glamorous Serena St. Clair and wedding plans, the village is instantly captivated.

Elsewhere, Anne Patterson's determination to see Hamish as the perfect policeman leads to some of the episode's best comedic moments.

Although the Hamish/Isobel relationship was central in the second series, it's been set aside here, perhaps to avoid giving Hamish too settled a personal life (and to keep the drama coming). Seeing Hamish trying to dodge a relationship with Anne makes a change from earlier episodes, when he seemed happy to pursue whoever took his fancy in the moment.

As an opener, this episode reintroduces themes—belonging, community and the peculiar justice of close-knit villages—that will resonate across *Hamish Macbeth*'s final run. Yet familiar territory still yields surprises, like Edie's accidental heroism and the Major's surprising reinvention as a romantic lead, proving Lochdubh has more than enough tales left to tell, even as the series nears its end.

2. DEFERRED SENTENCE

Writer: Daniel Boyle
Director: Nicholas Renton
Original broadcast: 23rd March 1997, 8pm

Guest cast

Caroline Paterson (Laura McDuff), Alan MacNaughtan (Father McPhail), Tom Watson (Enoch McDuff), Michael Byrne (Duncan Scott), Colette O'Neil (Rhona Lindsay), Amanda Walker (Barbara Scott), Annie Louise Ross (Claire Fleming), Daniel Boyle (Handsome Sailor).

Summary

Hamish Macbeth's holiday to Laggan-Laggan takes an unexpected turn when he meets Laura McDuff disembarking from the ferry. After being redirected from Columba's Guesthouse to St Columba's Church, which doubles as accommodation run by Catholic priest Father McPhail and Protestant landlord Enoch McDuff, Hamish finds himself caught in their ongoing religious feud.

The tension between the two men is immediately apparent during dinner, where Hamish improvises a claim to be Jewish to avoid taking sides in their theological disputes. That night, a window is smashed at the church.

As Hamish explores, he learns from Father McPhail that 20 years ago, Enoch's wife Fiona was found dead at the foot of cliffs, and that most islanders believe Enoch murdered her. Laura, who turns out to be Enoch's estranged daughter, confirms these suspicions when Hamish encounters her at the ruins of her childhood home. She reveals she burned the house down as a teenager, unable to live with her father after her mother's death.

Hamish's 'holiday' façade crumbles as his police instincts take over. He questions special constable Duncan Scott, who is also

Enoch's brother-in-law, about the original investigation. Duncan maintains Enoch's innocence, despite the central piece of evidence: a valuable family pocket watch that Fiona had planned to sell on the mainland, which disappeared after her death while the money she'd borrowed remained.

When Hamish visits Rhona Lindsay, Fiona's sister, someone takes shots at him in the hills. At the church, Claire Fleming, the housekeeper who found Fiona's body, offers to collect mussels for Hamish, a detail that later proves significant.

Examining old police photographs with Laura, Hamish notices a discrepancy in the tide times. Claire claimed to have found the body at 3pm while gathering shellfish at low tide, but the photographs show the tide was already coming in by then. This contradiction suggests Claire lied about when she discovered the body.

Breaking into Claire's home, they find damning evidence: a letter from Fiona to Enoch announcing she was leaving him, and a statement from Claire witnessing the murder. The murderer wasn't Enoch, but Duncan Scott, who killed Fiona when she threatened to tell his mentally ill wife Barbara about their affair.

The truth unravels when Duncan confronts Claire and admits his guilt, revealing he only remained silent to protect Barbara from the truth. Enoch had known all along but promised silence for Barbara's sake. Now that Barbara has died (discovered by Hamish and Laura), Enoch is ready to clear his name. Off-screen, Duncan jumps from a cliff to his death.

As Father McPhail prepares for a service, Enoch and Laura begin a tentative reconciliation. Laura's father asks her to stay and rebuild their home together, leaving open the possibility of healing their long-fractured relationship. Hamish departs the island, the mystery solved and justice finally possible after two decades.

COMMENTARY

'Deferred Sentence' represented the kind of storytelling that best suited Robert Carlyle, with the actor telling *The Herald* in March 1997 that the series 'worked best when it was at its darkest, in those episodes where Hamish maybe goes off to some remote island and meets these strange, strange people,' adding that 'sometimes I thought they softened it too much when they could have gone much further with the black comedy.'

Ming Ho: The originality of Daniel Boyle's imagination was the driving force of the show and he had pretty much free rein, as I recall. We did have to be judicious about giving notes on the execution... Unevenness of tone across the series was sometimes an issue. 'Deferred Sentence' in particular was a bit of a surprise when the first draft came in, stylistically quite different to the others, at first glance much more of a traditional whodunnit. We spent a lot of time honing the plot of that episode and discussing the subtext.

IN HIS REVIEW for *The Stage*, Harry Venning described the episode as 'wit, whimsy and wickedness neatly packaged into ideal Sunday night entertainment.' But even this professional critic found himself slightly bewildered, revealing, 'I have to admit I lost the plot at some point in Sunday's episode and have no idea why three craggy Jocks were trying to push each other over a cliff at the end.'

Ralph Riach: It was a great period of my life, the three years that we had doing it. I think there was only one episode I wasn't in, the one where Hamish went off to an island. None of the regulars were in it, apart from him.

Charles Salmon: It was great going off to Skye for that one because I hadn't been there before, and so that was quite nice to take the audience there as well.

Ming Ho: It was also set mostly away from Lochdubh, and it's always a challenge to retain the style and focus when an episode leaves its locational roots.

Charles Salmon: A lot of the storyline was about this community and their relationships. It was interesting to pluck them out of that and give them a new environment to work in. It's an extraordinary place. On a Sunday I used to drive around to discover these areas, so it was important to take the show a little further out.

FINAL THOUGHTS

Following a broadly comic premiere about disastrous honeymoon plans, Hamish's arrival at St. Columba's guesthouse on Laggan-Laggan plunges him into a 20-year-old mystery the locals would much rather keep hidden.

Separated from his usual Lochdubh allies, with no TV John or villagers to lean on, Hamish must navigate an island where everyone harbours secrets, including Caroline Paterson's Laura. Paterson, a co-founder of the Raindog theatre company with Robert Carlyle and Stuart Davids, was also a familiar face on the BBC's *EastEnders* in 1997, and had been in a long-term relationship with Carlyle until around the time of filming her episode of *Hamish* in 1996.

With so many new faces (eight including Daniel Boyle's second cameo of the series, this time as 'Handsome Sailor') and a complicated backstory introduced in just under an hour, 'Deferred Sentence' could have felt overstuffed, but instead it expands Hamish's world in an interesting way.

3. THE LOCHDUBH ASSASSIN

Writer: Daniel Boyle
Director: Nicholas Renton
Original broadcast: 30th March 1997, 8pm

GUEST CAST

Stephen Henderson (Frankie), Sandy McDade (Jean Foley), Forbes Masson (Tam Flood), David McKay (Tony McCreary), Stewart Porter (Andy Glass), James Ryland (Joe Scrimegour), Michael Mackenzie (Ferdinand McLopez).

SUMMARY

'The Lochdubh Assassin' opens in the back streets of Glasgow, where Jean Foley and her nephew Frankie Brice are escaping with Isobel after Frankie's father stole from Tam Flood's organisation. With the help of Frankie's best friend, Flood is soon hot on their trail alongside fellow gangsters Tony McCreary, Andy Glass and Joe Scrimegour.

When the gangsters follow Jean and Frankie to Lochdubh in their camper van, they attract the attention of Hamish, who gives them a friendly warning to stay out of trouble.

Isobel relocates Jean and Frankie to Cnothan and into the care of McCrae & McCrae Funeral Directors and General Handymen, where Lachie Jr takes an immediate liking to Jean and Lachlan Sr offers Frankie a job and (Lachie's old boiler suit). Hamish calls to let them know Flood has arrived in the area.

The gang attempts to intimidate the locals at the Stag Bar, but their efforts backfire when TV John, insulted by Andy Glass, produces eggs from nowhere and smashes them on Tam's face. When Andy threatens John, Hamish intervenes.

When Andy and Tony then attempt to ambush TV John in the woods, their plan goes horribly wrong. Tony is accidentally shot by Andy, who then lies to Flood, claiming TV John killed Tony. To cover their tracks, they bury Tony on a hillside, with his mobile phone still in his pocket. The phone later starts ringing as Major Maclean passes by, alerting Hamish to Tony's death.

It's revealed that Frankie's father stole £208,000 from Flood, but before disappearing he gave half the money to his son, who promptly donated it to 52 different charities. Flood's team then found Frankie's father and dealt with him.

TV John mentions in passing to Frankie that he's not concerned about threats from Flood because he didn't smell pomade, a type of hair oil, when he encountered them at the Stag.

While the community prepares for Ferdinand McLopez's annual sherry tasting festival, Flood orders his remaining men to target TV John. With Hamish distracted, TV John takes Jean and Frankie to Wee McPhee's bog, a place with dark historical significance—in 1897, a 'bad hat' named Wee McPhee was lured into the bog by villagers and left to die.

The gangsters follow but quickly find themselves trapped in the same bog. After TV John extracts a confession about their involvement in the shooting of Lachlan Sr (who had been hospitalised earlier in the episode), he and Jean prepare to leave the criminals to Wee McPhee's fate. Hamish arrives just in time to rescue Andy and Joe, arresting them while learning that Tony's death was actually an accidental shooting.

As the McLopez sherry festival reaches its climax, Flood makes one final attempt to get revenge. He hides in a cave and tries to shoot Frankie, but his gun fails. When his next shot ricochets and causes a cave-in, Flood finds himself trapped, shouting for help as the villagers continue their celebration, unheard amid the festivities.

COMMENTARY

Ming Ho: I don't remember much of the thinking behind [introducing Frankie and his aunt]. It was a guest strand, not intended to be integrated long term; one of Daniel's spontaneous inventions.

Stuart Davids: They asked me at the interview if I was gay, and I am, and they always played about with his sexuality a bit. There was always a kind of not-quite-sure [with Lachie Jr] and I liked that. It was the fact that he was a bit simplistic, called his father Daddy and was afraid of women. It was nice that he got that [relationship with Jean] and that he accepted her and her nephew, I liked that about Lachie Jr.

Forbes Masson (Tam Flood): I'd always loved the show, so when I got the chance to be in it, I thought, *Oh, great*. I was at drama school in Glasgow and shared a flat with Bobby Carlyle in my second year. He kept to himself but was obsessed with film, with lots of film books—that's where he wanted his career to go. Before this, I'd been doing *The High Life*, so it was interesting to take on a darker, tougher role. The script was bonkers, and the character was great fun to play. By the end of the series, the scripts were getting madder and madder.

We only did one season of *The High Life*, and there was one script where the producers said, 'It's a bit second season,' because they got nervous about things being too mad. It was quite clear that by that point with *Hamish Macbeth*, anything goes. What I loved was how well-drawn and eccentric the characters were—it was that kind of surreal Scotland we all understood.

WHEN FILMING ENDED, concern grew about Stephen Henderson's performance as Frankie. His strong Glaswegian accent spurred a dubbing debate that left cast and crew with mixed feelings.

Ralph Riach: They dubbed that boy completely because you could hardly make out a word he said. It wasn't the best dubbing, sadly.

Forbes Masson: It was an important series for Scottish actors being able to speak in their own accents, although in my episode there's a kid in it and I think they rather sadly dubbed him. There was nothing wrong, but I think there was a bit of, 'Oh, we can't understand it,' because you used to get a lot of that. When we were writing *The High Life* it was BBC London that commissioned us and we were putting things in scripts and they had no idea some of the words that we were saying or how rude it was.

Nicholas Renton: The wee boy was delightful but nobody could understand him.

Julia Duff: The point was that it was such a different accent to our normal accent.

It wasn't just those involved in the series that had an opinion on Frankie's accent. Channel 4's viewer feedback programme, *Right to Reply* (1982–2001), followed up a complaint from a student of Phonetics & Phonology, while the *Daily Record*'s John Millar also waded into the discussion on 12th April while reviewing Frankie's second episode, 'The Good Thief'.

'One voice also ruined the latest edition of *Hamish Macbeth* (BBC1) which was about a youngster who could sing like an angel,' wrote Millar. 'Unfortunately, it was horribly obvious that the sounds that came from the lips of Frankie whenever he spoke were not his. It actually seemed as though the lad had been dubbed by a woman! Whatever went on behind the scenes spoiled my enjoyment of the entire episode.'

Forbes Masson: When Alan [Cumming] and I were at drama school the voice teachers would say, 'If you want to be an actor, you have to lose your Scottishness. You have to be able to not speak in the Scottish accent and to extend your range,' and we were one of the first years at the Scottish drama school who said 'No.' We wanted to just use our own voice. [Our characters] Victor and Barry were not in our own voice, but it was in a Scottish voice. With *The High Life*, they tried to change things, but we stuck to our guns, our Scottish voice. *Hamish* was very much in a Scottish voice, unashamedly so. There's a classic line, 'It's not my accent, it's your ears.' The nation warmed to it and it wasn't like you have to pander to it or anglicise it or change it.

Jonas Grimås (Director, 'The Good Thief'): I worked with quite a few young actors over the years. All acting is about a controlled form of play. The actor knows their character, where they come from and what they want. The difference between the younger and the older is the control they have over their performance. This control allows the more experienced actor to repeat the same performance over and over again while with the less experienced actor it can be hit and miss. The beauty of film is that you preserve a moment, a here and now, which means the inexperienced actor can end up being just as good in the final film as the more experienced one. All it takes, at times, is a bit of patience and to embrace those limitations.

The two young actors in my episode were very professional when on set. They both came from a drama club in Glasgow and knew each other well, and we cast them as a duo. The problem with Stephen Henderson was that his Glaswegian accent was so 'thick' that it was impossible for the untrained ear to understand what he was saying. The decision to re-voice him with a female actor was a pragmatic one, since it's hard to find a teenager who is so in tune with their craft to do the job.

Charles Salmon: I did struggle at times [with the Scottish accent] and sometimes said, 'We've got to make sure that everyone can understand.' We had to honour the local accent, but at the same time you don't want to have subtitles.

Sarah Bruce: I had to shepherd the boys a bit, though they both had chaperones. They were young and played up a bit, but were fun and talented. I felt so upset when that episode aired and I saw they'd dubbed over Stephen Henderson's voice. The voice they used was terrible and sounded like a middle-aged woman. Although his accent was quite strong Glaswegian, which is why I imagined they'd dubbed him, for the wider audience, it sounded far worse than his own voice.

A FEW WEEKS before the episode was broadcast, the *Wolverhampton Express and Star* revealed that *Hamish Macbeth* had 'caused a bit of a storm in Australia' and that a debate was held 'on national TV and radio as to whether or not the show should feature subtitles for those unfamiliar with the Scottish accents'.

Toby Hefferman: At the time, I don't remember the accent being a problem. Those conversations would have been had quietly, as opposed to bandied around, because it would have been a little sensitive. But I remember the boy, he was a bit of a scallywag actually, full of confidence.

A TWIST IN the mystery behind Frankie's voice came from *The Scotsman* on 19th April 1997, in an article that touched on viewer confusion over the 'boychild from Glasgow' who resembled 'one of [Scottish photographer] Oscar Marzaroli's urchins, yet jabbered like somebody's mum.' The paper debunked the theory that Stephen Henderson's accent couldn't be understood and stated that it was during the editing process that 'the men with the fluffy earmuffs had technical difficulties with the nipper', but that when it came time to redub him, 'matey was nowhere to be found'.

Forbes Masson: *Hamish Macbeth* was groundbreaking. Looking at the progression of Scottish TV, I remember working with Alan [Cumming] on *The Terry Neason Show* [1987] for STV. We were saying to them, 'Come on, this is a real chance for a Scottish show on the ITV network,' but the Powers That Be said, 'There's no point, it's too Scottish.' *Hamish* was unashamedly Scottish and worked on the network without subtitles. It had surreality and kookiness, with a touch of sentimentality, but it didn't rely on its beautiful landscape. It had grit and truth, and Bobby's incredible central performance. I remember seeing him on screen and thinking, *Oh my God, now I understand why he was so obsessed with film as a student—*

he's an amazing screen actor. It was a big break for him and a springboard, but everyone in it was fantastic.

Deirdre Keir: I was watching an episode last night and there were a couple of lines with Billy [Riddoch] where there were two or three words and I said to my husband, 'What did he say?' I thought *I've no idea what he just said, how did we get away with that?* Nobody toned it down.

Forbes Masson: Even though I knew Bobby, I was really nervous for my first scene with him. It had been eight or nine years since we'd shared a flat in Glasgow, and he'd had amazing success. I'd done *The High Life* and other bits and pieces, but this was a different kind of role. I'm quite a nervous performer, but everyone put me at ease on my first day. We had to bring in an armourer because I had to shoot a gun. Some scenes were filmed in Glasgow, and driving down a dark alley in a limo felt very gangster-y. It had an edge to it, even though it was comic. Someone told me at the time that I reminded them of Alec Guinness, maybe from *The Ladykillers* [1955] or *The Bridge on the River Kwai* [1957], which I took as a compliment.

We had such a laugh doing all those scenes in the black suits, including our *Reservoir Dogs'* [1992] slow-motion walk. The costume designer took me shopping in London for the suit—it was expensive and felt really cool. There's a bit where one of my cohorts is buried with his mobile phone, and we had a lot of fun filming all that stuff.

Nicholas Renton: The gag I love most is the phone that goes off in the grave. I don't know whether it had been done before. I'm sure it's been done since, but that's what good writing gets you to.

Michael Mackenzie: That was in the very, very early days of mobile phones and it was hysterical. And all that stuff with TV John, the sort of ambivalence of it all, that was what was great about being under the radar of the watershed. Because people were like, 'Did he say that? What does he mean by that? What? How have they got away with that?' It was clever and intelligent, but it was also very funny, moving and very watchable. It appealed to all kinds of different people.

Forbes Masson: Nick Renton was great, I really loved working with him. I watched it a wee while back and there's a nice shot of me, I think I'm on the phone, and I was quite pleased with what I did with that. I haven't done a lot on screen, I'm mainly a theatre actor, and it's always like, 'Oh God, the camera's really close,' but I thought I did that quite well. I believed what I was doing. There was a scene where we were running about the mountainside, and we were all laughing, including the director. We were encouraged to sort of muck about. Some people weren't happy with the wee doggies, there were several West Highland Terriers and they were a bit temperamental.

Michael Mackenzie: When it was time to release the McLopez sherry out of these huge casks, they dressed me up in this outrageous costume, which was part Spanish and part Scottish. I had a sommelier cup around my neck. Everyone, including Hamish, made their way guiltily through the trees and into the depths of somewhere to find this amazing area with all these great big hog stands and everyone having a party and having a great time. It was such fun, except for the midges.

Forbes Masson: The midges were an absolute nightmare. The crew had these amazing net costume things that they'd put on. They were like beekeepers, completely covered. We were filming in the forest and it was just terrible. I'm not really bothered by them, but others were, it was just too much. There was a big run on Skin So Soft.

Michael Mackenzie: Oh, the midges were awful. Because we were cast, we tended to get given lots of midge repellent. All the crew went around in those sort of nets over their heads, but I remember one extra, an old guy who was in a kilt, and his knees and his thighs were completely covered in midge bites. Eventually he passed out, he had to be taken to hospital because the midges were just unspeakable.

Toby Hefferman: You'd say, 'I'm not gonna wear this net on my head,' and then after a day with the midges... I've got a vivid memory of the smell of the citronella spray that you put all over yourself. Nick Renton used to get lemon pith and rub it into his face. He was always a bit stubbly, and it would always remain there. He was the director, so I was too scared to go up to him and say 'You've got a little pith on your face.'

Final Thoughts

Three series in, *Hamish Macbeth*'s world has grown far beyond its original premise. The McCraes, once mere comic relief, become something richer here, particularly Lachie Jr, who wrestles with sharing his father's attention when Frankie Brice arrives on the scene.

At the same time, Glasgow gangsters in black suits and shades inject both danger and pitch-black humour. Even the comedic set pieces bristle with undercurrents of danger. Forbes Masson's Tam Flood radiates a restless kind of menace, even in his dressing gown serving Bellinis, culminating in his fourth-wall-breaking demise.

Amid all the chaos, the budding romance between Jean and Lachie Jr adds an unexpected tenderness, while Lachlan Sr's plans to hire Frankie point to uncharted territory for father and son alike.

It's Lochdubh's tried-and-true mix of folklore, local trickery and communal policing that wins the day, exemplified when TV John orchestrates Wee McPhee's bog as a trap for the unwary. Yet one glaring flaw remains: Frankie's jarringly dubbed voice, which pulls viewers out of the story.

Despite that hiccup, the episode's lively cast of criminals, undertakers and hopeless romantics proves just how adaptable this small Highland village can be, while TV John's mention of pomade sows seeds for the final episode.

4. THE GOOD THIEF

Writer: Daniel Boyle
Director: Jonas Grimås
Original broadcast: 6th April 1997, 8.10pm

GUEST CAST

Sandy McDade (Jean Foley), Stephen Henderson (Frankie Brice), James Young (Tusker Gray), Bill Murdoch (McClintock), Tam Dean Burn (Black Bob Roberts), Campbell Morrison (Harry Balfour), Ruaridh Hepburn (Alfie Balfour).

SUMMARY

Hamish arrives at Lochdubh station to collect Frankie Brice's best friend, Tommy 'Tusker' Gray, catching him pretending to be blind to avoid paying the train fare. Tusker displays a mischievous, sometimes cynical, attitude that contrasts with Frankie's earnest nature.

In Lochdubh, music fills the air as young Frankie rehearses for the Willie McGraw Memorial Trophy singing competition, a prestigious local event pitting Lochdubh against rival village Dunbracken. The contest, which Dunbracken has won for the last 26 years, is a matter of village pride and substantial betting, with locals placing wagers worth hundreds of pounds.

Complications arise when Harry Balfour from Dunbracken reveals that Frankie, being from Glasgow, is ineligible to represent Lochdubh according to competition rules requiring contestants to be natives of their villages. The Lochdubh residents counter by invoking rule eight, which states contestants should also show 'depth of intellect'.

They propose adding a general knowledge component to the competition, knowing Dunbracken's champion, Alfie Balfour, would likely fail such a test. Both villages agree to drop these additional requirements, allowing Frankie to compete. However, the night before the contest, disaster strikes when someone breaks into the Stag Bar, stealing both the trophy and the betting money. Initial suspicions fall on the Dunbracken men, leading to a confrontation that ends with both sides covered in sheep dip.

Hamish finds Tommy's penknife at the scene and discovers the stolen items hidden among Frankie's possessions. Tommy confesses to the theft, leading to his expulsion from Jean's home. But Hamish senses something isn't right about the case, especially when Doc Brown reveals that Tommy is seriously ill and unlikely to see his 18th birthday.

Hamish uncovers the truth: the boy deliberately set himself up as the thief to make Frankie hate him. Knowing he's dying, Tommy believes making his friend despise him will soften the eventual blow of his death. He's been methodically trying to alienate Frankie through increasingly offensive behaviour.

The episode culminates at the singing competition, where Frankie delivers a stunning performance that outshines Alfie Balfour's, with Tommy suggesting 'it's in the bag'.

COMMENTARY

Jonas Grimås (Director): When I arrived in Plockton it had rained for as long as anyone could remember and at times, when filming the episodes before mine, the clouds had been so low that you could touch them with your hands. In other words, a constant, merciless and persistent downfall of rain from day one; except for Sundays, when the sun often came out. This part of Scotland is deeply religious, and I suppose the sunny Sundays were there in support of their faith. Me and my family hanging our laundry in this sunshine was not taken kindly by the population of Drumbuie where I rented a cottage, so we had our wrists slapped a few times... However, we never filmed on a Sunday so when planning my shots I assumed it would rain and integrated this in my plans.

Then, on my first day of shooting, the strangest thing happened. The rain, inexplicably, stopped. It stopped not only for a day, but for the entire period of my filming, which was four weeks. This caused me some problems since the opening sequence of my first episode, 'The Good Thief', was built on the idea of a pouring rain that would cease when the silvery voice of Frankie Brice in all its glory would part the clouds and bring out the sunshine. We decided to 'make rain', a bizarre idea, and called up a special effects company who, with the support of the fire department, could pump water from tanks through specially designed pipe systems aligned with the camera to achieve the desired effect.

After an hour of filming, the tank engine ran out of water. The nearest filling station was too far away, so they attached a long hose to a pump and dropped it into the loch some fifty yards away. After another half hour of filming, the rain suddenly stopped again. The confusion was total. Could we possibly have emptied the sea...?

After some stressful minutes of speculation, one of the firemen went down to the loch to take a look. We hadn't emptied the sea, it was just the tide that had gone out. As I mentioned earlier, the sun kept shining for the next four weeks. Only on my last day, at lunchtime, it started to rain again. I was doing interiors for the rest of the day, so I didn't mind. I was, however, asked to leave a lock of hair behind, since the assumption was that I had something to do with the weather. We shall never know.

Ming Ho: I helped Jonas to choose the song for the Mòd [festival of Scottish Gaelic song, arts and culture] competition in 'The Good Thief' from a selection of Gaelic folk songs. I can see us playing the tapes in Jonas' room in the production office, Duncraig Castle, an imposing building, somewhat dilapidated at that time; bits of plaster from the ceiling periodically fell down on us as we worked.

Tam Dean Burn (Black Bob Roberts): It was really idyllic filming up there in Plockton, and it was great to have this double act with Campbell Morrison. He was the sort of the hotel owner and I was his sidekick who would do his business. Campbell had quite a scary reputation, but he was such a lovely guy. You were sort of parachuted in alongside the core cast. There were only 20 episodes and that's what's really interesting, it meant so much to people. The singing competition was filmed in the mountains.

Stuart McGugan: I wasn't thrilled with the other village stuff. If I may be so bold, the villagers were playing a different series, an old style of Scots pantomimic, and the two didn't gel.

Sarah Bruce: While shooting the outdoor singing competition, I was stopping traffic during filming of a wide shot of the location that day (this was often my job) and was stationed at the crew base, quite a distance from the camera crew. The assistant director radioed after the first take to say that one of the crew HGVs was in the shot. It was bright yellow, so no disguising it. It would have taken several minutes for someone to drive round to where I was and deal with it and the keys were in it, so they talked me through how to reverse an HGV on the radio! I almost considered a career as a trucker after I stopped pursuing TV. I was pulled into the make-up department for that episode, as there were so many people to paint up to look like they'd been in the sheep dip.

FINAL THOUGHTS

The Willie McGraw Memorial Trophy singing competition transforms a routine village rivalry into one of the series' more moving stories. Frankie Brice emerges as Lochdubh's unexpected vocal champion, turning the episode into a reflection on friendship, jealousy and small-town pride.

The interplay of broad comedy (the attempt to impose a 'general knowledge' rule to sabotage rival village Dunbracken) and emotional stakes exemplifies the show's gift for blending whimsy with sincerity. Ultimately, Tommy's painful confession and the community's rallying behind Frankie deliver an ending that refuses easy sentimentality.

5. THE TROUBLE WITH RORY

Writer: Stuart Hepburn
Director: Mandie Fletcher
Original broadcast: 13th April 1997, 8.10pm

GUEST CAST

Ronnie Letham (Peter the Fireman), Stuart Hepburn (Eric Clelland), Mona Bruce (Edie), Alyxis Daly (Alma Mathers), Eilidh MacLean (Veronica), Kay McLean (Kay), Gordon Munro (Archie the Cameraman).

SUMMARY

The episode begins with TV John, Doc Brown, Barney and Rory taking part in a fitness test for the voluntary fire brigade under the watchful eye of fire chief Peter, one which Rory fails.

At Lochdubh Primary School, teacher Esme discusses the Highland Clearances with her pupils. That evening at the pub, Barney regales the locals with an embarrassing story about Rory, which is interrupted when Lachlan Sr notices that the school is on fire.

The village rushes to help, but the school burns down despite their efforts. Peter suspects an electrical fault caused by a 30-amp fuse in a five-amp socket, though Rory initially believes it was arson after smelling turpentine. Hamish discovers that local builder Eric Clelland had recently carried out roof repairs on the school.

The next day, Esme visits the Education Department, where she's shocked to learn the school was already scheduled for closure, with students to be transferred to nearby Cnothan. She confronts Rory, who is revealed to be a local councillor who knew about the closure plans but kept them secret from her. Furious, she ends their relationship and launches a community campaign to save the school.

Isobel Sutherland returns to Lochdubh to cover the story for Highland Television, creating tension with Hamish. At a heated public meeting, Education Officer Mrs Mathers reveals the closure will happen the following Friday, with the land being sold for development. The villagers are outraged, especially at Rory for his betrayal.

The next morning, Esme discovers a fire in the equipment shed behind her house. Hamish suspects arson and confronts Clelland, having overheard a tense exchange between him and Rory about money. That night, Hamish organises a surveillance operation with TV John, Lachlan, Lachie, Doc Brown and Barney, with Esme joining despite Hamish's concerns.

While staking out Clelland, they discover he's having an affair with Mrs Mathers rather than starting fires. Meanwhile, another fire is discovered at the school and Esme knocks out a masked man who turns out to be Peter, who is deliberately setting the fires to play hero and impress Esme.

When confronted, Rory confesses that he lent money to Clelland, who was supposed to build a kitchen extension for Esme's house at cost. Despite his misguided actions, Esme forgives him.

COMMENTARY

Behind the scenes of 'The Trouble with Rory,' the production team faced a sobering reality when tragedy struck the small Scottish town of Dunblane on 13th March 1996. The Dunblane Massacre was Britain's deadliest mass shooting, when a gunman entered Dunblane Primary School and killed 16 children and one teacher and injured 15 others before taking his own life. The tragedy led to significant changes in British gun laws, including the banning of most handguns.

This national trauma cast an unexpected shadow over the production of *Hamish Macbeth*, impacting both the creative team and the content of an episode already in development.

Ming Ho: Stuart Hepburn lived in Dunblane, where we had visited him for script meetings, and he was working on this episode at the time of the Dunblane Massacre. When the news started to come through that day about what had happened, we were fearful for him and his family, as we knew his children attended the school. Thankfully, they were safe, but of course, it deeply affected him. Everyone in that small town knew someone whose child had not come home, and the class teacher, Gwen Mayor, was killed.

By terrible coincidence, the storyline of 'The Trouble With Rory', which was already well on its way to production, centred on Esme and featured a gun-man, a fire at the school and the school being bulldozed. While we instantly took steps to minimise any resemblance to the real-life event, Stuart also had to amend the seemingly innocuous bulldozer incident in the script, explaining to us that in Dunblane the image of a bulldozer had become synonymous with the school gym being razed to the ground after the atrocity.

It was too close to shooting to pull the episode completely, so we did what we could to change any elements that might remind viewers or risk upset to the people of Dunblane. Even so, there remained some nervousness about scheduling when it went out and there were delicate negotiations with the BBC about this. In itself, it is a typically warm and affectionate comic tale, giving the spotlight to well-loved characters Esme and Rory and progressing their romance, so it would have been a pity to lose it. A sad footnote to an otherwise happy show.

Stuart Hepburn: In the fire episode, what was interesting to me was Anne Lacey's character and her progression rather than that idiot fireman that was in love with her. I'm always more interested in female characters because they're the ones that want to talk about feelings and men kind of 'do' things. Plus, the whole thing was built around a male character, so why not have the females?

Anne Lacey: The writers got to know us and almost wrote around us. Stuart Hepburn said he wanted to write an episode about Rory and Esme because he loved the characters. We didn't have input into the stories.

Jon Older (First Assistant Director): Mandie was a big fan of Anne and I think she really enjoyed doing that episode because Esme had that much more to do. There was a really good scene in the village hall when they get everybody together and they're all protesting about what's going to happen. I thought that went really well. We actually got some decent performances out of all the supporting players as well.

Toby Hefferman: Brian Pettifer was a beautiful man. He turned up on *Shakespeare in Love* [1998]. He came in for a day and it was really weird because it was a whole different world. We were at Shepperton Studios, it was a big movie, and Brian got a day on it. It felt so funny to see him out of Plockton. It was almost like they really lived there, they were really residents.

FINAL THOUGHTS

Stuart Hepburn's penultimate script thrusts primary-school teacher Esme Murray into the spotlight. Her scenes at the village hall, where she challenges both official indifference and her own boyfriend's betrayal, showcases how well Mandie Fletcher handles heightened emotions.

Meanwhile, the heartbreak of seeing a cherished institution closed down underlines the episode's thematic thrust: rural communities are more than numbers on a balance sheet.

By exploring not just the mechanics of local politics but also the personal cost to Esme, Rory and the children, 'The Trouble with Rory' is a testament to what happens when a seemingly small plot point like a school's closure resonates through a tight-knit village.

Stuart Hepburn is the second writer to appear in an episode following Daniel Boyle's earlier cameos, though as Hepburn is also an actor, he's given the more substantive role of Eric Clelland.

The episode also gives us some more information on some of the regular cast, specifically the full names of TV John, Doc Brown, Barney and Rory: John James McIver, Dougal Alexander Fleming Brown M.D. PhD, Bernard Keir Hardie Meldrum and Rory Duncan Campbell.

6. MORE THAN A GAME

Writer: Stuart Hepburn
Director: Mandie Fletcher
First broadcast: 20th April 1997, 8.10pm

GUEST CAST

Morag Hood (Doloris Balfour), Brian Alexander (Jubel McBean), Mona Bruce (Edie), Iain McColl (Neil the Bus), Tam Dean Burn (Black Bob Roberts), Campbell Morrison (Harry Balfour), Neil MacRae (Dunbracken Captain), Mabel Aitken (Cathy), Sandy McDade (Jean Foley), Dallas Young (Houston Old).

SUMMARY

'More Than a Game' centres on the annual shinty [an ancient Highland sport played with curved sticks, predating both hockey and hurling] match between Lochdubh and Dunbracken, with tensions running especially high as Dunbracken has won for 19 consecutive years—one more victory would let them keep the Angus McNichol Memorial Cup permanently.

The episode opens with Lachlan Sr coaching the team, while Lachie shows little enthusiasm. Their already strained relationship deteriorates further when they argue during practice, leading to Lachie quitting the team. Without their star player, Lochdubh's chances look even bleaker, with Jubel reluctantly drafted as goalkeeper.

Meanwhile, Lachlan has placed a personal ad describing himself as a 'fun-filled, cuddly landowning gent' and receives a response from Doloris. As their romance blossoms, Hamish grows suspicious and discovers she's actually the sister of Harry Balfour in Dunbracken, sent to distract Lachlan from his coaching duties.

The community rallies behind their team despite the setbacks. When match day arrives, the team's bus breaks down, but they're saved by Doloris, who fixes it. At the match, Lochdubh falls behind quickly, and matters worsen when Jubel is injured. In a dramatic halftime confrontation, Hamish reveals Doloris' deception to Lachlan.

Rather than being crushed, Lachlan explains he has a plan. He reconciles with Lachie, who rejoins the team, and they unveil their secret weapon: Houston Old, a legendary shinty player who arrives by helicopter to the tune of *Simply the Best*. Though Dunbracken protests Houston's eligibility, it's revealed his mother is the Major's housekeeper, Edie from Lochdubh, making him a legitimate player.

The match goes to penalties, with Lachie Jr making crucial saves as goalkeeper. Houston scores the winning goal and Lochdubh finally breaks their losing streak. The episode ends with hints that Houston might be looking for a business partner when he leaves his job on the oil rigs, suggesting a potential new chapter for Lachlan Sr.

COMMENTARY

Stuart Hepburn: I've been sacked from more shows than I've been successful in. It's not easy. Danny's the man, not me. Danny's just an idea machine. He'd have had a separate conversation with Scott and I'd get asked if I had any ideas, by that time they just trust you. So if I say I have an interest in shinty, Scott said, 'Oh great.'

Mandie Fletcher (Director): I had great fun with that because I had to learn the rules and on my day off I went to watch a shinty match. The other thing was that I wanted it to be funny. I loved the fact Brian fell over anytime he had to do anything. Then there was that extraordinary, glamorous shinty player who was flown up.

Stuart Hepburn: I went to [broadcaster and shinty expert] Hugh Dan MacLennan and said 'I want to bring on a shinty player halfway through the match,' it was straight from *M*A*S*H* [1970], Spearchucker Jones. You get Spearchucker Jones and bring him on in the second half and win the game. We went and found Dallas Young of Kingussie and his flowing golden locks. Those were the days when you said 'We want to bring him in on a helicopter,' and they said 'Aye,' and we called him Houston Old.

Dallas Young (Houston Old; Shinty Player): I got a phone call and was asked to do it. They had contacted me because it was a shinty-themed episode, and I had this wild look with a headband and long hair, which caught their attention right away. That seemed to fit the kind of flamboyant character they were looking for, someone who comes in and wins the game.

THE HIRING OF Dallas Young was big news in the Scottish press, with *The Herald* noting on 7th October 1996 that 'the Gazza of the shinty world', was a Scotland internationalist 'who has helped Kingussie to many championships and cups'.

Dallas Young: The comparison to Gazza, that was my character back then. I used to wear a helmet with 'I'll be back' written on it, referencing Arnold Schwarzenegger. It was part of my personality, especially during games. That was directed at a Newtonmore player, Angus MacRae, who I had legendary battles with during games. No matter how hard he hit me, I'd put the helmet back on as if to say, 'I'll be back.' Everything I did was a bit like that.

My wife and I had an argument about it recently. She said, 'You'd rather have not got the injuries and had more trophies.' And I said, 'No, I wouldn't.' It's in your DNA, it's part of what you are. I wouldn't trade my success for anyone else's, and I know others wouldn't trade theirs for *Hamish Macbeth*, but I think *Hamish Macbeth* probably went with my character, so I was really lucky and privileged to be part of it.

THE HERALD WENT on to interview Young in 1996, who said: 'I thought it was a total wind-up at first... I am really quite scared. The last time I had this many butterflies in my stomach was before a Camanachd Cup Final.'

Dallas Young: I think the Camanachd Cup Final was actually easier. With that, you're in an environment you know and can handle. But going into this was different, especially with Robert Carlyle, who was a big star. But he made it so easy. He was class, you couldn't ask for a nicer person. The day I arrived, he came in before we went on set and said, 'Hi, I'm Bobby. Make sure you enjoy yourself and have a great time.' He didn't have to do that.

THE *DAILY RECORD* also reported on Young's new role, adding that 'Old men weep and young girls swoon as broad shouldered six-footer Young walks proudly onto the field carrying his caman—shinty stick, that is—wearing his now infamous red and blue Wild Thing headband. Filming of the episode begins today [7th October] at Balmacara on the west coast of Scotland.'

Dallas Young: I don't know how we came up with Wild Thing. I think it was one night in the pub and one of the local girls made the headband. It was beautifully done and became part of my persona.

Stuart Hepburn: Mandie had done a football match before and she said, 'You've got to write every shot.' So every fucking shot had to be choreographed. I had to speak to Hugh Dan MacLennan and met Johnny Ach [real name John MacRae], who was the head of Scottish shinty. His brother was Ian MacRae, the boatman. Johnny was a wonderful man. He was the harbour master at Kyle of Lochalsh and we went to the Camanachd Cup Final. If you can understand football you can understand shinty and Hugh Dan got me Dallas Young. I went up to Kingussie and asked if he'd do it.

Dallas Young: The first thing I did when I arrived on set was celebrate, getting carried off the pitch. It was weird because that was actually the last scene, but it was the first thing I filmed. There wasn't much rhyme or reason to it, but when you see it all put together, it works like clockwork.

Sarah Bruce: The shinty episode had so many locals in it, you never knew who was going to turn up on set.

Colin Finlay (Local resident): I was an extra, and we had to wait in the changing rooms until our scenes. Whilst in there, somebody knocked over one of the whisky barrels that were used as props. When we heard liquid inside, we investigated further to find it was the original whisky which had seeped out of the cask sides. After 'testing' the fluid, it was found to be of exquisite strength. We then conducted further tests and filled every container we could with the liquid to take home. Nobody was drunk *per se*, but it made for merry days filming.

Dallas Young: I wasn't in the helicopter as it came over the hill, I wasn't insured to go up in it. The helicopter was sitting on the ground. I got in and it moved off about three or four inches and then sat back down and I got out.

Mandie Fletcher: The shinty match was done in a Force 8 gale. I even heard that they'd asked a submarine to stay underside in case they got blown over. We had to keep working and they parked these coaches that everyone could sit in out of the wind and the rain, except me of course, who was shooting. Everyone came out of the coaches so slowly and I stormed in shouting, 'I need you out there, I need you to shoot the bloody... get out!' And they all dragged their sticks.

Dallas Young: The bit where they played *Simply the Best*, that couldn't have been worse! I'm a Celtic fan and first they said 'They think it's all over,' which is the England World Cup Final 1966, then they play *Simply the Best*, which is Rangers' anthem. For my father, that was horrendous. But it was a perfect week.

Jon Older (First Assistant Director): Mandie was a very strong personality, but I'm very fond of her because she knew what she was doing. She had an impatient side to her, but as an AD, the only thing you ever need a director to do is to know what they want. The director becomes a nightmare when they haven't got a clue what they want until they see something. That's the wrong way around. But that's not the case with Mandie, she'd always go into something with a clear idea of what she wanted to see.

Mandie Fletcher: It was great in the end, but the actual shooting of it I have never known such hell. I even remember taking my hat off, throwing it on the floor and stamping on it as I was so cross.

Dallas Young: Mandie was really flamboyant. She had such a presence, but was so lovely. It was a great example of how to treat people. Even though I was a nobody and just a small part of the production, they had time for me and made me feel included. Sitting in the bar with all the main cast and not feeling excluded, I couldn't have asked for a better experience.

Sarah Bruce: I remember them getting the helicopter flying shot and Mandie was a bit emotional over it. I think it was one take.

Jon Older: I was really pleased with the timing of the final shot, it was down to the timing of me cueing the bus and the helicopter. It wasn't my idea, but I made it work. I had a walkie talkie for the chopper and a radio to my assistant, who spoke to the bus driver. We positioned the camera at the side of the road and got the helicopter hovering, waiting for the perfect moment. Honestly, it was more about the pilot's skill in keeping steady. I think we only did it once, and it's a really nice shot.

Charles Salmon: Every episode was different and had its own character. With Mandie, it was the difficulties of filming sports as a drama. It wasn't like a procedural show, where you run a certain style and know when something's going to happen. Though there was a continuity of the series, the directors could run with their particular stories.

Dallas Young: It was a massive thing for shinty. I remember back when it was on, sitting in the house with my wife and she was laughing when it came on. The Monday after was just madness. Everyone was taken aback by it.

Tam Dean Burn: My episodes were filmed back to back in consecutive weeks. I think they were the only two that Campbell Morrison did as well. They sort of concentrated on the hotel and both stories were outdoors, a shinty match and the singing competition centred around the hotel.

Mandie Fletcher: It was that perfect Sunday night fare, it wasn't too serious. Maybe we're in a different world now, where you have to be quite serious and threatening, but I get rather tired of turning on my TV and seeing some poor woman being murdered in some ghastly way. I don't know why we do it. But I like comedy and I like fun and I loved the fact there was comedy in it. I loved the fact there was a lightness to it. I'm not sure you could make it now. I'm not sure anyone would give you the money.

Dallas Young: The long hair was my trademark, then I shaved it off for charity after we won the Scottish Cup. I've never grown it back. My wife says I'd look ridiculous without hair now, so I've kept what's left. [The headband] came up again a couple of weeks ago. Someone called me to ask if I still had the strip because a young lad wanted to dress up as me for a fancy dress event. I found the headband and sent it to him along with the strip. His mum put a wee thank-you post on Facebook, which was lovely.

I've got a photo from the end of the day of all of us, Bobby and the rest of the cast. I couldn't say enough good things about him or the rest of them. They made me feel at home and wanted. It was a total pleasure to spend time with them all.

FINAL THOUGHTS

In the ancient sport of shinty, local pride runs deep. 'More Than a Game' uses Lochdubh's annual match against

Dunbracken to explore both sporting tradition and family dynamics.

At the episode's heart is Lachlan Sr's dual crisis: trying to coach an underperforming team while falling victim to a honey trap scheme orchestrated by Harry Balfour, though as the episode ends it looks like Lachlan might find romance with Edie.

The introduction of Dallas Young as Houston Old adds some authenticity to the proceedings, an in-joke for shinty fans who aren't used to seeing the game represented in prime time TV dramas. His helicopter arrival for the climactic penalty shootout elevates what could have been just another sporting underdog story.

In the end, writer Stuart Hepburn shows that in small communities, sport is never just about winning and losing.

7 & 8. DESTINY PARTS I & II

Writer: Daniel Boyle
Director: Nicholas Renton
Original broadcast: Part I: 27th April 1997, 8.10pm; Part II: 4th May 1997, 8.10pm

Guest cast

Sean Scanlan (Kenneth McIver), Richard Marsella (The Comandante), Kenny Ireland (Torquil McFarquar), Caroline Loncq (Ava Grimm), Stephen Henderson (Frankie Brice), Brendan Conroy (Cruiser Captain), Sandy McDade (Jean Foley), John Grieve (Herman), Joseph Greig (Dugal Finlay), Ray De-Haan (Coxswain).

Part I summary

Somewhere in South America, March 1996: Torquil Farquar McFarquar and his companion Ava Grimm arrange the release of Kenneth McIver, TV John's long-lost brother, from a South American prison. Kenneth, sporting a metal leg and hook hand (the results of his accident-prone criminal career), reveals he knows the location of the Stone of Destiny, Scotland's ancient coronation stone.

A flashback reveals a young Kenneth spying on TV John and other members of the Lochdubh community as they discuss the Stone of Destiny. During World War II, the parents of current Lochdubh residents stole the real Stone of Destiny from Westminster Abbey, replacing it with a replica. Each family was given a line of verse as a clue to the Stone's location, with no single person knowing the complete directions.

In the present day, Torquil offers Kenneth half a million pounds to retrieve the Stone.

Back in Lochdubh, TV John begins organising his possessions, telling a concerned Hamish he believes he's about to die, though Hamish dismisses this premonition. The community rallies around TV John, with each villager attempting to distract him from thoughts of his impending death. Lachie Jr discusses embalming techniques, while Hamish prepares TV John's favourite plum duff pudding.

Kenneth McIver arrives in Lochdubh with Ava Grimm, displaying bitter resentment toward his brother and the village he left 35 years ago.

Later, Isobel races back to Lochdubh after receiving a false message about Hamish being seriously ill, suggesting someone is manipulating the community. During a hill walk, TV John reveals the secret of the Stone of Destiny to Hamish, noting that he knows its location and shows Hamish the Stone hidden behind a waterfall.

Through hypnosis of the Major, Rory and Isobel, Ava helps Kenneth piece together the coded verses about the Stone's location: 'Look in the place where the monarch soars and the young go to bask in the sun.' Kenneth deduces this refers to a waterfall where salmon (the 'monarch' of fish) swim upstream, and where children once swam on hot summer days.

As a thunderstorm builds, tensions escalate. Doc Brown begins to understand what's happening to the affected villagers, while Kenneth and Ava prepare to claim the Stone, armed with horses and a gun. The episode ends with Kenneth confronting his brother, revealing he knows the Stone's location and has come for something more than just directions.

Part II summary

Having been kidnapped by Kenneth, TV John is forced to help locate the Stone of Destiny.

When Doc Brown announces that a hypnotist is on the loose in Lochdubh, Hamish and Isobel race to John's empty caravan and find horse manure outside. With the help of Lachlan, Rory, Doc Brown and the Major, Hamish realises Kenneth is transporting the Stone on horseback to Rubha na Fearna, a promontory where a boat waits nearby.

As the villagers set off by truck to intercept them, Hamish and Isobel take a treacherous shortcut over the high pass. Their journey becomes life-threatening when a blizzard strikes, leaving them freezing and disoriented until a mysterious hermit named Herman rescues them.

Meanwhile, John tries to reason with his brother, revealing that their parents loved Kenneth and suggesting that Kenneth himself possesses powerful psychic abilities that manifest negatively. When Ava is bitten by an adder, John refuses to leave her behind despite Kenneth's threats.

Believing they might die, Hamish and Isobel finally confront their feelings. Hamish admits he never told Isobel he loved her, having assumed she would know without being told. The pair find their way out of the cave to help their friends.

As dawn breaks, both parties converge on the beach. Kenneth forces John onto Torquil's boat, with the latter offering half a million pounds for the Stone. But John has secretly swapped the real Stone for a rock. As the boat loses control in rough seas, John reveals to Kenneth that he knew his own death was imminent but came anyway out of brotherly love.

The brothers face their fate together, with TV John uttering his final word, 'Pomade', just before a massive explosion engulfs the vessel. Afterwards, Hamish recovers only Kenneth's prosthetic leg from the water.

Back at the Stag Bar, the villagers mourn TV John while dedicating a corner of the pub to his memory. Their solemn tribute is interrupted by a news broadcast announcing that, after 700 years, the Stone of Destiny will be officially returned to Scotland. The group immediately begins planning to break into the sewers beneath Westminster Abbey to retrieve their stone, certain the authorities will renege on their promise.

The episode concludes with a supernatural visitation from TV John's father, who apologises for John's incorrect prediction about the Stone never being returned to Scotland and brings personal messages, including a startling prophecy for Hamish: despite their agreement to remain childless, Hamish and Isobel's encounter in the snow cave will soon require 'thousands of Pampers'. The series ends with Hamish, Isobel and Wee Jock joining the others as they return the Stone.

COMMENTARY

Scott Meek: We'd always said, 'If we're going to go out, let's go out with the maddest kind of *Hamish* episode we can,' and that had to be written by Dan. We were basically saying, 'Fuck it, it's the last two episodes ever, just do what you want and make it a mad Scottish *Gone With the Wind* [1939].'

Toby Hefferman: The final two episodes were epic. We had a special effects supervisor, Stuart [Brisdon], and we had stunt people: Ray De-Haan, who was one of the drivers on the James Bond movies, and Sy Hollands, who was also a big stunt person at the time. I spoke to some of the crew members that had done bigger jobs, and they said, 'This is like working on a movie.' We had fake snow and action sequences. It was really exciting and at the time it was as big as it got.

Andrea Calderwood: There was definitely a feeling of 'Let's go out on a high and do something bold and spectacular.' That's what I always thought was interesting about series rather than one-offs. People were forever trying to do films about the Stone of Destiny, but in an expansive show like *Hamish* you could put in storylines that would never get made as films and avoid setting up an entire production around it.

Duncan Duff: It did get very weird towards the end with the

Stone of Destiny. It was like they were on LSD rather than dope.

Toby Hefferman: When you're making something, you never know if it's going to be good or not. Everyone was a little cautious with 'Destiny'. There were definitely questions about, 'Where is this going?' It wasn't the norm. But because it was the final two episodes, everyone threw caution to the wind, and it was like, 'Well, they know what they're doing. We're just going to go out with a bang.'

Charles Salmon: I supported the episodes because I had come from a small town, and I knew that some pretty crazy things could happen. It's a reflection of those sorts of communities, but you still look after each other. It's not sinister or destructive, but they're things that people get passionate about. I was up for pushing the boundaries within the parameters of Sunday evening entertainment. That was part of the fun of the show, the unexpected. It was at the end of the season, and we wanted a finale that was impactful, so we decided to go with it.

Ming Ho: I researched the background of the Stone of Scone [another name for the Stone of Destiny]. The storyline of 'Destiny' was based on the attempted theft of the Stone from Westminster Abbey by Scottish Nationalists in 1950 and its wartime concealment in a place of safety. The Coronation Chair (though not the Stone) was moved to Gloucester Cathedral for the duration of the war, and as Gloucester was near my home town, I visited the Cathedral out of interest one weekend, though it was not directly related to the story as it turned out in Daniel's scripts.

Daniel Boyle: I wanted to end it on a high. I thought if you could heighten it, it could work well. I was casting around and then the idea popped into my head. We said it was taken by forbears in Lochdubh, then [secretary of state for Scotland] Michael Forsyth gets it back.

Deirdre Keir: I was working on the development of scripts and I was standing at the sink listening to BBC Radio Four thinking at least they're all going out there and getting geared up to do it, it felt really weird not to be part of it. The 11 o'clock news came on and said, 'The government has decided to return the Stone of Scone to Scotland.'

Duncan Duff: John Major, in a desperate effort to buy votes in Scotland and buy a single Conservative seat in Scotland, returned the Stone of Scone. It was returned from Westminster Abbey to Edinburgh Castle, I think that was around that time. It was very topical. And the joke was that it wasn't the real one that was returned to Westminster Abbey. They just returned a fake.

Scott Meek: Things were happening that we couldn't control. We had written all of that with the absolute certainty that the Stone wasn't going to be returned to Scotland. We were filming it when they stood up in the Houses of Parliament and said it would be returned to Scotland, at which point we were like, 'For fuck's sake, what are we meant to do with that?'

Deirdre Keir: [I was on the phone to Daniel saying] 'Have you heard the news? They're going to send the Stone of Scone back to Scotland.' He said, 'Oh, fuck, what are we going to do?' I'm standing there thinking this is terrible because this two-parter is going to close the series. 'Daniel, put the phone down, have a walk about and if needs be, I'll come back up and sit with you.' Of course Daniel being Daniel he just worked his way through it, [effectively saying] 'This is what really happened.'

Daniel Boyle: I had to tag on a scene with a radio. I loved it. Ghosts walking around, cut them off at the pass... I was [always thinking] *How can I push it further?*

Ralph Riach: A funny thing that happened during the filming of that episode, that's when John Major decided to give the Stone back to Scotland. We were driving into the castle one day and somebody said, 'It's just been on the news that the Stone of Destiny is coming back to Scotland.' Oh, fuck!

Stuart Davids: The final episodes were great fun to do. I liked the idea that the Stone of Destiny was in Lochdubh and that it was a shared secret. I loved the idea of making TV John psychic and of Ralph foreseeing his own death. There was something epic about it, and that was before the Stone did come home. I liked it a lot.

Ming Ho: The two-part finale was substantially shot on Skye. Quite a challenging shoot for the crew, involving stunts. I stayed back at the production base in Plockton. I wasn't up there for the whole series shoot, being based at Zenith's office in London; I just went up to Plockton periodically for a few days at a time to issue scripts and work on amendments.

Stuart Davids: I remember being in a cave and it was tough to do. We had to do those episodes in Skye because of the tourist season. It rained the whole time. They would pay you to be there because of weather cover and the schedule would have to change and my abiding memory is of sitting around and waiting in a room with the rain lashing against the window. You were always waiting to get back to Glasgow, but they wouldn't let you leave because of the weather cover.

David Ashton: We were all discussing whatever it was and it was bucketing down and I looked at the film crew and you couldn't see them, they were covered in waterproofs. You could see little slits where their eyes were peeping out, and I said, 'What are we doing in kilts, freezing our butts off and these buggers are giving us directions?' We were quite indignant about that.

Ming Ho: I recall there was some debate about the portrayal of the hook-armed, tin-legged, eye-patched villain, TV John's estranged brother, Kenneth McIver, played by Sean Scanlan: was it OTT? And was the portrayal potentially offensive to people with disabilities? I also had to write a synopsis for Range Rover, who supplied the vehicle Kenneth drove in these episodes and wanted to know how their car would feature.

Stuart Davids: Sean Scanlan was terrific, the courage with which he played it. The character was nuts.

Nicholas Renton: Sean was a very exotic actor. He always played it big and there was that long scene at the beginning, that was done in Plockton. He was great fun to work with. He's kind of in the tradition of Robert Newton, he kind of had that slant.

Scott Meek: Sean is absolutely fantastic. Whether it's in feature films or television, there's one constant with actors. Actors like acting and like acting with other good actors. If you're making something, if you've established you've got a really good gang, actors want to be in that gang, because there's real pleasure in it for them.

Toby Hefferman: I remember going out to the boat in waders with a plank of wood with tea on it. We weren't shooting in the town, so it felt like we were doing something slightly different. It wasn't *Hamish Macbeth*. They had the same characters and mostly the same crew, but it definitely felt like something else, like a sort of special edition. I ended up meeting an assistant director called Gareth Tandy, who then took me on as an assistant on *The Borrowers* [1997] at Shepperton Studios. If I hadn't done *Hamish*, I wouldn't have met Gareth, and I ended up meeting Deborah Saban, who took me onto *Shakespeare in Love*... it's a sort of chain reaction.

Charles Salmon: We took a great deal of trouble to make a replica of the Stone of Destiny. We were on that set for quite a few days, so we put it in position and it would be left there overnight. I'm sure we had some security on it, but when we wrapped filming, it was left in the location. The next morning it had gone. Someone had taken the Stone of Destiny. Whether it was an inside job, I don't know. Maybe they knew that we'd finished filming, so there was no harm to the shooting schedule. But it was pretty funny that the Stone had actually been stolen. BBC Radio Four asked me to do an interview on it, and they were really serious about the fact that it had been stolen. I never did find out what happened to our prop.

David Ashton: It was crazy, but early on some people thought it was a joke about the Stone of Destiny, and Nick was on us like a flash that it was totally serious. This means everything to these people. They live up in the Highlands. This is Prince Charlie, Jacobites, this is totally serious to them. So we said, 'OK, we play it like it's a serious kind of Sir Walter Scott adventure.' That's what made it work. He only had to give us notes once.

Nicholas Renton: Some of it went into areas I'm just not sure about, Kenny Ireland's character and all that. Because it was simply like a road movie, there are bits of it I find filmically really interesting. We were doing a shot where the girl who came out of the water and mesmerised everyone was on a horse and I said, 'Go round in a circle,' and I could see the horse going nearer and nearer to the edge of the frame and I said, 'Please don't go out of the frame,' and she turned the horse around. It's a bit shot in Skye and Scott said, 'Well, that's that then. I can't possibly match any of that. Move on.' We had bits in the cave, we had to do the cave twice for some reason. There was something wrong with the first cave. I think I had no handle on that story at all and I think that's kind of good. It's where it deserved to go.

Stuart Davids: There was a scene in the two last episodes where they're priming me to tell John that he won't die, and I'm in the bar with various implements used in embalming. On the page it's about two-and-a-half pages of dialogue, and I always say that this is the reason why I've never acted again. I was obsessed by the length of this dialogue and was quite nervous.

I knew [Nick Renton] wasn't going to let me off with it and that he'd shoot it in one shot. I was so aware of what I was doing as an actor that I could hear the film in the camera turning and it was the moment I said I wasn't acting again. I've never really acted again, but not in a regretful way. It's just that something happened to me as an actor. Once it's gone, you can't get it back.

Ralph Riach: I've no idea how they did that trick at the end when I walk into the mirror. All I had to do was walk into the cupboard, turn around and stand there. That was crazy. People still ask if we're doing more.

Final Thoughts

The two-part series finale wraps its story around one of Scotland's most potent national symbols: the Stone of Destiny, the ancient coronation stone stolen by Edward I in 1296 and taken to Westminster Abbey.

As Hamish and Isobel chase clues, they also wrestle with long-simmering feelings and unresolved guilt over Alex's death. That they would end up a couple was never really in doubt, though nobody could have foreseen quite how much Daniel Boyle would put them through the emotional wringer across three series.

Though it diverges drastically from a standard police drama—Hamish spends most of his time out of uniform, and the biggest 'crime' is the theft of the Stone itself—the two-parter feels like a natural culmination of everything the show embodies: dark humour, Highland mysticism and the unbreakable bond of community.

TV John's death, heralded by the smell of pomade, and the entire village's plan to break into Westminster Abbey, blend into a finale that is, by turns, heartbreaking, hilarious and unapologetically Scottish.

If *Hamish Macbeth* had to end, at least it went out in a suitably bold and brazen style.

SEVENTEEN
LEAVING LOCHDUBH

AUTUMN 1996

In his production caravan in Portree, Robert Carlyle studied the script for the day's scenes filmed on Skye but set on Laggan-Laggan. The episode was taking Hamish far from the familiar comfort of Lochdubh, into another of those remote island mysteries the actor had grown to relish.

When he'd first taken on the role, he'd been known for intense dramatic parts like Albie in *Cracker*. Hamish had offered something different; not straight comedy, but a more nuanced character who could navigate between light and dark.

Over time, Hamish had emerged as something entirely his own: a man who thought far more than he spoke, whose struggles with communication had become not just a character trait but the heart of who he was. Even now, approaching the end, Hamish thought far more than he said, especially when it came to women.

From kicking in headlights in that first episode to what lay ahead—a two-part finale dealing with mysticism, the Stone of Destiny and the death of a friend—the show had evolved into something far bolder than anyone had anticipated.

The Australian fan mail was already flooding in through this new thing called the internet, not that he understood much about that. There was talk of Christmas specials, perhaps even another series at some other time. The show's blend of mystery and character-driven drama had found its audience, even if that audience was often halfway around the world.

Three series felt right, enough time to find *Hamish Macbeth*'s unique voice, but not so long that they'd start recycling stories or resenting the constraints of Sunday night TV. He'd told the press he might consider Christmas specials, but the truth was more complicated.

With Begbie in *Trainspotting* changing how people saw him and *The Full Monty* waiting in the wings, it was time to move on.

Downing the last of his coffee, he headed out to film. The BBC might have their own plans for Lochdubh's future, but that was a story for another day. Right now, there were still mysteries to solve, characters to inhabit and a few more chances to show what made this corner of Scotland so different from anything else on TV.

FUTURE PLANS

It was in the autumn of 1996 that journalist Alison Graham had found herself in Plockton's village hall, watching the cast and crew of *Hamish Macbeth* attempt their final ceilidh.

The (largely) English production team's earnest but awkward attempts at the Gay Gordons and Strip the Willow provided an unintentionally perfect metaphor for their three-year relationship with this remote coastal village. Initially outsiders, they were gradually absorbed 'by a process of osmosis' into the fabric of Highland life.

Robert Carlyle reflected on three years that had transformed both the village and his career. Despite tabloid speculation about his departure, he remained characteristically direct about the show's future. 'Myself and Danny Boyle [the writer] always agreed that three was enough,' he told Graham, though he left the door open for one-off Christmas specials.

Graham wrote about her visit for the 22nd–28th March 1997 issue of *Radio Times*, which saw *Hamish Macbeth* secure its second front cover, this time featuring Robert Carlyle in his police uniform alongside Dex as Wee Jock.

Ratings for *Hamish Macbeth*'s third series started on a high with 10.46 million for 'The Honourable Policeman' against ITV's *Poirot* (1989–2013) with 11.18 million, but they soon took a tumble.

Unfortunately for *Hamish*, ITV scheduled the pilot episode of police drama *Midsomer Murders* (1997–) against 'Deferred Sentence' on 23rd March. While 13.53 million watched *Midsomer*, *Hamish* only managed 8.53 million. Another new ITV drama, *Where the Heart Is* (1997–2006) secured 11.98 million for its first episode on 6th April against *Hamish*'s 7.28 million for 'The Good Thief'. As *The Stage* put it, *Hamish Macbeth* was being 'knocked all over the pitch by whatever ITV bowls at it'.

Kind courtesy of Radio Times Archives

Series three's arrival on BBC One in March 1997 coincided with the publication of *The Box*, a new British magazine devoted to TV. Issue one placed *Hamish Macbeth* at number five on its list of 'Must see TV', just behind *The X-Files*. 'Quirky, dark, puzzling, *Hamish Macbeth* is the thinking man's

Ballykissangel,' announced the magazine, adding that Robert Carlyle's performance was 'a masterpiece of laconic cool' and that it was 'TV you can't watch in background mode.' The article ended on a bittersweet note: 'Hamish will ride off into the Lochdubh sunset just as the word finally gets out about what an authentically bizarre curio this show really is.'

The conclusion of the final two-part story, 'Destiny' in spring 1997, left viewers wondering if they had truly seen the last of Hamish and Lochdubh. Gavin Docherty pushed Carlyle on his reasons for quitting in the *Sunday Express* on 16th March, with the actor telling him he'd made the decision to leave after three series even before the first series had begun.

Daniel Boyle told *The Box* he had always envisioned the series as a finite story of 18-20 episodes and that they had resolved the storyline exactly as planned. But during the promotion of series three, he went back on a previous statement that he'd run out of ideas, telling the *Sunday Express,* 'Yeah, I was all written out, but that was last year. I'd love to do more. There's life in the old boy yet.'

It was clear that the show's success had created something larger than its original concept, a world rich with characters and possibilities that many felt could sustain countless more stories.

Speaking to *The Herald* in 1997, Robert Carlyle revealed that the BBC would happily have continued making *Hamish Macbeth,* but that he simply didn't want to do it anymore. 'I knew that, if I did, I would start to hate it; that I'd begin to resent the character. As it is, it has been a pleasure right up to the very last day.'

Scott Meek: Bobby wouldn't have [done a fourth series] I don't think, but the BBC would have quite happily gone on with *Tales of Lochdubh*, *Hamish Macbeth* without Bobby. But we were very firmly of the idea that we didn't want to continue, which is commercially foolhardy but we felt we didn't have enough left to make a series four or five that would be as good as the first three series. We wanted to get out while the going was good and be fondly remembered rather than making money, not particularly enjoying ourselves and people saying, 'I remember that when it was good.'

Andrea Calderwood: It was very much the approach at the time. It was the same with *Cardiac Arrest*. [Producer] Tony Garnett had a mantra about how after three series, a show outlives its freshness and its relevance. There was a feeling that you shouldn't keep milking things. Now, that's not brilliant business sense, obviously, and *Hamish* could have been milked. It wasn't cancelled. It was much more a creative decision to quit while we were ahead. I was very gung-ho and I think Scott is the same.

DESPITE HIS DESIRE to leave the series behind, Robert Carlyle told *The Herald* that he'd 'miss it, for the very selfish reason that I won't get four months in the Highlands every year. Everyone concerned is quite content to finish up now. I think that, because the stories were often so extreme, that there are only so many tales you can tell before you start dropping your standards.'

Daniel Boyle: If you aim for run of the mill you can keep going forever. But when it's tonally distinct it becomes harder. I knew three series would be all because of Bobby. We could perhaps have carried on with Gerard Kelly.

Ralph Riach: The man before the man before Macbeth could've been in it.

Stuart Hepburn: I didn't know Bobby all that well, but I wasn't that surprised. We were due to do many more episodes of *McCallum* [1995] and John Hannah decided to do *The Love Bug* [1997] in the US. The talent goes and that's it. Robbie Coltrane did *The Planman* [2003] then went on to do Harry Potter. You would need another cop. People watch something and they don't understand what it is. I understood what it was, Scott Meek did and Danny Boyle certainly understood what it was. You had a cop who didn't want to solve crime, didn't want to be promoted and didn't want to be successful. It's almost unprecedented. How do you bring in another cop who's exactly the same? I'd have been part of the planning to make series four work, and I'd only have done it if Scott and Deirdre would've done it.

Shirley Henderson: It was a surprise it came to an end. I wasn't doing lots of films, I just had a couple of wee bits in stuff; films for me were still a long, long way away. I think we were all a bit surprised, but in some ways I suppose you leave people wanting. Maybe it was a natural thing?

Andrea Calderwood: I felt it had a natural arc to it.

Stuart Davids: If it had kept going I probably wouldn't have done other things. I directed an episode of *Heartbeat* and saw people who had done it for 10 years. I think if you do it for five series the bar would have got lower because it's hard to maintain the quality with Christmas specials, going abroad... it's nice that people still remember it as it was.

Barbara Rafferty: For a long time there was talk of carrying on the series with the locals, like they did with *Ballykissangel*. People lived in hope for a long time, but nothing ever came of it. Then they brought in *Two Thousand Acres of Sky* [2001–03], which wasn't bad, but it didn't have that edge.

Ralph Riach: When we finished the third series, we got the impression that because it had been so successful, they couldn't just let it die. I suggested that we do it pre-*Hamish* called *Waiting for Hamish*, it could have gone on for years and years.

Deirdre Keir: Had there been the spin-off, [TV John] would have been back.

Nicholas Renton: If you do a fourth it really does have to change, so structuring something around TV John would make total sense because the whole idea is changing, but you can't sell it as *Hamish Macbeth* anymore. They managed it on *Taggart*. We stopped just in time. Series three was very tough.

Ming Ho: If we were starting now, no doubt there would be an imperative to build in some recasting or a spin-off for the village or other characters, but it wasn't an option then. It was too quirky to be produced on an industrial scale. We could probably have set it up to last longer by going down a more mainstream commercial route and keeping more storyline control within the production unit, which would enable more writers to be brought on as journeymen, but that's not the show any of us wanted to make at the time.

Stuart Hepburn: I was part of refocusing *Taggart*. It was a painful process, but we made the right decisions. I don't know if I'd want to go through that trauma again. I'd want to be at the centre of it because TV ideas are far more fragile than you'd imagine. People might think it was the dog, the landscape... actually it was the psychological truth at the centre of a man who didn't want to be successful. That's what it was really about, in my humble opinion.

Andrea Calderwood: It was three good seasons and done. Maybe at another time in broadcasting or another time in independent production, you would just keep going and going. You would recast and get whole new creative teams in because it's a brand.

Ralph Riach: I also had an idea for a sequel, where we could all get together without Bobby, because he wasn't going to do it, where the locals go in search of TV John, because his body was never found. He's maybe washed up on some exotic desert island or he's lost his memory and they all go looking for him.

Stuart Hepburn: Ralph wanted to create it and everyone would have come back. Zoot would've come back.

Ron Donachie: If they'd asked me back I would have done it. I had such great fun doing it I would've gone back. I think they missed a trick there, because although Bobby was essential to it and was a terrific central performance, I think in fairness to the way it was written and created, the other characters were so well rounded and such an ensemble group, you could really have done what they did on *Heartbeat* and bring in another copper every few years, or just dispense with the copper altogether and just called it *Tales of Lochdubh*. There was enough going on and the writing was strong enough to make strong stories out of that.

Duncan Duff: I know there was talk about doing *Tales of Lochdubh* or whatever, which would have been a post-*Hamish* sort of thing. Whilst it would've been appealing in some ways, I think, *Thank God it didn't happen*. The show ended on a high when people still were fond of it and looked forward to watching it.

David Ashton: We did a lot of canvassing for it to come back, but we got the impression that whoever had made that decision it was a closed door, and nobody closes a door faster and more secure than the BBC.

Shirley Henderson: It is what it is. Whoever makes these decisions, they made that and you move on from it and you just have to get your head around it.

David Ashton: I felt that if we could have retained Danny, I think we could have done at least one more series. Although it was an awful lot to ask him to write all the episodes. Perhaps if we'd done a shorter series, not so many episodes, maybe four and really let him have his head but not stretch it out too far. I don't think anyone in the cast was particularly pleased that they called a halt to it. If they'd played their cards differently, they could have got him back, even if it was for a 90 minute special, *Christmas in Lochdubh*, it would have been terrific and Bobby would have done it. But a lot of his loyalty was to the cast and Danny Boyle's writing.

Stuart McGugan: I thought the series had legs even after three years, even without Bobby and if the will had been there. Brian Pettifer said that *The Grocer of Lochdubh* would be a great series. I thought Barney and the bar would be great.

Forbes Masson: I knew Bobby didn't want to do it anymore. It was quite understandable, but I thought it could have lasted. It's like what they've done with *Shetland* [2013–]. They brought other people on. *Shetland* is different, darker, not comic at all, but there's that sort of Scottishness... I don't think *Shetland* would have happened if *Hamish Macbeth* hadn't happened all those years ago.

It was a shame that they didn't take a risk and carry on with it. It was probably too early, but it could have been a woman, they could have completely shifted it. Because the stories were great, you could have had limitless stories in that world. And lovely, warm characters. It was so well crafted and beautiful, the area was so gorgeous. I still think there's mileage for that sort of small community Scottish thing. It's nice to be part of something like that and nice that it's remembered.

Ming Ho: You could perhaps say that Dominic Minghella took elements of it on into *Doc Martin* [2004–22]; the father and son Lachies from *Hamish* resurface in *Doc Martin*'s Bert and Al Large...

Deirdre Keir: Dominic said, 'We've taken *Hamish* down to Cornwall.'

Dominic Minghella: Arguably *Doc Martin*, which I developed later for ITV, is a kind of *Hamish*, in the medical rather than policing arena, and I was able to apply lessons learned to that material.

Duncan Duff: I'm not saying that *Hamish Macbeth* caused this sort of thing, but in the wake of it you got *Ballykissangel*, *Doc Martin* and *Monarch of the Glen*, this whole slew of Sunday evening sort of 'Celtic feel good' series. What was brilliant about *Hamish Macbeth*, and they still retained it even when these other things came along, is that it was so much more than that. It was very, very sophisticated. It was silly and whimsical and, while some episodes were definitely better than others, I think it was very cleverly conceived.

Forbes Masson: When *Hamish* sadly left the screens, it was replaced by that sort of shortbread-y tin *Monarch of the Glen*. I felt as though it had stepped back a bit, because what I loved about *Hamish Macbeth* was it felt real, not that it was inherently working class, but it was real people and funny characters.

Andrea Calderwood: I turned down *Monarch of the Glen* three times, and then it got made and was a big hit. I wanted to do something that was more about contemporary Scotland.

Duncan Duff: I remember hearing that it was based on the stories written by Compton Mackenzie and my ears pricked up and I thought, *Oh, that sounds interesting.* I tried to get seen for it and the word was they were not going to see anybody who had any connection with *Hamish Macbeth*, and if you look, certainly initially, there's not a single crossover.

It was very much an English view, and the focus was on the completely anglicised Richard Briers and Susan Hampshire characters, though nothing against them whatsoever. It was very much looking at things from the laird's point of view. What's brilliant about *Hamish Macbeth* is that it was completely subversive. It's very much the other side, the Clearances side, of the Highland experience.

Michael Mackenzie: *Hamish* was in the great tradition of German film or Australian film in the 1970s, which is, 'This is us, this is what we do. We're doing it well. If you like it, join in with us'. *Monarch of the Glen* was, 'Oh look, we're in Scotland, we're going to show you lots of tartan and lovely hills, because that's what the tourists expect.'

Ralph Riach: *Hamish* is a world apart from *Monarch*, which looked nice but had no substance. Most, if not all, of the writing was done by English writers and it seemed to me that the humorous lines that were put into the mouths of the Scottish characters didn't ring true. I didn't believe it. I couldn't believe that the son of the house would marry Lexie. Having said that, working on it was lovely. Richard Briers was lovely to work with.

Michael Mackenzie: *Hamish* was created by people who wanted to tell those really peculiar, absurd, quirky stories with a very Scottish, straight-faced sense of humour. That very, very dry sense of humour, which is peculiarly Scottish, which I think really works for us. And because it worked for us, and because it was made with that integrity, it's been sold all over the world and everybody loves it, in exactly the same way as the Australian films of the 1970s, *Picnic at Hanging Rock* [1975] and all those others.

Toby Hefferman: I think if you tried to do it now, it would be a lot different. When you watch it, there's an innocence to it. I think that sort of sums up the general philosophy of how we made it. There was a beautiful innocence about the whole thing. If you did it now... well, they don't make shows like that anymore. It was so eclectic and there was a continuity to it. It wasn't just luck. There was a definite sort of magic dust on that series.

Ming Ho: Although *Hamish* was successful, it has remained a cult show; arguably it might have got a bigger audience and continued for longer, had it been a more straightforward family Sunday night drama, as *Monarch of the Glen* later became.

Charlie MacRae: Apart from the money stopping, most people in Plockton were pleased the series was ending. Three years was enough as we had visitors anyway. I think I was pleased too. The location manager came to my house at 5pm daily asking if it was OK to go certain places the next day. Villagers thought I was getting well paid; I think I got a bottle of whisky when they left. I also got the General Manager's Award for the Highland Area from Royal Mail for my involvement and a trip to Edinburgh.

Sarah Bruce: It's hard to speak from a village perspective [on the series ending] as I was working six days a week, up to 11 hour days on the show. You end up quite immersed in that world. The tourists were definitely coming anyway, but the season was shorter. I'm not sure if *Hamish* affected that or if it would have naturally happened anyway. By the end of series three airing, there was a definite tourism increase. It felt very busy and everyone wanted to know about the show. Anyone working in hospitality eventually got sick of being asked how to find Hamish's house and where Wee Jock was.

Toby Hefferman: We all had the best experience on *Hamish*. There are some brilliant technicians who've come from there, like Mark Sanger, he was a location assistant and he's now an Oscar-winning editor for *Gravity* [2013]. Siobhan Lyons, who was the production assistant, she was a unit production manager on *Dumbo* [2019] and other things. There were some other people who fell into the film side of it.

Andrea Calderwood: I'm really, really fond and proud of it. When I started out I'd get in a taxi and drivers would say 'What do you do?' 'BBC Scotland drama.' 'Have you made anything I've heard of?' At that time, everybody talked about things like *Doctor Finlay* or *Taggart*. Then later I'd get in taxis and I could say *Hamish Macbeth*. That felt like a real achievement, to have a show that everybody recognised and everybody was watching. It became one of the stalwart shows that everybody knew about.

Anne Lacey: It was lovely to be there with great people. It finished on a high and became a classic.

Duncan Duff: It was a really special show, and it has a special place for me professionally, also in my life. Without getting overblown about it, I think that's the thing for many of the people who were involved in *Hamish Macbeth*, it was more than just another job. It was mainly because you were there for extended periods of time. It really took up an important part of people's lives. To see the same people for three years in that weird separate location and really get to know them quite well and see how different people's lives went in that time, for better or worse.

Shirley Henderson: Looking back, it never ran out of steam; it finished before that happened. It was a complete thing. You got them together and everybody's story was tied up. Not every drama has to go on for years and years. Maybe that's not a bad thing.

THE MOST INTRIGUING revelation about how *Hamish Macbeth* might have concluded came from Daniel Boyle. He shared, possibly with tongue-in-cheek, that he had once contemplated an ending where Lochdubh 'didn't exist, almost like Brigadoon'. In the closing seconds, the episode would have revealed the entire community as existing only in Hamish's imagination, the Glasgow policeman never having left the city. According to Boyle, 'You'd realise he'd dreamed the whole thing.'

For a series that had always danced between reality and fantasy, it would have been a fittingly audacious way to end it. Perhaps *Hamish Macbeth*'s greatest achievement was creating a world so vivid that viewers, like Hamish himself, never wanted to leave, whether it was real or not.

EIGHTEEN
MOVING ON

HAMISH MACBETH officially ended on 4th May 1997, sandwiched between an episode of *The Great Antiques Hunt* (1994–) and part one of a two-part drama, *The Heart Surgeon* (1997).

Audiences would next see Robert Carlyle in *The Full Monty* in August, a film that grossed more than $250 million from a budget of $3.5 million and won both BAFTAs and an Oscar.

The Mirror (6th August 1997): In his latest role, Robert [Carlyle] swaps his Highland bobby Hamish Macbeth for that of an unemployed Sheffield steelworker who becomes a male stripper. And the reaction to a nude Hamish MACBUFF in *The Full Monty*—earning a big thumbs up from fans. Jan Gray from Musselburgh said: 'Robert Carlyle was hot in his police uniform, but without his clothes he's scorching.'

London Evening Standard (September 1997): [*The Full Monty*] has remained London's most popular film for nearly two weeks. Last weekend, the weekend of [Diana, Princess of

Wales's] funeral, it took £1.6 million in ticket sales, £400,000 more than *Mrs Brown* and *Austin Powers* put together.

IN SEPTEMBER THAT year, Carlyle could also be seen in Antonia Bird's gangster drama, *Face* (1997), before he reunited with many *Hamish* alumni, including producer Deirdre Keir and actors Ron Donachie and Michael Mackenzie, in the BBC Scotland crime drama *Looking After Jo Jo* (1998).

Roles in films such as *Ravenous* (1999), *The World is Not Enough* (1999) and *Angela's Ashes* (1999) saw the actor take the noughties by storm, working consistently in British film and TV before moving to America for lead roles in *Stargate Universe* (2009–11) and *Once Upon a Time* (2011–18). Though he seemed happy to revisit old characters for *T2 Trainspotting* (2017) and *The Full Monty* (2023) mini-series, no mention has ever been made of a return to Lochdubh.

Just as they had done before *Hamish Macbeth*, the rest of the cast and crew continued to carve out diverse careers between TV, film and theatre. What had started as a close-knit ensemble in a remote Highland village dispersed into a diaspora of talent, their shared experience in Plockton serving as a creative spring-board that launched them into everything from Hollywood blockbusters to acclaimed stage productions.

Duncan Duff: I went up for *Skins* [2007–13, Channel 4 series created by Bryan Elsley] and it was the first time I'd met Bryan since *Hamish Macbeth*. There's definitely a little bond whenever you run into people that are connected with it. There's a nice feeling of having been involved in something that was a wee bit special, that everybody holds in a sort of treasured part of their memory.

On Sunday 23RD March 2008, BBC Four broadcast an episode of *The Cult of Sunday Night* devoted to *Hamish Macbeth*, 13 years to the weekend since *Hamish*'s BBC One premiere. Focusing solely on programmes broadcast on the BBC, each episode was a chance to revisit the likes of *All Creatures Great & Small*, *The Onedin Line* (1971–80) and *Howard's Way* (1985–90) in the company of cast and crew, with Ralph Riach, Valerie Gogan and Daniel Boyle among those reminiscing about their time in Lochdubh.

The BBC iPlayer streaming service added all episodes of *Hamish Macbeth* (except 'West Coast Story') in September 2023, a homecoming of sorts for the series.

A WRITER'S REVENGE

M.C. Beaton may have publicly praised both Robert Carlyle and the show in 1996, but two years later she published a new Hamish Macbeth novel, *Death of a Scriptwriter*, in which a TV company arrives in the village of Drim to adapt a series of cosy crime novels. When the author discovers her detective heroine has been transformed into a pot-smoking hippy, the show's screenwriter meets an untimely end. It was perhaps the ultimate act of creative revenge, a way for Beaton to reclaim her creation and remind readers that, in her world, it was always the author who had the last word.

By the time of her death on 30th December 2019 aged 83, Beaton had established herself as one of Britain's most successful crime writers, with 179 novels and short works to her name, including 33 *Hamish Macbeth* books and 30 featuring amateur sleuth Agatha Raisin, the basis for the TV series starring Ashley Jensen. For a period, she was the most borrowed

UK adult fiction author in British libraries, with her crime novels selling over 21 million copies worldwide.

FAREWELL, TV JOHN

Ralph Riach died on 20th March 2022 aged 86, prompting renewed appreciation for an actor whose career had spanned almost four decades.

It was after serving five years as an apprentice draughtsman in an architect's office ('People always say I was an architect, but I was a draughtsman!'), that he finally pursued his true calling.

'At that time you didn't do that,' he recalled of his early acting ambitions, mimicking his parents' reaction: 'Dinnae be silly Ralphie, you cannae do that!' But the performing bug had caught him early through the local boys' drama club, where he worked with Harry Robertson, better known as Lord Rockingham of the chart-topping Lord Rockingham's XI, who had a 1958 hit with *Hoots Mon*.

Riach admitted that he'd never planned to be on TV. 'When I was young, there was no television, so that was never my ambition. I would listen to the radio and watch the cinema. Some people say it's an insecurity thing, but I never felt insecure about myself. I wanted to pretend to be someone else. I just enjoyed it.'

He also maintained connections with Plockton long after saying goodbye to Lochdubh.

Charlie MacRae: Our Post Office had been closed for five years, but it was reopened in 1998 and Ralph Riach came back to open it.

Alasdair MacQuarrie: I spoke to Ralph a few times after the series ended. I had a couple of video calls from him and Calum. I got married in Perthshire and Ralph was doing a play nearby. He heard about the wedding from Calum, and a few dances in he made a surprise appearance. It was lovely to see him.

WHILE RIACH'S FUNERAL was streamed online, allowing many fans and villagers to attend virtually, at least one attended in person.

Calum Mackenzie: TV John became a very good friend of ours. He was in my boat a few times after the series finished. I was at his funeral and got a mention because I used to phone Ralph from the boat. Passengers would say they loved *Hamish Macbeth* and I'd ask who their favourite character was. A lot of them said TV John. Unknown to them, I'd phone up Ralph and he'd say, 'Who have you got to speak to me now?' So quite a few people would end up speaking to him. He was a lovely man.

I've actually got his *Hamish Macbeth* jacket. We went to visit him one time in Perth and as we were going out the back door his jacket was hanging up. I mentioned it to him and he gave it to me.

WRITING ON TWITTER on the day of Ralph Riach's death, Robert Carlyle captured what made his old friend special both on and off screen:

 One of the nicest, kindest, funniest men I've ever had the pleasure of working with. Ralph took me in for my audition at RSAMD in 1983. I loved my time with him on *Hamish Macbeth* and feel blessed that I had that opportunity. Farewell 'TV John' 🩶

EPILOGUE

THE PALM TREES still line Harbour Street in Plockton, their presence as striking now as when they first surprised Deirdre Keir during her location scout in 1994.

Like the series, they represent something that shouldn't work but somehow does: exotic trees flourishing in Scottish soil, just as a Sunday night drama featuring cannibalistic lobsters, a pot-smoking copper and the supernatural found its way into millions of homes.

When *Hamish Macbeth* debuted, it appeared to be following a well-worn path. A quirky police officer in a rural setting suggested another comfort drama in the vein of *Heartbeat* or *The Darling Buds of May*.

Yet over three series and 20 episodes, the show developed into something far more distinctive, blending comedy with tragedy, the mystical with the mundane, even weaving in occasional Gaelic dialogue that reminded viewers this was a world with its own language and traditions.

That evolution mirrors the transformation of Plockton itself.

Where once TV cameras captured a bustling community life, both real and imagined, the location that doubled as Lochdubh's Main Street now tells a different story. A visit to the village in March 2024 by *The Herald* found two-year-old Sorley Mackenzie and his five-year-old sister Alice as the only children living among its 43 homes, a stark contrast to the two dozen youngsters who called this street home during the series' heyday. The village's population has dwindled from an estimated 400–500 in 1995 to fewer than 350 today.

By its second series, *Hamish* had found its rhythm. TV John's second sight became more prominent, the village itself emerged as a protagonist and Hamish's police work became almost incidental. The third series saw both show and character venture into new territory.

After Alex's death, Robert Carlyle's portrayal deepened as Hamish navigated grief, his complicated relationship with Isobel and his growing acceptance of his place in the community.

By the time the Stone of Destiny appeared in the finale, Hamish had become less the reluctant village policeman and more a part of Lochdubh's fabric, as integral to the community as TV John's prophecies or the village's endless supply of secrets.

Plockton's spirit endures beyond its TV fame. It now hosts the National Centre For Excellence in Traditional Music at the High School, while the Am Bàta project teaches pupils the art of boat building. At the primary school, real life imitates fiction; the roof leaks, just as in 'The Trouble with Rory', and the pupils have been moved to the secondary school.

Alexander Mackenzie revives traditions like oyster fishing, while his partner Fiona's father, Calum, still offers boat trips with his famous guarantee of a refund if no seals are spotted. The waters of Loch Carron, designated a Marine Protected Area in 2019, host the world's largest known flame shell reef, along with extensive maerl beds and seagrass meadows.

After a 15-year ban, Highland cattle now roam freely through Plockton's streets and beach once more; VisitScotland's popular #Coosday social media posts sometimes share their images worldwide. Influencers now rub shoulders with families and coach tours, many oblivious of the old TV show that brought fame to the area.

At the nearby Balmacara Hotel, the saloon doors may have gone, but the old Stag Bar interior has remained intact for three decades, though change is on the way; the owners plan to convert it into more bedrooms by the end of 2025.

The Plockton Hotel remains a family affair under the Pearson family's stewardship. Where once it might have closed from October to April, tourists now come year-round, drawn by the same timeless appeal that first brought BBC cameras to its door. Properties that would have sold for approximately £80,000 in 1995 now command upwards of £450,000, even those in need of substantial renovation.

The village may be 'creaking', as one resident puts it, but its future isn't written yet. Plockton embodies a similar spirit of resilience to its fictional counterpart. Visitors still come searching for Hamish's world. While they may not find Rory's shop or the police house exactly as they remember them, they discover something equally valuable: a community that continues to surprise.

As chairman of the Community Council in 1994, Charlie MacRae helped broker the deal that made his village a global TV star. He's watched the place change from fishing community to TV location to tourist destination. Now in his 80s, Charlie very much lives in present-day Plockton, but it seems he'll never really leave Lochdubh behind: 'Not a day goes past without someone mentioning *Hamish Macbeth*. They want to know where Wee Jock was killed and buried. People send them to me because I was involved.'

While today's Plockton grapples with housing affordability and demographic shifts, its essential character remains unchanged: palm trees still stand sentinel, boats still bob on Loch Carron and tourists still pay tribute to a wee dog and his best pal, Hamish.

Perhaps that's the final legacy of *Hamish Macbeth*, a reminder that even the smallest communities can leave the deepest impressions. Stories of resilience, humour and belonging continue to echo through Plockton's streets, proving that some tales never truly end. They simply become part of the landscape, waiting to be discovered by those who come looking.

AUTHOR'S NOTE

Thank you for reading *Hamish Macbeth: The Making of a BBC TV Classic*.

Unlike Hamish, independent authors can't avoid promotion, so I'm asking for your help. Reviews are incredibly valuable and if you enjoyed this book, please consider sharing your thoughts on your preferred online book platform or social media. Even a few words or a photo can make a huge difference.

My newsletter may not be as comprehensive as the *Lochdubh and District Listener*, but you can sign up jonathanmelville. substack.com for updates and extra content.

Feel free to contact me direct for speaking opportunities or to buy copies of the book in bulk: linktr.ee/jonathanmelville

ACKNOWLEDGMENTS

Thanks to everyone who took the time to discuss their connection to *Hamish Macbeth* for this book—please see the 'Interviewees' section for the full list.

Special thanks to Scott Meek and Deirdre Keir for replying to my numerous emails through the years and waiting so patiently for the end result.

Thanks to Ross Maclean, Ron MacKenzie, Ian Hoey, Catherine Aitken and Sarah Bruce for their feedback on the manuscript, fact-checking and for catching all those spelling mistakes.

Thanks to Deirdre Keir, Sarah Bruce, Charlie MacRae, Morag Mackenzie and Kay Herbert for the use of their photos/ephemera, to *Radio Times* and *The List* for allowing me to publish their covers, and to VisitScotland and Paul Tomkins for their Plockton photos. All other photos were taken by me during visits to Plockton.

Thanks to the moderators and members of the Plockton Past and Present Facebook group for all their help. Thanks also to the Hamish Macbeth International Fan Group on Facebook for their spirited discussions of the TV series and M.C. Beaton's novels.

Finally, huge thanks to Ben Morris for the book's stunning cover.

ABOUT THE AUTHOR

Jonathan Melville is an author, development researcher and freelance arts journalist based in Edinburgh. His work delves into the creation and legacy of classic films and TV series, offering comprehensive behind-the-scenes insights from the creatives involved.

Seeking Perfection: The Unofficial Guide to Tremors examined the horror-comedy franchise through interviews with 50 cast and crew, including Kevin Bacon and executive producer Gale Anne Hurd.

A Kind of Magic: Making the Original Highlander looked at the 1986 classic and featured new interviews with Christopher Lambert and Clancy Brown, Queen's Brian May and Roger Taylor and many more.

Local Hero: Making a Scottish Classic, provided an in-depth look at the making of the 1983 film, with contributions from Bill Forsyth, Peter Riegert, Denis Lawson and more.

Currently, Jonathan is working on a book of interviews with creatives who worked on projects from the worlds of Jim Henson.

BIBLIOGRAPHY

Chapter One

Marion Chesney Gibbons background:
- Official M.C. Beaton website
- John Dingwall, 'Hamish Macbeth author MC Beaton on how Highland bobby was born on Fifth Avenue', *Daily Record*, 30th July 2011
- Mary Campbell, 'Beaton uses journalistic skills to create memorable sleuths', *The Daily Gazette*, 6th September 1998

It was never: Tom Lappin interview with Robert Carlyle, *Scotland on Sunday*, 16th March 1997

When later asked: Paul Simpson, 'Shortbread & Cannabis' *The Box*, April/May 1997

Veteran playwright Peter McDougall: 'Surprise and anger at BBC's selection for head of drama', *The Herald*, 5th November 1993

Hamish Macbeth's future: 'Fresh talent', *The Herald*, 9th November 1993

Every time: Paul Simpson, 'Shortbread & Cannabis'

Calderwood announced: 'Ghost story tops BBC list', *The Herald*, 27th November 1993

Chapter Two

I wasn't really interested it: Stephanie Bunbury, 'At home with Hamish', *Sydney Morning Herald: The Guide*, 28th July–3rd August 1997

I thought long and hard: Fiona Morrow, 'Brave Heart', *Time Out*, Issue 1334, 13th–20th March 1996

I don't find it difficult: *Radio Times*, March 1995, issue number unknown

If you went looking: Eddie Gibb, 'The Polis Man', *The List*, 24th March 1995

Hamish could not: Paul Simpson, 'Shortbread & Cannabis'

[Bobby] asks you questions: Katharine Viner, 'Hard man, soft man', *The Guardian*, 31st January 1997

The most important thing: Ibid.

The stuff I've been doing: Eddie Gibb, 'The Polis Man'

When Hamish first: Robert Carlyle at Belfast Film Festival, 12th April 2019

I would never really: Alison Graham, 'Everyone's Local Hero', *Radio Times*, 30th March–5th April 1996

'Big softie at heart': 'A fair cop for Macbeth without a witch in sight', *Daily Record*, 25th March 1995

noting that once: *Bristol Evening Post*, 21st March 1995

Chapter Three

The fee seemed: 'TV Star sent my bobby all to pot', *Daily Record*, 17th February 2013

I wrote about a 6 foot: *BBC Woman's Hour*, 10th December 2014

I had to let go of [my Hamish]: Cordell Marks, 'How I created Hamish Macbeth', *Radio Times*, 3rd–9th May 1997

Speaking at the: Robert Carlyle at Belfast Film Festival, 12th April 2019

Hamish Macbeth sees himself: 'TV's Macbeth has Highland police in a stooshie', *The Herald*, 28th March

Robert Carlyle discussed: Allan Laing, 'Now on to his next beat', *The Herald*, 12th March 1997

The actor expanded: Gavin Docherty, 'Laid-back lawman', *Daily Express*, date unknown

I've always said: Stephanie Bunbury, 'At home with Hamish'

BIBLIOGRAPHY

Chapter Four

'People who don't: Paul Simpson, 'Shortbread & Cannabis'

The show uses its tartanry: *The Herald*, 1st April 1995

Chapter Five

Biographical information on Duncraig via http://www.lochalsh.co.uk/duncraig_castle.shtml and https://en.wikipedia.org/wiki/Duncraig_Castle

Charlie MacRae, chairman: William Greaves, 'Local Hero', *Radio Times*, 25th–31st March.

Chapter Six

Chapter introduction research:
- William Greaves, 'Local Hero', *Radio Times*, 25th–31st March
- Hilary Bonner, 'Mac's a law unto himself, *Daily Mirror*, 25th March 1995
- 'Yes, Hamish is great for business', circa 1996, unknown newspaper [clipping], from the personal collection of Jonathan Melville.

Robert Carlyle always: 'Robert slept on the beach for 18 months', Unknown newspaper [clipping], 1996. From the collection of Jonathan Melville.

I've travelled: Cordell Marks, 'How I created Hamish Macbeth'

It was important: Ibid.

We used to say: Laurence Ford, 'Villagers bite back at midges', *Sunday Mirror*, 16th May 2004

The worst thing: Robert Carlyle at Belfast Film Festival, 12th April 2019

The recently appointed Head of Drama: 'Woman who can swing her own hammer', *The Herald*, 20th February 1995

Scottish culture: Eddie Gibb, 'The Polis Man', *The List*, 24th March 1995

Speaking ahead of: Gavin Docherty, 'Laid-back lawman'

The Herald turned: 'TV or not TV - that's the hamlet's question', *The Herald*, 25th March 1995

Chapter Seven

I hate dogs: Fiona Morrow, 'Brave Heart'

While the BBC's: *Points of View*, BBC One, 29th March 1995

Northern Constabulary: 'TV's Macbeth has Highland police in a stooshie'

A Northern force officer: Ibid.

Cheeky cops: Charles Lavery, 'Cop this for a laugh', *Daily Record*, 9th April 1995

Hamish was written: *The List*, 7th–20th March 1997

With Hamish: Paul Simpson, 'Shortbread & Cannabis'

He also touched: Gavin Docherty, 'Laid-back lawman'

playing with caricatures: 'Tartanry used to subvert, not stereotype', *The Herald*, 1st April 1995

As Robert Carlyle: Allan Laing, 'Now on to his next beat'

Years later: Demetrios Matheou, 'The outsider with an OBE', *The Telegraph*, 12th September 2002

Incomers were also: Ian Black, 'Real life meets make-believe in a media village', unknown newspaper [clipping], circa winter 1995.

who was replaced: *North Star and Farmers' Chronicle*, 1st April 1995

Writing for *CST Online*: Dr Melissa Beattie, 'A Good Place with Good People: *Hamish Macbeth* and the Highlands', *CST Online*, 2nd February 2024, Available at: https://cstonline.net/a-good-place-with-good-people-hamish-macbeth-and-the-highlands-by-melissa-beattie/

On the one hand: 'MacBeth's No Tragedy', *TV Week Australia*, 1996

Chapter Eight

Averaged around 10 million: 'Another play for Macbeth', *The Herald*, 13th April 1995

Reviewing 'The Great: John Millar, 'Record TV—Oscar Bravos', *Daily Record*, March 27th 1995

Charlie MacRae told: Jackie Mackenzie, 'Thumbs up from village for new TV cop', *The Press & Journal*, 28th March 1995

Douglas Hamilton of: Ibid.

The Scottish Tourist Board: 'Film cameras focus tourist attention north of the Border', *The Herald*, 26th April 1995

In Caithness, Lochdhu Lodge: 'Film cameras focus tourist attention north of the Border', *The Herald*, 26th April 1995

Ratings remained relatively: 'Royals fail to win the TV war', *The Herald*, 10th May 1995

On the eve: George Hume, 'Fair cop as Hamish pulls 'em in', *The Herald*, 29th April

One Plockton resident: 'Hollywood must wait', *The Herald*, 28th April 1995

Mini property boom: 'Rush to Plockton', *The Herald*, 23rd August 1995

Unscrupulous breeders: 'Fears over 'mass production' of TV puppies', *The Herald*, 4th December 1995

BBC One's *Points of View*: Sarah Hodell, 'Highland police give their verdict on TV's crime programmes', *North Star and Farmers' Chronicle*, 6th May 1995

At the 1995 BAFTA Scotland: 'BBC wins 12 Bafta awards', *The Herald*, 6th November 1995

Around this time: 'They seek him here, they seek him there, directors that is', *HQ Magazine*

Chapter Nine

One other cast change: Aidan Smith, 'My Stars Take a Bow Wow Wow—Creature Comforts: Scotland's answer to Dr Dolittle on the secrets of his success', *Daily Record*, 29th March 1996

Chapter Ten

Opening narrative derived from:
-Alison Graham, 'Everyone's Local Hero'
- Unknown newspaper [clipping], 'Yes, Hamish is great for business', circa 1996

a constant struggle: Fiona Morrow, 'Brave Heart'

My father was: William Greaves, 'Local Hero'

Angry villagers: 'Hamish angers the villagers - Bloody Macbeth 2', *Daily Record*, 8th September 1996

Chapter Eleven

Ahead of *Hamish Macbeth*'s return: 'Tartan telly clash', *Daily Record*, 9th March 1996

The *Daily Record*'s John Millar: John Millar, 'Telly ratings war Macs me so mad', *Daily Record*, 6th April 1996

She succumbed to: Alison Graham, 'Everyone's Local Hero'

At the March: Stephen McGinty, 'Mum's the word over MacBeth's bride', *The Herald*, 6th March 1996

Not everyone welcomed: Julie Davidson, 'Trading virtues for five-minute fame', *The Herald*, 12th April 1996

Reader W.R. Anderson: 'Elitist attitude to extra visitors', *The Herald*, 20th April 1996

Some publicity: Tony Purnell, *The Mirror*, 23rd February 1996

Chapter Twelve

Comparing 'paratextual' partners: Dr Melissa Beattie, 'A Good Place with Good People: *Hamish Macbeth* and the Highlands'

As the second: *The List*, 7th–20th March 1997

Whether at the centre: Lisa Rohumaa, 'Hamish Macbeth review', *The Stage*, 4th April 1996

I've no need: Press information relating to 'In Search of a Rose', Spring 1997

It was a bit hairy: *Irish Independent*, 1st April 1996

After Alex died: Paul Simpson, 'Cannabis & Shortbread'

The hash smoking: Stephanie Bunbury, 'At home with Hamish'

A spokesman said: 'Caution for TV's Hamish Macbeth', *The Herald*, 29th August 1996

Other programmes: John Millar, 'Hamish's ash and carry out', *Daily Record*, 4th May 1996

Chapter Thirteen

By early 1996: 'Leading role for Scottish drama', *The Herald*, 28th March 1996

Sunday evenings: Tara Conlan, 'Ratings Watch', *The Stage*, 16th May 1996

ITV's decision: 'Telly doc is axed', *Daily Record*, 18th June 1996

Author M.C. Beaton's: *Points of View*, BBC One, 3rd April 1996

That May: 'Acting award for 'Hamish Macbeth', *The Herald*, 24th May 1996

Chapter Fourteen

There are just: Fiona Morrow, 'Brave Heart'

Chapter Fifteen

Opening narrative derived from:
- Stephanie Bunbury, 'At home with Hamish'

- It was on 25th June: 'Macbeth us do part says TV cop writer', *Daily Record*, 25th June 1996

One month later: Richard Wallace, 'Bye Bye Hamish', *Daily Record*, 24th July 1996

Charles Salmon explained: 'Teaching a new dog old tricks', *Radio Times*, 22nd-28th March 1997

Chapter Sixteen

Comedy isn't something: John Millar, 'I was scared I'd be like PC Plod', *Daily Record*, 15th March 1997

worked best when: Allan Laing, 'Now on to his next beat'

In his review: Harry Venning, *The Stage*, 3rd April 1997

Channel 4's viewer: Anecdotal information from an individual involved at the time

One voice also: John Millar, 'Chilled by this grate accent', *Daily Record*, 12th April 1997

caused a bit: *Wolverhampton Express and Star*, 15th March 1997

A twist in the mystery: 'Teuchs', *The Scotsman*, 19th April 1997

The Gazza of: 'Fame beckons shinty's Gazza', *The Herald,* 7th October 1996

I thought it: Ibid.

Old men weep: 'Shinty 'Gazza' is telly star', *Daily Record*, 7th October 1996

Chapter Seventeen

Narrative derived from Alison Graham, 'Haste ye back Hamish'

It was in the autumn: Ibid.

Ratings data: Tara Conlan, 'Ratings watch', *The Stage*, various issues

Series three's arrival: 'Must see TV', *The Box*, April/May 1997

Gavin Docherty pushed: Gavin Docherty, 'Macbeth: the biggest mystery of them all', *Sunday Express*, 16th March 1997

Daniel Boyle told: Paul Simpson, 'Cannabis & Shortbread'

Yeah, I was all: Gavin Docherty, 'Macbeth: the biggest mystery of them all'

I knew that: Allan Laing, 'Now on to his next beat'

miss it, for: Ibid.

Chapter Eighteen

In his latest role: Steve King, *The Mirror*, 6th August 1997

[*The Full Monty*]: Andrew Billen, 'The Andrew Billen interview', *London Evening Standard*, September 1997

By the time of her death: Details from the official M.C. Beaton website: https://www.mcbeaton.com/

For a period: Kirsty McKenzie, 'Renowned Glasgow writer MC Beaton dies aged 83', *Glasgow Live*, 2nd January 2020, Available at: https://www.glasgowlive.co.uk/news/glasgow-news/renowned-glasgow-writer-mc-beaton-17503562

One of the nicest: Robert Carlyle on Twitter, 20th March 2022

Epilogue

Sources:
- Caroline Wilson, 'Plockton second homes leaves village facing housing crisis', *The Herald*, 2nd March 2024
- 'Outrage as cows given right to roam Highland village of Plockton', *The Scotsman*, 10th October 2018
- Craig Williams, 'How Highland Coos are helping promote Scotland round the world', *The Herald*, 30th November 2024
- The waters of: 'A Lesson from Loch Carron', *Open Seas*, 27th May 2019, https://www.openseas.org.uk/news/a-lesson-from-loch-carron/